Valitut Palat

Finland

Land of the Midnight Sun

Chosen
Book of the Year
by the
World Wildlife Fund Finland

This book is a work in which beautiful pictures combine with informative texts in a harmonious union. With the aid of this combination, the book describes the factors that have influenced the Finnish landscape, are still visible in it or that threaten to alter it. It reveals with striking clarity the importance of the areas recently proposed for inclusion in a network of national parks. Most of the areas recommended by the state committee on national parks are presented, including those unique natural and cultured areas so important to the Finnish nation as preserves of nature and the living environment. This book gives much information about these areas as well as about the dangers that threaten them. Information is essential if the objectives of the nature conservationists are to be understood, appreciated and achieved. Their objectives coincide exactly with those of the World Wildlife Fund, both in Finland and at international level. Therefore the Fund has chosen Finland — Land of the Midnight Sun as its Book of the Year for 1978 on the grounds that book makes its own contribution to supporting the work of the World Wildlife Fund to save our threatened environment, and to preserve in as untouched a state as possible our national natural heritage.

World Wildlife Fund Finland

Valitut Palat

Finnland

Land der Mitternachtssonne

Vom
World Wildlife Fund Finnland
gewählt zum
Buch des Jahres

Dieses Buch ist ein Werk, in dem die Schönheit der Bilder und die Informationen der Texte eine harmonische Verbindung eingehen. Mit Hilfe dieses Zusammenspiels beschreibt es jene Faktoren, die auf Finnlands Landschaft Einfluss genommen haben, die immer noch in ihr zu sehen sind oder die sie zu verändern drohen. Dieses Werk zeigt treffend, wie bedeutend gerade jene Gebiete sind, die für die Gründung von Nationalparks vorgeschlagen worden sind. Es stellt die meisten vom Nationalparkkomitee vorgeschlagenen Gebiete vor, unter ihnen die wertvollsten Natur- und Kulturlandschaften des Landes, denen als Bewahrer der Natur und der Lebensumwelt der Nation eine wesentliche Bedeutung zukommt. Über sie vermittelt dieses Werk Wissen, ebenso über die Gefahren, von denen sie bedroht sind. Wissen ist notwendig, um die Ziele der Naturschützer verstehen, schätzen und verwirklichen zu können. Die gleichen Ziele verfolgt auch der World Wildlife Fund (Weltnaturfonds) — auf finnischer und auf internationaler Ebene. Daher hat er das vorliegende Werk zu seinem Buch des Jahres 1978 gewählt. Dieses Werk unterstützt seinerseits die Arbeit des World Wildlife Fund zur Rettung der bedrohten Natur und zur Erhaltung des nationalen Naturerbes Finnlands.

World Wildlife Fund Finnland

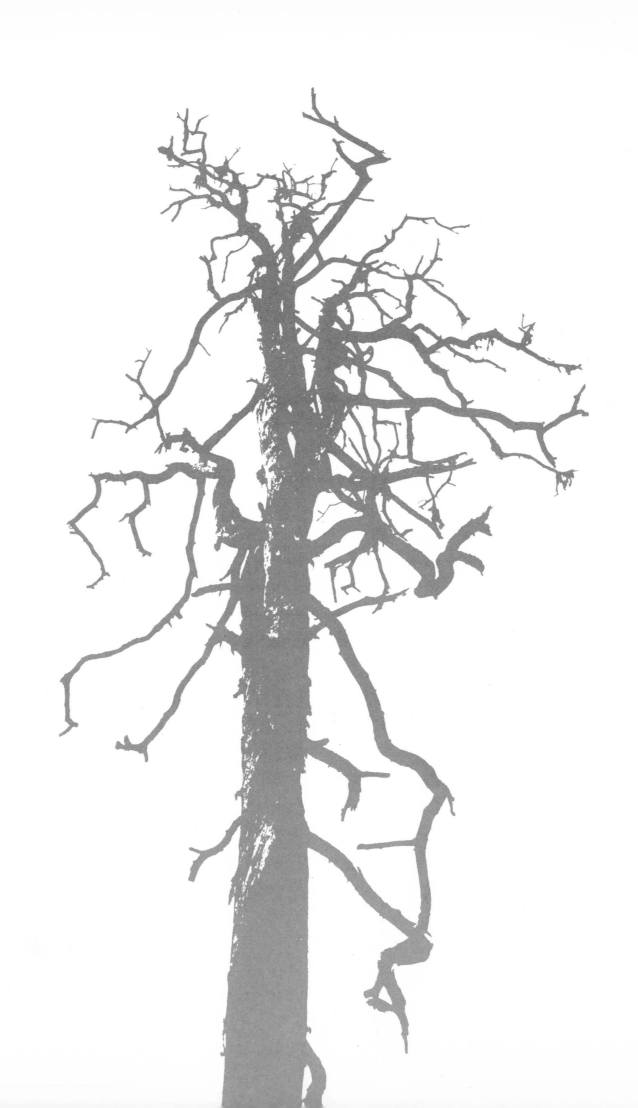

FINLAND

Land of the Midnight Sun

Land der Mitternachtssonne

FINNLAND

Oy Valitut Palat – Reader's Digest Ab   Helsinki

EDITORIAL BOARD/REDAKTIONSKOMITEE
Veikko M. Neuvonen
Matti A. Pitkänen
Arno Rautavaara
Teuvo Suominen

RESPONSIBLE EDITOR/VERANTWORTLICHER REDAKTEUR
Pertti Kosonen

TEXTS/TEXTE
Bo Carpelan   Elina Karjalainen   Pertti Ranta   Raimo Uusinoka
Matti Eronen   Venny Kontturi   Arno Rautavaara   Nils-Aslak Valkeapää
Sauvo Henttonen   Perttu Koski   Reino Rinne   Erkki Vanninen
Juha Hämäläinen   Martti Linkola   Juhani Santanen   Seppo Vuokko
Asko Kaikusalo   Ari Lyytikäinen   Matti Sippola
Päiviö Kangas   Jaakko Napola   Teuvo Suominen
Annikki Kariniemi Veikko M. Neuvonen   Heikki Turunen

PHOTOGRAPHS/FOTOS
Matti A. Pitkänen Seppo Keränen   Jorma Luhta   Rauno Ruuhijärvi
Hannu Hautala   Juhani Koivusaari   Martti Montonen   Kari Soveri
Lasse Holmström   Mauri Korhonen   Pertti Nikkari   Teuvo Suominen
Reijo Juurinen   Heikki Kotilainen   Arno Rautavaara

DIAGRAMS/GRAFISCHE DARSTELLUNGEN
Teuvo Berggren

PICTORIAL DESIGN/FOTOGRAFISCHE GESTALTUNG
Matti A. Pitkänen

PICTURE PROCESSING/FOTOGRAFISCHE BEARBEITUNG
Pauli Hiltunen

LAYOUT AND TYPOGRAPHY/LAYOUT UND TYPOGRAPHIE
Pauli Hiltunen

TRANSLATION/ÜBERSETZUNG
Oy Wortexport Ltd.:
English:
Gregory Coogan
Deutsch:
Hans-Joachim Zimmering

ISBN 951-9078-55-X
© 1978 Oy Valitut Palat — Reader's Digest Ab
Typesetting and Printing/Satz und Druck: Sanomapaino, Helsinki
Binding/Einband: Arvi A. Karisto Osakeyhtiö, Hämeenlinna
Printed in Finland

Foreword

The foreigner knows Finland — if at all — as a land of midnight sun, pine forests, a thousand lakes or cold winters. By all means, but we believe that the Finnish landscape has much more to show. Even when we began planning this work, our basic idea was to present the richness of our country's natural beauty to foreign readers. Above all, we wished to create a record of the Finnish natural and cultivated landscapes, since it is a regrettable fact that also in our country these original and harmonic landscapes are endangered by the actions of man, urbanisation, industrialisation and traffic facilities.

A decisive contribution to the success of this task was made by the experience and skill of the main photographer, Matti A. Pitkänen. His objective coincided with that of the publisher: to erect a milestone in the photographical representation of the Finnish landscape. In the foreword to the original Finnish edition of this work, Matti A. Pitkänen states: "I accepted the task of illustrating this work as a major gesture of confidence on the part of Valitut Palat. With the aid of my pictures, I can give the reader some glimpses of the natural beauty of our native country. We can consider ourselves very fortunate that our living environment consists of virtually unpolluted waters, extensive forests, a rich island world and northerly wildernesses. As the inhabitants of a country with bright summer nights, blue lakes and glistening snow-covered slopes, we are surrounded by a natural beauty that is granted to few other nations. We must only remember that nature is the common property of all generations; today's generation may derive benefit from their natural surroundings, but they may not be damaged in any way."

This book, which was published during the celebrations marking the diamond anniversary of Finnish independence, was very positively received by the public and the entire Finnish-language edition was soon sold out. We are happy to be able to state that this was more than a fleeting success — six months after it had been published, the book was chosen by The Committee on Finnish Book Art, as one of "the most beautiful landscape and picture collections in Finland", for inclusion in the "Collection of Élite Books". Because of this, and encouraged by numerous inquiries, Valitut Palat Oy decided to publish an English-German version. The photographs and all other illustrations remain unchanged, but the text had to be condensed and adapted. For this work, in which the interests of foreign readers were taken into account, Valitut Palat expresses its sincerest thanks to Veikko M. Neuvonen and Arno Rautavaara.

Special thanks is due to the translators, Gregory Coogan and Hans-Joachim Zimmering, for their successful interpretation of the text, a task in which they had to overcome the additional problem of matching translations of two different lengths together and into the exact space provided.

We hope that the pictures and information in this book will help the readers to form a conception of the beauty of our country in the remote North.

Helsinki, 1. 8. 1978
The Editorial Board

Vorwort

Dem Ausländer ist Finnland — falls überhaupt — als Land der Mitternachtssonne, der Wälder, der Tausend Seen oder des kalten Winters bekannt. Warum nicht, aber wir meinen, dass die finnische Landschaft viel mehr vorzuzeigen hat. Den Reichtum der Natur unseres Landes vorzustellen war schon bei der Planung des vorliegenden Werks unser Leitgedanke. Vor allem wollten wir in ihm die finnische Natur- und Kulturlandschaft festhalten. Denn leider sind diese ursprünglichen und harmonischen Landschaftstypen auch in unserem Lande von menschlicher Tätigkeit, Verstädterung, Industrie und Verkehr bedroht.

Zum Gelingen dieses Projekts hat entscheidend die einschlägige Erfahrung und das Können des Hauptfotografen des Werks, Matti A. Pitkänen, beigetragen. Seine Zielstellung war mit der des Verlegers identisch: in der fotografischen Darstellung der finnischen Landschaft einen Meilenstein zu errichten. Im Vorwort zur finnischsprachigen Ausgabe dieses Werks schreibt Matti A. Pitkänen: "Ich habe die Illustrationsaufgabe für dieses Werk als grossen Vertrauensbeweis seitens Valitut Palat entgegengenommen. Mit meinen Landschaftsfotos kann ich dem Betrachter Streiflichter von der Schönheit der Natur unseres Heimatlandes zeigen. Wir können uns sehr glücklich schätzen, dass wir als Lebensumwelt an sich saubere Gewässer, weitläufige Wälder, eine reiche Inselwelt und die nordischen Wildnisse erhalten haben. Als Bewohner eines Landes mit hellen Sommernächten, blauen Seen und leuchtendweissen Schneehängen erfahren wir in unserer Umgebung eine Naturschönheit, wie sie nur wenigen Völkern vergönnt ist. Nur dürfen wir nicht vergessen, dass die Natur gemeinsames Eigentum aller Generationen ist; die heutige Generation darf Nutzen aus ihr ziehen, aber sie darf nichts von ihr zerstören."

Das vorliegende Werk, das während der 60-Jahr-Feiern der Selbständigkeit Finnlands erschienen ist, hat bei den Lesern ein positives Echo gefunden: die gesamte finnischsprachige Auflage war in kurzer Zeit ausverkauft. Wir freuen uns festzustellen, dass dies nicht nur ein flüchtiger Erfolg war — ein halbes Jahr nach seinem Erscheinen wurde dieses Werk vom Ausschuss für finnische Buchkunst als einer der *schönsten Landschafts- und Bildbände Finnlands* in die "Kollektion der Elitebücher" aufgenommen. Aus diesen Gründen und ermutigt durch zahlreiche Anfragen beschloss Valitut Palat, das Werk in einer englisch-deutschen Version herauszugeben. Die Illustration blieb unverändert, aber der Text muste gekürzt werden, wobei das Interesse der ausländischen Leser berücksichtigt wurde. Für diese Arbeit bedankt sich der Verleger Valitut Palat herzlichst bei Veikko M. Neuvonen und Arno Rautavaara.

Besonderen Dank verdienen die Übersetzer dieses Buchs, Gregory Coogan und Hans-Joachim Zimmering, für die gelungene Interpretation der Texte, wobei sie zusätzlich das Problem zu bewältigen hatten, zwei an sich verschieden lang ausfallende Übersetzungen auf ein vorgegebenes Mass abzustimmen.

Wir hoffen, dass dieses Werk dem Leser einen Begriff von der Schönheit unseres weitab im Norden gelegenen Landes vermittelt.

Helsinki, 1. 8. 1978
Die Redaktion

Contents
Inhalt

The Genesis of the Finnish Landscape

Die Entstehung der finnischen Landschaft

The Bedrock

Der Felsgrund

10 The bedrock of Finland consists of granites crystallised from magma as well as gneiss and various schists. Although exposed rocks cover only 3 % of Finland's land area, rock is met everywhere at a maximum depth of about twenty metres. Finland's bedrock is a well-worn part of the ancient Fennoscandian Shield. The oldest rocks, granite-gneiss specimens about 2,700 million years old, are found in Eastern and Northern Finland. The granulites in the Lapland area are about 800 million years younger.

The greatest part of our bedrock originated 1,900—1,800 million years ago. These mountain ranges — long since levelled out — included two components: the Svecofennides crossing South and Southwestern Finland and the Karelides crossing Eastern and Northern Finland.

The easily-crumbling "rapakivi" granites of the Åland Islands, Southwestern Finland and Kymenlaakso are about 200 million years younger than the Svecokarelides. The youngest, about 600—400 million years old, are the stones of the Koli edge zone, which make up the arctic fells of Halti and Saana.

A couple of million years ago, rock movements occurred in the area that had worn flat, producing the arctic fells of Lapland's granulate areas. The forces of erosion also intensified, producing the present typography of Finland's bedrock, with fold valleys and relict mountains. This was completed by the Pleistocene ice sheets, which finally covered our bedrock almost completely with loose soil.

Finnlands Felsgrund besteht aus Tiefengesteinen, die sich aus Magma kristallisiert haben, sowie aus Gneissen und verschiedenen Schieferarten. Obwohl blossliegender Fels nur drei Prozent der Oberfläche ausmacht, stösst man im ganzen Lande spätestens in einigen Dutzend Metern Tiefe auf Fels. Der finnische Felsgrund gehört zum uralten, tief abgetragenen Baltischen Schild. Das älteste Gestein, rund 2700 Millionen Jahre alte Granitgneisse, findet man in Ost- und Nordfinnland. Lapplands Granulite sind etwa 800 Millionen Jahre jünger.

Der Hauptteil des Felsgrundes entstand vor 1900 bis 1800 Millionen Jahren. Zu den damals eingeebneten Bergkettengürteln gehören zwei Gebirgszüge: die Svekofenniden verlaufen durch Süd- und Westfinnland, die Kareliden durch Ost- und Mittelfinnland.

Die Rapakivi-Granite der Ålandinseln, Südwestfinnlands und des Kymitals sind rund 200 Millionen Jahre jünger als die Svekokareliden. Am jüngsten, rund 600 bis 400 Millionen Jahre alt, ist das Randgürtelgestein des Kjölen-Gebirges.

Vor einigen Millionen Jahren kam es in durch Erosion abgeflachten Gebieten zu Verwerfungen, in deren Folge unter anderem die Fjälls des lappländischen Granulitgebirges aufstiegen. Auch die Erosionskräfte belebten sich, und als Resultat entstand das heutige Relief des finnischen Felsgrundes mit seinen Tälern und Restbergen. Intensiviert wurde diese Entwicklung durch das Inlandeis, welches den Felsgrund schliesslich fast vollständig mit losen Bodenarten abdeckte.

Soil Cover

Finland's most common kind of mineral soil is moraine, which covers the bedrock to a depth of a couple of metres. Moraine was produced by the great ice sheet during the Pleistocene. As the glaciers slowly moved they scoured the earth and carried the loose material along. Moraine contains all kinds of soil: alluvium, silt, sand, gravel and stone, in considerably varying proportions.

In many regions, the moraine is covered by layers of younger soil. In Southern Finland, alluvial land is common. This was created by sedimentation in deep water during the lifetime of the Baltic. Isostatic recovery has uplifted the seabed, forming dry land.

Finnish moraine ridges are sand and gravel washed out by the meltwaters of the glaciers. This material was deposited in those places where the water flow weakened as the ice sheet retreated. As the glaciers shrunk, the delta area situated close to the edge was transferred and thus the moraines formed long eskers.

Mineral soil formations also include beach layers and areas of drifted sand. The former can be found on today's coasts as well as on ancient beaches. The latter are also very common in association with strand formations but one can also find drifted sand areas or dunes in places where the land was without plant cover for some time after the Ice Age had come to an end.

Peat is the most common organogenic type of soil in Finland. It is composed of semi-decayed vegetation.

Die Bodendecke

Finnlands häufigster Bodentyp ist die Moräne. Sie bedeckt den Felsgrund in mehrere Meter starken Schichten. Die Moränen enstanden unter Einwirkung des Inlandeises. Indem es langsam wanderte, löste das Inlandeis Materie aus dem Erdboden und führte sie mit sich. Die Moräne enthält alle Korngrössen: Ton, Treibsand, Sand, Kies und Steine. Ihr Mischverhältnis in der Moräne kann stark schwanken.

Vielerorts bedecken die Moränen Erdschichten, welche jünger sind als die Moränen selbst. In Südfinnland ist der Ton weit verbreitet. Er entstand während der verschiedenen Entwicklungsphasen der Ostsee durch Sedimentierung und wurde durch die Landhebung freigelegt. Finnlands Oser sind von den Schmelzströmen des Inlandeises sortierte Sand- und Kiesmassen, die sich in der Rückzugsphase des Eises bis zu jenen Stellen aufschichteten, an denen der Wasserstrom abschwachte.

Zu den Mineralbodenformationen gehören weiterhin Uferterrassen und Flugsandfelder. Uferterrassen findet man an heutigen wie auch an vorzeitlichen Ufern. Flugsandfelder erstrecken sich über gewöhnliche Uferformationen, aber man findet Flugsandverwehungen — Dünen — auch an einigen Stellen, an denen das Land nach der Eiszeit keine Pflanzendecke hatte, so dass der Wind die feine Materie der Erdoberfläche aufwirbeln konnte.

Die verbreitetste organische Bodenart Finnlands ist der Torf. Dieser entsteht, wenn Sumpfpflanzen absterben und von jüngeren Vegetationsschichten überdeckt werden.

Traces of the Ice Age

Die Spuren der Eiszeit

12 The centre of the vast ice sheet that covered Finland during the last Ice Age was in Northern Sweden. From here, the glacier advanced slowly across Southern and central Finland. The glaciers have left clear marks in the morphology of the country. Everywhere the summits of hills have been rounded. Moraine ridges, eskers and drumlins, were formed, giving the landscape viewed from the air a stripy appearance. This is clearly visible in Finland's Lake District and Kuusamo.

The action of the glaciers can be seen in the smooth rock formations and the signs of wear on the surface. The ice gave the rocks a smooth, gently-sloping shape on the side it arrived, while the end from which it departed is rough. Boulders (erratics) show how the glacier transferred material. Some of them were carried hundreds of kilometres before they were deposited.

The ridges were created by the floods from the melting glaciers. They run in the direction of the glacier's retreat. The gravel and sand forming them piled up in the areas where sub-glacial rivers emerged. These deltas moved along with the retreating edge of the glacier. The Salpausselkä ridges and other terminal moraines are vertical ridges stratified by meltwater. They were formed in front of the glacier's edge after it had stayed in the same place for some time.

Strong flows of water were able to wear out unbroken rock. This is indicated by the "devil's churns" which are pot-holes worn out by swirling water.

Das Zentrum des Inlandeises, das Finnland während der letzten Eiszeit bedeckte, lag in Nordschweden. Von dort wanderte der langsam strömende Gletscher in Nordwest-Südostrichtung über Süd- und Mittelfinnland. Das Inlandeis hat in der Landschaft deutlich erkennbare Spuren hinterlassen. Überall sind die Gipfel der Bodenerhebungen glattgeschliffen. Das Eis liess langgestreckte Moränenrücken — Drumlins — entstehen, welche die Landschaft von oben streifig aussehen lassen.

Die Auswirkungen des Inlandeises erkennt man an den Formen der Rundhöcker und an Abtragungsspuren an der Erdoberfläche. Das Eis hat die Rundhöcker in Zuflussrichtung flachgehobelt. In Abflussrichtung ist der Fels schroff. Findlinge — erratische Blöcke — geben Aufschluss über die Transporttätigkeit des Eises. Die Findlinge sind vom Eis vereinzelt über Hunderte von Kilometern mitgeführt worden, in den meisten Fällen jedoch nur wenige Kilometer.

Das Eis hat Landrücken — Oser — entstehen lassen. Sie verlaufen quer zur Rückzugsrichtung des Eises. Der Os-Kies und Os-Sand haben sich in den Mündungsgebieten der Schmelzwasserströme abgelagert. Derartige Oser haben sich in Zeiten langen Stillstandes des Inlandeises vor den Gletscherrändern gebildet.

Die Schmelzwasserströme waren stellenweise so stark, dass sie massiven Fels verschleissen konnten. Hiervon zeugen die hier und da anzutreffenden Gletschermühlen, vom Wasser ausgewaschene topfartige Vertiefungen in der Felsoberfläche.

The Development of the Baltic

Die Entwicklung der Ostsee

Most of Southern and central Finland was covered by the waters of the Baltic Basin after the Ice Age, but isostatic forces have gradually raised this land above sea level. The Baltic itself has gone through many stages of development since the end of the Ice Age. Land upheaval has also changed the connection between the Baltic Basin and the ocean, which accounts for the fluctuations in the salinity of the water.

The oldest stage in the development of the Baltic was the Baltic Ice Sea, which was bounded by the edge of the glacier in the Salpausselkä zone. This ended about 10,200 years ago and was followed by the brackish Yoldia stage and after that by the completely fresh-water Ancylus Lake. Via the Mastogloia stage, the Baltic changed into the Litorina Sea about 7,000—7,500 years ago. Since the beginning of the Litorina Sea there have been no great changes in the history of the Baltic. The salinity has declined somewhat and land upheaval has altered the shape of the coastline.

For the greatest part of the Baltic's history the coastal waters have been becoming shallower. Land upheaval has exposed new land. This development has twice been temporarily interrupted by rises in the sea level, transgressions, on the southern Finnish coast. The last transgression ended about 6,000 years ago. In Ostrobothnia, however, land upheaval has been so rapid that there the coastal waters have continued to grow shallower throughout the period since the Ice Age and the coastline is constantly moving seawards.

Der grösste Teil Süd- und Mittelfinnlands lag nach der Eiszeit unter der Ostsee. Die Landhebung hat dieses Gebiet allmählich aus dem Meer ans Trockene steigen lassen. Die Ostsee selbst hat vom Ende der Eiszeit bis zur Gegenwart eine mehrphasige Entwicklung durchgemacht. Aufgrund der Landhebung ist auch die Verbindung der Ostsee mit dem Atlantik Veränderungen unterworfen gewesen, weshalb es im Salzgehalt des Wassers Schwankungen gegeben hat.

Die erste Phase der Ostsee war der Baltische Eissee, der im Salpausselkä-Gürtel an den Rand des Inlandeises grenzte. Diese Phase endete vor etwa 10 000 Jahren. Es folgte die teilweise salzhaltige Yoldia-Phase und darauf der rein süsswässrige Ancylussee. Über die Mastogloia-Phase wandelte sich die Ostsee vor 7500—7000 Jahren zum deutlich salzhaltigen Litorinameer. Seither hat die Ostsee keine grösseren Änderungen mehr durchgemacht. Der Salzgehalt ist gesunken und die Landhebung hat die Uferlinie zum offenen Meer hinaus verschoben.

Die meiste Zeit der Ostseegeschichte hindurch ist die Uferlinie im Vormarsch gewesen. Die Landhebung hat Neuland blossgelegt. Zweimal jedoch wurde diese Entwicklung der südfinnischen Küste vorübergehend durch ein Steigen des Meeresspiegels, eine sog. Transgression, unterbrochen. Die letzte Transgression endete, als vor 6000 Jahren das Ansteigen des Ostseespiegels aufhörte. In Österbotten war und ist die Landhebung so stark, dass dort die Uferlinie seit der Eiszeit unausgesetzt vorgedrungen ist.

The Lakes and Rivers are Born

14 The development of most Finnish lakes began with the contraction of the Baltic Basin. Land upheaval led to the Lake District of Finland being separated from the waters of the Baltic about 8,000—8,500 years ago. The great lakes formed in central Finland began to flow towards the Gulf of Bothnia. However, the land upheaval strongly influenced the development of the water bodies in the Lake District. It was stronger in the North West and South West than in the South East. The North Western flow basin to the Gulf of Bothnia became shallower, while lakes flooded dry land in the South and South East.

Just as it has altered the coastline, land upheaval has changed the shapes of all the great Finnish lakes and this development is still continuing. However, where the small lakes are concerned, the tilting of the land has not led to any great changes because elevation differences remain quite small over short distances.

Geologically, the Finnish water bodies are very young. The lakes, which are often joined into chainlike systems, are to a great extent in basins scoured out of clefts along faults in the earth's crust. This accounts for their shallowness and labyrinthine form. The rivers have not yet had time to level out their courses and flow unevenly forming smallish rapids ever so often. The great rivers in Lapland flow in old valleys which were created before the last glacial period and then deepened by the action of the ice. But the rivers near the south coast wind along over young alluvial strata.

Die Seen und Flüsse entstehen

Die Entwicklung der meisten finnischen Seen begann mit ihrer Abschnürung vom Ostseebecken. Die finnische Seenplatte entstieg im Zuge der Landhebung vor 8500 bis 8000 Jahren der Ostsee. Die in Mittelfinnland entstandenen grossen Seen begannen zum Bottnischen Meerbusen abzufliessen. Jedoch hatte die Landhebung von Anfang an einen grossen Einfluss auf die Entwicklung der Binnengewässer. Im Nordwesten ging die Landhebung schneller vor sich als im Südosten. Die nordwestliche Abflussrinne zum Bottnischen Meerbusen flachte ab, und die Seen traten im Süden und Südosten über ihre Ufer.

Die Landhebung hat die Umrisse aller grossen Seen Finnlands geändert. Die Entwicklung der Seen dauert auch weiterhin an. Auf die Formen der kleinen selbständigen Seen hat sich die unterschiedliche Landhebung nicht sehr stark ausgewirkt, da das Kippen auf kurzen Strekken nur geringe Höhenveränderungen des Wasserspiegels bewirkt.

Die finnischen Gewässer sind geologisch sehr jung. Die Seen befinden sich grösstenteils in Senkungen, die in Bruchlinien der Erdkruste enstanden sind. Dies ist der Grund für die zersplitterte und labyrinthähnliche Gestalt der Seen. Die Flüsse haben es noch nicht geschafft, ihre Betten einzuebnen, sondern sie fliessen ungleichmässig und bilden immer wieder kleine Stromschnellen. Während die Ströme Lapplands in alten Tälern fliessen, die schon vor der Eiszeit entstanden sind, schlängeln sich die Flüsse an der südfinnischen Küste über junge Tonschichten.

Finland Becomes Covered with Vegetation

About 9,000 years ago Finland was freed of its ice cover and the last of the glaciers melted in Western Lapland. Vegetation immediately started to spread to the areas now liberated from the ice. Herbaceous plants were the first to establish themselves. The most common were grasses and sedges as well as artemesia-related species. After these "pioneers" came birch. The first birch forests slightly resembled today's arctic fell birch woods in Lapland. The tundra-type vegetation and birch forests followed the trailing edge of the ice sheet in a fairly wide belt. Pine arrived after birch. In Southern Finland it became common about 9,000 years ago and largely displaced birch, becoming the dominant type of tree. The climate was relatively mild at that time and apparently fairly dry.

About 8,000 years ago the climate had become warmer and humidity had increased. The common alder spread into Finland. About 8,000—5,000 years ago was the warmest period since the Ice Age and rare deciduous trees spread north of their present distribution areas. About 5,000 years ago the climate began to cool and fir began to spread into Finland from the east. About 3,000 years ago it was a common type of tree in Southern Finland. By about 2,000 years ago it had spread to the area in which it is now found. Fir took living space from rare deciduous trees, especially. The spread of fir was the last major change in the development of Finnish vegetation during the prehistoric era.

Finnland erhält seine Pflanzendecke

Vor etwa 9000 Jahren befreite Finnland sich von seiner Eisdecke. Sofort begann Vegetation sich über die trockenen Gebiete auszubreiten. Die ersten Eroberer des blossgelegten Landes waren krautstengelige Pflanzen. Am häufigsten waren Gräser und Ried sowie mit dem Gemeinen Beifuss verwandte Arten. Diesen "Pionierarten" folgte die Birke. Die Gebiete tundraähnlicher Vegetation und der Birkenwälder folgten in breiten Gürteln dem Rande des zurückweichenden Inlandeises. Nach der Birke hielt die Kiefer Einzug. Über Südfinnland verbreitete sie sich vor 9000 Jahren. Die Kiefer verdrängte weitgehend die Birke und wurde zur dominierenden Baumart. Das Klima war zu jener Zeit relativ warm und offenbar recht trocken.

Vor rund 8000 Jahren wurde das Klima wärmer und die Luftfeuchtigkeit nahm zu. Damals breitete sich die Rot-Erle in Südfinnland aus. Der wärmste Zeitabschnitt der nacheiszeitlichen Geschichte datiert um 8000 bis 5000 Jahre zurück. Zu jenen Zeiten kamen viele edle Laubhölzer über ihre heutigen Verbreitungsgrenzen hinaus nach Finnland. Vor etwa 5000 Jahren begann das Klima sich abzukühlen. Gleichzeitig breitete sich auch die Fichte von Osten nach Finnland aus. Vor 3000 Jahren hatte sie in Südfinnland schon weitgehend Wurzel gefasst. Zu Beginn unserer Zeitrechnung erreichte sie ihre heutige Ausbreitung. Die Fichte beraubte vor allem die edlen Laubhölzer ihres Lebensraums. Die Ausbreitung der Fichte war die letzte grosse Umwälzung in der vorgeschichtlichen Vegetationsentwicklung Finnlands.

The Return of the Fauna

16 The development of Finland's fauna is not known so exactly as that of her flora. The history of the forests can be explained with the aid of pollen analysis, but in studying the fauna's development one has to rely on casual finds. Recognisable bones of vertebrates and remains of invertebrates, e.g. wings of coleopters, have been preserved in peat strata. Shells of ancient molluscs and bivalves can be found in places by the sea.

The Finnish soil is so acidic that bones buried in it dissolve in a couple of centuries. Only in some special cases can bones thousands of years old be preserved. Important information has been obtained from the middens of stone-age dwellings, where the cooked bones of game animals have survived.

The bones of the following mammals have been found near dwelling places 6,000—8,500 years old: ringed seals, beavers, elk, wild forest reindeer, bears, foxes and dogs. The bones of swans, red-throated loons, dabchicks, ducks and heath grouse have also been identified. The fishbones found include those of perch, pike, pike-perch, bream and roach. Thus all these stone-age people cooked their food. Quite a lot of seal bones have been found, indicating that they have been in the Baltic for a very long time. Many relicts, i.e. species of fauna that were left in isolation outside their actual distribution area, also inform us about the fauna's development. These include the Saimaa ringed seal and a species of bullhead or sculpin known as the four-horned cottus.

Die Tiere kehren zurück

Die Entwicklung der finnischen Fauna ist nicht so gut bekannt wie die der Flora. Die Geschichte des Waldes kann mittels der Pollenanalyse erhellt werden, aber beim Zurückverfolgen der zoologischen Entwicklung ist man auf zufällige Funde angewiesen. Von Wirbeltieren sind identifizierbare Knochen erhalten geblieben, von Weichtieren unter anderem im Moor konservierte Insektenflügel. Am Rande von Mooren kann man die Schalen vorzeitlicher Muscheln und Schnecken finden.

Der finnische Boden ist derart säurehaltig, dass die in ihm begrabenen Knochen gewöhnlich innerhalb weniger hundert Jahre zerfallen. Nur in einigen Ausnahmefällen konnten Jahrtausende alte Knochen dem Zahn der Zeit widerstehen.

Nahe den etwa 8500 bis 6000 Jahre alten Wohnplätzen hat man die Knochen folgender Wirbeltiere gefunden: Robbe, Biber, Elch, Wildren, Bär, Fuchs und Hund. Aufgrund der Vogelknochen konnten Schwan, Sterntaucher, Haubentaucher, Ente und Birkhuhn identifiziert werden. Die gefundenen Fischgräten stammen von Barsch, Hecht, Zander, Brachse und Plötze. All diese Tieren haben also den Steinzeitmenschen als Nahrung gedient. Man hat sehr viele Robbenknochen gefunden, ein Beweis dafür, dass die Robbe schon vor langer Zeit in der Ostsee weit verbreitet war.

Von der Entwicklung der Tierwelt erzählen viele Relikttiere, die ausserhalb ihres eigentlichen Verbreitungsgebiets isoliert vorkommen, so die Saimaa-Ringelrobbe und der Vierhörnige Seeskorpion.

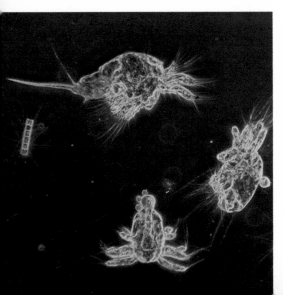

Man Settles Finland

Finland's first postglacial inhabitants arrived about 10,000 years ago. They had a neolithic culture and formed small hunting communities. Throughout the Stone and Bronze Ages the population was small and the source of livelihood was hunting and fishing, ultimately also small-scale cattle raising. The early hunter adapted to nature and preserved the landscape unchanged. His activities were determined by the annual rhythm of land and water animals, the salmon's upstream migration, the whitefish's mating period, the seal's littering and the migration of elk and deer.

The Iron-age agricultural population first established a bridgehead in South-Western Finland from where settlements spread into parts of Häme and Southern Savo. Another dwelling settlement was in Karelia, mainly east of the present border of Finland and the third was in Southern Ostrobothnia. The coastal area in the province of Uusimaa was populated by Swedish-speaking settlers in the Middle Ages. North of the agricultural settlements lived the Lapps.

Using slash-and-burn agricultural methods, people from Savo settled major parts of central Finland, Northern Savo, central Ostrobothnia, Kainuu and Northern Karelia during the 16th and 17th centuries and they also settled in Southern Karelia.

The prosperity of the farming population increased considerably during the 19th century. It was then that the handsome rural houses that dot the landscape were built.

Der Mensch kommt nach Finnland

Die ersten nacheiszeitlichen Menschen kamen vor rund 10 000 Jahren nach Finnland. Damals begannen zur frühsteinzeitlichen Kultur gehörende kleine Jägergemeinschaften das Land zu besiedeln. Die ganze Stein- und Bronzezeit über siedelten nur wenige Menschen in Finnland, die sich von Jagd und Fischfang, später auch von Viehzucht kleineren Umfangs ernährten. Das Verschmelzen mit der Natur und ihre Erhaltung im Urzustand charakterisierten das Leben des Wildnisbewohners. Er war ein Nomade, dessen Wanderung sich nach dem Lebensrhythmus der zu Wasser und zu Lande lebenden Tiere richtete. Diesen Rhythmus bestimmten die Lachswanderung, das Laichen der Renke, das Kalben der Robbe und das Wandern des Elchs und des Wildrentiers.

Brückenkopf der eisenzeitlichen Agrarkultur was Südwestfinnland, von wo sie sich nach Häme und Süd-Savo ausdehnte. Ein weiteres Zentrum der Agrarbesiedlung befand sich in Karelien jenseits der heutigen Landesgrenze und ein drittes in Süd-Österbotten. Im Mittelalter liess sich an der Küste von Uusimaa schwedischsprachige Bevölkerung nieder. Nördlich der Agrarbesiedlung lebten die Samen.

Indem sie durch Brandrodung neues Land urbar machte, besiedelte im 16. und 17. Jahrhundert eine savo-stämmige Bevölkerung grosse Teile Mittelfinnlands, Nord-Savos, Mittel-Österbottens, Kainuus und Nordkareliens. Im 19. Jahrhundert wurde die Bauernbevölkerung zunehmend wohlhabender. Damals entstanden die prächtigen Landhaustypen, die sich äusserlich so gut der finnischen Landschaft anpassen.

The Finnish Archipelago

Schären-Finnland

My Archipelago   by/von Bo Carpelan

My archipelago is a summer place. It has bays, lush islands, thorough-fares through the sea rushes, smells of clay and sunshade. I'm a stranger in this world, like most of those who slice through the narrow sounds in their fast motorboats, or leave their cars atop hills between pine trees to seek their way to their summer homes, shoreside saunas, to their strip of shore, perhaps where a bulldozer has ploughed a path towards the glittering water and the freedom of the summer. My own experience of the intermediate and outer archipelagoes is casual: mo-mentary flashes, marginal notes. What would I know of the hard life once the rule in these waters, but I can well remember the abundance of fish in the 30s...

During the years of my boyhood I contemplated completely different scenery. Peace reigned here. Narrow paths twisted among the rocks, picnic baskets were carried to desolate shores and children punted themselves on ice floes to quietly waiting uninhabited islands. There it was: adventure, a wonderful picture of the archipelago, an uninhabited island. There is a little bit of Robinson Crusoe in all of us. Those thousands of islands, foci of the longing for freedom which we delicately keep secret, the most hidden of our desires in a world of banal char-acteristics. If only one could conquer a whole island by oneself: does not this childhood dream live in all those who each summer Friday join endless queues to seek the glittering water, the tranquilly reflected moment of evening, at least one sheltered interlude in one's hard every-day life...

The archipelago: a great, free system of movement and co-operation, contrasts and solitude to suit everybody's character. An angler tranquilly waiting by a shallow bay, the quick movements of a fisherman casting his spinner at the end of a promontory, the heavy nets of the professional rising close to the horizon. Later in the evening, warming light through the windows; filtering through bushes and trees standing fragrant and bleached by the dusk after the bright, hot day...

The fragrance of sun-warmed rock, the fragrance of skin. The smell of the salt from the sea, the fragrance of the heat waves from the sound, the fragrance of the grass's verdure: this is how you want it to be. But summer is treacherous, and particularly so close to the sea, where chilly winds, grey expanses of open water, deciduous trees teased by the wind and pale summer visitors behind rain-striped windows are the other side of the gleaming summer coin. The smell of smoke leaking in from the fireplace; or, stink rather... The smell of dampness.

Where would the delightful mental image of Ilmarinen's masterpiece, the vault of heaven described in the Kalevala as the place where "Yet we find no trace of hammer, Nor the trace of tongs discover," be more di-rectly realized than at the moment of dawn on a clear archipelago morning, when space is so bright that it draws the one resting on the shore upwards, into the bottomless gulf of space? One stands up and feels dizzy...

The morning mist rises from the water and drifts along the dark edge of the forest. Its undulating veils obscure the limits between sky and water, sea and land. A beautiful, enchanting, listening moment. You row through the mist, letting the oars rest, you glide into the unknown. Nobody can see you. You are happily forgotten...

LANDING FORBIDDEN, and somebody has scribbled a continua-tion: AN UGLY VILLA ON A SPOILT PIECE OF LAND...

Finding one's way from the inner coves to the outer archipelago is a gradual process of unloading oneself of burdens and selfishness; step by step, one is freed from oneself and lets one's eyes be cleansed of what has clung to them, of endless details. The sea and the sky: who wouldn't dream of such solitude as when the summer mist has gone — and how many achieve and bear it? We live in a thicket which is the perspective from which we view our lives; it protects us from all that is great, simple and lonely...

The young people leave the old people alone and move from the

loneliness of the archipelago to the city, to an even more severe lone-liness, to the loneliness of the dormitory suburbs, asphalt and masses of people. The islands are abandoned. The cottages stand empty and slowly decay. The children of the city, in turn, move to the archipelago and bless it with all their modern tricks and equipment: a glass house on top of a rock, cars in lines among the pines, fast motorboats, tape recorders, radios, fridges, grills, waterskis, coca cola and plastic. Exhaust fumes shimmer like thin chiffon above the cars queuing for the ferries. Mini motorbikes buzz angrily along paths where nobody even dreamt of driving before and in the bays plant exuberance gradually fills the waters with a choking growth. The Swedish of the natives is mixed with the Finnish of the newcomers. On the main island, the chimneys of factories and power plants rise behind the skerries. Like a grotesque, gigantic house, an iceberg filled with junk, a caricature of a ship, some "Finnjet" vessel glides along its course, and the islands seem to make room for it and slowly draw aside. On a bare crag, a cubicle made of glass and metal tries to keep in balance — an aquarium to hold strange fish, which now abound in the outer archipelago as well. Bearded long-distance sailors eagerly snap pictures of an old fisherman standing in front of his boathouse. The rich life of summer in the archipelago! Nature undergoing a process of change...

The wind may blow long and without pause, persistently and treacher-ously, or, in the outer archipelago, openly with an endless thundering. The autumn rains have come to stay and the wind blows inexhaustibly from North to South. Everything begins to get ready for the bleakness of the coming winter...

When the summer mist has gone, bright days begin, with rain washing the rocks and light quickly penetrating through and being reflected from the empty open waters. And on the grey days the few and faint noises sound soft and distant: the call of a sea bird and the chugging of a fishing boat. The shores are empty. One stands by oneself and sees everything that is familiar and odd in a strange light. Was it here that summer and I paid a brief visit such a short time ago?

Snow billows over the black waters and blankets the crags in white. Bare rocks and boulders, which still hold some of the warmth of the setting sun, are left bare. Gingerly the trees accept their snowy burden. As evening draws in the wind rises and the snow races. Black silhouettes, the black archipelago...

Winter storms, endless wandering on the ice, weeks of complete isolation while the ice is growing strong and again melting away, waiting, reports of missing persons, drownings. A grey, lonely, hard life, nothing but fishing, scarcity and the four elements. A foot that froze fast in a boot during a night of fishing, but was nevertheless saved. Some old people still cling tooth and nail to their homesteads, their home turf, or at least they return from the old folk's home on the main island when early summer brings its abundance of light. And the waves murmur with the voices of all those who lived their lives out here in the open and gave their lives, were shipwrecked, disappeared from the world of which the summer visitor glimpses but a fraction in passing: he's a stranger no matter how hard he tries to take root...

Meine Schärenwelt

Meine Schärenwelt ist die sommerliche Schärenwelt mit ihren Buchten, laubbewachsenen Inseln, Strassen inmitten von Schilfdickichten, dem Duft von Lehm und Sonnenschatten. Ich bin Gast in dieser Welt, wie die meisten derjenigen, die mit ihren schnellen Motorbooten durch die Sunde rasen oder ihre Autos zwischen Kiefern auf einem Hügel parken, um ihre Sommergrundstücke, Strandsaunas, Uferstreifen aufzusuchen, wo vielleicht ein Bagger einen Weg freigeräumt hat, hin zum glitzernden Wasser und zur Freiheit des Sommers. Meine Erfahrungen mit den Mittel- und Aussenschären sind eher zufälliger Natur: augenblickliche Eindrücke, Randnotizen. Was könnte ich schon vom harten Leben wissen, das einst Alltag in diesen Gewässern war, aber zumindest kann ich mich an den Fischreichtum der dreissiger Jahre erinnern.

Damals, in meiner Kindheit, lag vor mir eine völlig andere Landschaft. In ihr war die Ruhe zu Hause. Schmale Pfade schlängelten sich die Ufer entlang, Picknickkörbe wurden zu den einsamen Stränden mitgeschleppt, und auf schwankenden Eisschollen stakten sich die Kinder zu unbewohnten Schären, die schweigend warteten. Dort war es: das Abenteuer, ein herrliches Bild von der Schärenwelt, eine unbewohnte Insel. Ein bisschen Robinson Crusoe lebt in uns allen. Diese Abertausenden von Inseln: Fixpunkte unserer geheimen Hoffnungen, unserer versteckten Freiheitssehnsüchte in dieser Welt trivialer Eigenschaften. Allein eine ganze Insel erobern: lebt etwa dieser Kindheitstraum nicht in all jenen fort, die an jedem Sommerfreitag in endlosen Autokarawanen dem glitzernden Meer, den Spiegelungen eines stillen Sommerabends, wenigstens für einen Augenblick der Geborgenheit vor dem harten Alltag zustreben...

Die Schärenwelt: ein grosses freies System der Bewegung und des Zusammenspiels, der Kontraste und der jedem Charakter etwas bietenden Stille: das harmonische Ausharren des Anglers in einer seichten Bucht, die schnellen Bewegungen des Spinnfischers auf der felsigen Landspitze, das mühsame Netzeinholen der Schärenfischer unter dem Horizont. Später am Abend wärmendes Licht durch die Fenster, gesiebt von den Bäumen und Büschen, die nach einem blendenden, heissen Tag vom Dämmerlicht beleuchtet duftend vor dem Haus stehen...

Der Duft sonnenwarmer Klippen — der Duft der Haut. Der salzige Duft des Meeres, der Duft der Hitzewelle aus dem Sund, der Duft üppigen Grüns: so wünscht man es sich. Aber der Sommer ist trügerisch, und dies gilt besonders für die Meeresnähe, wo kalte Lüfte, graues Meer, vom Winde geplagte Laubbäume und bleiche Sommergäste hinter regenbespritzten Fensterscheiben die Kehrseite der glänzenden Medaille sind. Der Duft — oder vielmehr der Gestank — des Rauches, der einem aus dem qualmenden Kamin entgegenschlägt. Der Duft der Feuchtigkeit...

Wo könnte einem das im Kalevala beschriebene bezaubernde Gedankenbild von Ilmarinens Meisterwerk, der Lüfte Dach — "Nirgends sieht man Hammerspuren, nirgends eine Spur der Zange" —, spontaner einfallen als im Augenblick des Tagesanbruchs an einem hellen Schärenmorgen, wenn die Tiefe des Raums so klar ist, dass sie den am Strand Ruhenden aufwärts zum bodenlosen Himmelsmeer zieht. Du setzt dich auf und dir ist schwindelig...

Der Morgennebel steigt aus dem Meer und treibt die dunklen Waldränder entlang. Seine wabenden Schleier verwischen die Grenze zwischen Wasser und Himmel, zwischen Land und Meer. Ein schöner, betörender, lauschender Augenblick. Du ruderst im Nebel, lässt die Riemen ruhen, treibst irgendwohin ins Unbekannte. Niemand sieht dich. Du bist glücklich vergessen...

ANLANDGEHEN VERBOTEN. Und jemand hat daruntergeschrieben: HÄSSLICHE VILLA AUF VERDORBENEM STÜCK LAND...

Sich von den inneren Buchten den äusseren Schären zu nähern heisst, dass man sich Meter für Meter von einem Ballast und seiner Selbstsicherheit befreit, dass man sich Meter für Meter seiner selbst entledigt

und seine Augen von allem Hängengebliebenen, von den endlosen Details reinspült. Das Meer und der Himmel: wer träumt nicht von einer solchen Einsamkeit — und wie viele erreichen und ertragen sie? Wir leben in einem Dickicht, und das Dickicht ist unsere Lebensperspektive, es schützt uns vor allem Grossen, Einfachen und Einsamen...

Die Jungen lassen die Alten allein und ziehen aus der Einsamkeit der Schären in die Stadt, in eine noch strengere Einsamkeit, die Einsamkeit der Schlafstädte, des Asphalts, der Menschenmassen. Die Schären veröden, die Katen stehen leer und verfallen allmählich. Die Kinder der Städte wiederum ziehen in die Schärenwelt und segnen diese mit allen neuzeitlichen Finessen und Schikanen: Glashäuser auf Felskuppen, unter den Kiefern Auto an Auto, schnelle Motorboote, Kassettenrecorder, Radios, Kühlschränke, Grills, Wasserskier, Coke und Plastik. Wie ein dünner Schleier schweben die Abgaswolken über den Autos, die vor den Schärenfähren anstehen. Minimotorräder knattern böse über Pfade, auf denen zu fahren früher niemandem im Traum eingefallen wäre, und in den Buchten wächst das Wasser mit wuchernden Pflanzen allmählich dicht. Das Schwedisch der Ureinwohner vermischt sich mit dem Finnisch der Zugezogenen. Hinter den Inseln auf dem Festland ragen die Schornsteine der Kraftwerke und Fabriken auf. Wie ein groteskes Riesenhaus, ein mit Schrott gefüllter Eisberg, wie die Karikatur eines Schiffes rauscht irgendeine Finnjet in ihrer Fahrrinne vorbei, und die entgegenkommenden Inseln scheinen sich zurückzuziehen und langsam vorbeizugleiten. Auf einer kahlen Klippe balanciert ein Würfel aus Metall und Glas — ein Aquarium für neue, fremdartige Fische, die jetzt auch in den Aussenschären so zahlreich aufgetaucht sind. Ein alter Fischer vor seinem Bootsschuppen wird eifrig von bärtigen Freizeitseglern fotografiert. Das reiche Sommerleben der Schären! Die Natur in der Veränderung begriffen...

Manchmal bläst der Wind lange und ununterbrochen, zäh und hinterlistig, oder aber in den Aussenschären offen und ewig donnernd. Die Herbstregen sind gekommen, um zu bleiben, und der Wind weht unaufhörlich von Norden nach Süden. Die Natur bereitet sich auf die Dürftigkeit des kommenden Winters vor...

Wenn der Sommernebel gegangen ist, beginnen die klaren Tage, an denen der Wind die Felsen reinwäscht und das Licht schnell die Sphäre durchdringt und von der leeren, offenen See reflektiert wird. Und an grauen Tagen klingen die wenigen und geringen Geräusche — der Schrei eines Meeresvogels, das Tuckern eines Fischerkahns — weich, von weit herkommend. Die Ufer sind wie leergefegt. Du stehst allein und empfindest alles Vertraute als seltsam und fremd. War es hier, wo der Sommer und du eben noch zu Gast gewesen seid?

Schnee legt sich über das schwarze Wasser und kleidet die Klippen weiss ein. Ausgespart bleiben nur blanke Felsen und Blöcke, die noch einen Teil der Wärme der sinkenden Sonne speichern. Zögernd nehmen die Bäume die Last des Schnees auf sich. Gegend Abend kommt Wind auf und es beginnt zu schneien. Schwarze Schattenbilder, schwarze Schärenwelt...

Winterstürme, endlose Eiswanderungen, währen das Eis wächst und wieder schmilzt, Wochen totaler Isolation, Warten, Nachrichten über Verschollene, Ertrunkene. Ein graues, einsames, rauhes Leben, nur Fischen, die Notwendigkeiten des Lebens und die vier Elemente. Ein Fuss, der beim nächtlichen Fischen im Stiefel festgefroren war und dennoch gerettet werden konnte. Einige Alte klammern sich mit Händen und Füssen an ihr angestammtes Heim, ihre Scholle, oder zumindest zieht es sie aus ihren Altenheimen auf dem Festland zurück, wenn der Sommer und mit ihm die Lichtfülle beginnt. Und, im Brausen der Wellen, die Stimmen all jener, die hier draussen ihr Leben gelebt und gelassen, die hier Schiffbruch gelitten haben, hier verschwunden sind aus einer Welt, von welcher der Sommergast nur einen flüchtigen Blick erhascht; er ist ein Fremder, wie sehr er sich auch bemüht, Wurzel zu fassen...

The Archipelago
Die Inseln

The Finnish Archipelago was formed in the course of millions of years of geological developments. The earth's crust moved and shifted, mountain tops rose above sea level and were exposed to the fury of the waves and changing weathers. The most recent major change occurred during the Ice Age. The Pleisto-cene ice sheet acted like a file, levelling out heights and transferring loose elements. The archipelago's image is still changing as new reefs emerge from the sea.

Three zones can be distinguished in the archipelago: the outer, intermediate and inner zones. A journey from the open sea is like a journey through thousands of years. The inner archipelago is the present while the outer zone reveals what the inner was like thousands of years ago when the islands had just emerged from the sea. As one passes through the zones of the archipelago, the open sea gradually makes the transition into a continent.

Finnlands südwestliche Inselwelt ist ein einzigartiger Archipel mit Tausenden von Schären. Aus der Luft präsentiert sich dieses Gebiet als gewaltiges Labyrinth.

Die Inselwelt hat ihre heutige Gestalt als Ergebnis eines Jahrmillionen dauernden geologischen Entwicklungsprozesses angenommen. Die Erdrinde hat sich bewegt und verändert. Berggipfel sind aus dem Meer gestiegen, wurden den Wellen und dem Witterungswechsel ausgesetzt und erhielten durch die Eiszeit ihren letzten grossen Schliff. Das Inlandeis hat die Höhenunterschiede nivelliert und lose Materie verschoben. Indem das Meer neue Klippen freigibt, ändert sich das Archipel auch heute noch unaufhörlich.

In der Schärenwelt kann man drei Gürtel unterscheiden: die Aussen-, die Mittel- und die Innenschären. Eine Fahrt durch die Schären ist wie eine Reise durch die Jahrtausende: Die Innenschären repräsentieren die Gegenwart, die Aussenschären wiederum zeigen, wie die Innenschären vor Tausenden von Jahren, als sie gerade dem Meer entstiegen waren, ausgesehen haben. Mit den Schärengürteln geht das offene Meer stufenweise zum Festland über.

2

The southwestern archipelago is fragmented. The islands lie in parallel lines, which are even noticeable in places on the map shown below. In the outer zone vegetation is found only in some sheltered hollows (3). There are forests in the intermediate zone (2) and the inner zone is rich in farmlands and lush shores (1).

Die Schärenwelt ist zersplittert. Auf der Karte kann man erkennen, wie die Schären stellenweise parallel verlaufende Ketten bilden. In den Aussenschären sieht man Vegetation nur als kleine Flecken in Mulden (3). In den Mittelschären wächst Wald (2), und in den Innenschären findet man ausgedehnte Ackerflächen und verlandende Strände (1).

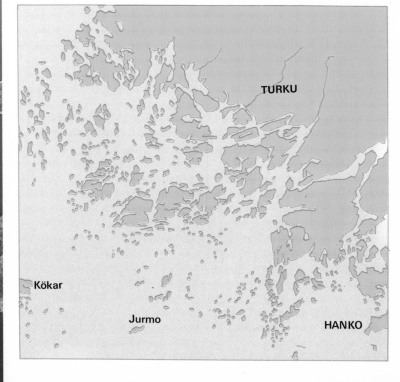

The Baltic Sea

The Baltic is an inland sea bounded by seven states. Its bays, the Gulf of Finland and the Gulf of Bothnia, reach far into northern Europe. Only beyond the outermost skerries do the waters of the Baltic open up. The sea is connected with the ocean by the narrow and shallow straits of Denmark. The rivers bring plenty of fresh water and since the Danish straits prevent the free influx of oceanic waters, the salt content of the Baltic is considerably lower than in the oceans. In the Gulfs of Finland and Bothnia the salinity drops close to zero.

The deepest point in the Baltic (459 m) is near Gotland. In Finnish waters, the deepest point is in the Åland Sea (285 m). The Gulf of Finland is a direct continuation of the Baltic, but the Gulf of Bothnia is more separated.

Both marine and freshwater flora and fauna flourish in the Baltic. Only during the most severe winters does it freeze completely, but most of Finland's coastal waters are covered with thick ice in winter.

The ecology of the Baltic is very delicate. Its low-oxygen deep layers do not mix with the surface layers, leading on occasion to severe oxygen deficiency in the deepest layers. Many toxic substances are also discharged into the sea.

Die Ostsee

Die Ostsee ist ein von sieben Anrainerstaaten umgebenes Binnenmeer, dessen grosse Buchten, der Finnische und der Bottnische Meerbusen, bis weit nach Nordeuropa vordringen. Erst südlich der südwestfinnischen Schärenwelt beginnt das offene Meer. Mit der Nordsee ist die Ostsee nur durch die schmalen und flachen dänischen Belte verbunden. Flüsse speisen die Ostsee mit Süsswasser, und da die Belte den freien Zutritt des Nordseewassers in die Ostsee behindern, ist der Salzgehalt der Ostsee überall geringer als in der Nordsee. Im Innersten des Finnischen und des Bottnischen Meerbusens nähert der Salzgehalt des Wassers sich dem Nullwert.

Die tiefste Stelle der Ostsee (459 m) liegt in der Nähe von Gotland, die grösste Tiefe des finnischen Ostseegebiets (285 m) im Schärenmeer. Der Finnische Meerbusen ist ein direkter Ausläufer der Ostsee, der nach Osten hin abflacht. Der Bottnische Meerbusen ist nicht mehr so direkt mit der restlichen Ostsee verbunden.

Die Ostsee ist ekologisch sehr anfällig, da ihre sauerstoffarmen Unterschichten sich nicht mit dem Oberflächenwasser vermischen. Die Folge kann ein Sauerstoffverlust in den tieferen Schichten sein. Zusätzlich werden von der industrie viele giftige Stoffe in die Ostsee abgelassen.

The Outermost Skerries

Die Aussenschären

The rugged outer archipelago is embraced by the open sea. Most of its islands are small treeless rocks. The sea dominates the scenery. The shores of the nearly bare islands are steep: smooth-worn rocks seem to glide into the depths of the sea. The islands are low, geologically only recently emerged from the deep. Some of the skerries are still struggling with the sea for their existence. Trees haven't had a chance to take root in the outer archipelago, and isolated bushes crouch in sheltered hollows. Sparse flora has found its way into cracks in the rocks and between stones where just enough loose soil has gathered.

The fauna is also distinctive. In summer the birds are the most noticeable. Even small skerries, provide homes for hundreds of pairs of birds: seagulls, terns, waders, ducks and razorbills.

The scenery of the outer archipelago is open and light. The seasonal changes of nature are emphasized by its lighting and the caprices of the weather.

Mitten im offenen Meer liegen die Aussenschären, zumeist kleine baumlose Klippen. In dieser Landschaft dominiert das Meer, hier gibt es mehr Wasser als Land. Die Ufer dieser fast vegetationslosen Schären sind steil, die blanken Felsen gehen fliessend ins Meer über.

Die Aussenschären sind hauptsächlich flache, nach geologischer Zeitrechnung erst kürzlich dem Meer entstiegene Felsen. Einige Klippen müssen noch immer gegen das Meer um ihre Existenz

kämpfen. Bäume haben in den Aussenschären noch nicht Wurzel fassen können, und nur vereinzelt wachsen Sträucher geduckt an geschützten Stellen. In Felsspalten und zwischen den Steinen hat sich gerade soviel Erde angesammelt, dass hier eine kärgliche Vegetation sesshaft werden konnte.

Auch die Tierwelt ist eigentümlich. Im Sommer fallen vor allem die Vögel ins Auge. Auch auf kleinen Klippen nisten oft Hunderte von Vögeln, so Möwen, Seeschwalben, Enten und Alke.

Dwarf cornel grows both in the archipelago and on Lapland's arctic fells (1). Razorbills and guillemot nest in communities on the rugged skerries of the outer archipelago (2). One can see seals sunbathing on the outer reefs (3 and 4).

Der Schwedische Hartlieger wächst sowohl in den Aussenschären wie auch in Lapplands Fjällandschaft. (1) Auf den kargen Klippen des äusseren Schärengürtels nisten Alk- und Stechentenkolonien. (2). Auf den glatten Aussenklippen sonnen sich oft Seehunde (3 und 4).

The World of the Eider   Das Reich der Eiderente

In the simple landscape of the marine archipelago individual species of birds and plants are more distinct as significant scenic factors than in the lush inland areas. In the summer of the archipelago, seagulls, terns, waders, guillemots, mergansers and eiders are just as essential a part of the scenery as rocks, scrub juniper, ponds or the sea surface.

The brackish basin of the Baltic is an interesting cross between a salty ocean and a freshwater lake. It is the low salinity of the Baltic that makes the marine biology of Finland's sea areas a mixture of oceanic and lake plankton.

Many typical sea birds thrive in the Baltic: razorbills and eider. Inland water birds also nest in Finland's marine archipelago. Both oceanic and freshwater fish are found in Finland's coastal waters. The same applies to the flora.

In der schlichten Natur der Aussenschären fallen die vereinzelt vorkommenden Vogel- und Pflanzenarten viel deutlicher als im üppigen Binnenland als landschaftlich prägnante Faktoren ins Auge. Im Sommer sind die Möwen, Seeschwalben, Stechenten, Sägetaucher und Eiderenten ebenso wichtige Landschaftselemente wie Felsen, Wacholdersträucher, Teiche oder auch das Meer selbst.

Das Brackwasser der Ostsee ist eine interessante Zwischenform von Ozean und Binnensee. Wegen ihres geringen Salzgehaltes ist das Plankton der finnischen Küstengewässer eine Mischung aus Binnensee- und Ozeanplankton. An der Ostsee sind viele typische Ozeanvögel heimisch, so Alk und Eiderente. Ebenso nisten auch Binnenseevögel in den Schären. In den finnischen Küstengewässern leben sowohl Salz- wie auch Süsswasserfische und -pflanzen.

Juniper bushes offer excellent protection for nesting waterbirds. A hatching hen eider blends perfectly into her surroundings.

Wacholderpolster bilden hervorragende Nistplätze für die Wasservögel. Die brütende Eiderente verschmilzt praktisch mit ihrer Umgebung.

The Island World

Three different zones can be distinguished in many of the sea areas off Finland's coast: outer, intermediate and inner archipelago. In the southwestern archipelago, the distinction between these three zones is not everywhere so clear, since there is a belt of open water between the outer and intermediate islands. In the area between the outer skerries and the lush inner islands there are groups of many islands separated by wide belts of open water which can have their own small-scale zones.

Rocky shores are the most typical in the archipelago, but where many islands group together even grassy shores or stone and sand shores can be found in sheltered spots. The highest islands in these individual groups rose from the sea so long ago that forests have had time to become established on them.

Here, in the open water zone of the southwestern archipelago,

a most distinctive island culture has developed. The groups of islands isolated by windblown waters used to be small worlds of their own and the people living on them seldom met. The holiday boater was an unknown concept while the pastor might pay a visit once a year. The island culture is rapidly disappearing. Fishing villages are changing into summer resorts and the youth have fled to the towns. Year round habitation will end with the last old people. What remain, fortunately are the stories of the lives and livelihood of people at the mercy of the sea on Vänö, Berghamn, Nötö, Björkö, Jurmo and hundreds of other islands. Descriptions of the earlier life in the archipelago are like exciting adventure stories to modern people.

Although the traditional island life is disappearing, idyllic villages with their buildings and harbours are still part of the archipelago scenery. Hard natural conditions, winds, rough seas, the power of the ice and the scarceness of arable land due to unevenness in the bedrock have dictated the places for buildings and harbours. Thus the old island architecture is in harmony with nature.

The harbour in Nagu on the island of Nötö represents island culture at its most beautiful (1). The southwestern archipelago is very rugged in places. Rocks rise from the sea as steep walls (2). The majestic sea eagle has rapidly become rare (3).

Schärenkultur: Hafen der Insel Nötö in der Gemeinde Nagu (1). Die Schärenwelt ist stellenweise sehr bergig. Wie Wände ragen die Felsen steil aus dem Meer auf (2). Der König der Schärenvögel, der Seeadler, ist selten geworden (3).

hat sich die eigentümlichste Insulanerkultur herausgebildet. Die durch stürmische Seenflächen voneinander getrennten Schärengruppen waren einst eigene kleine Welten, deren Bewohner einander nur selten trafen. Sommerliche Bootsausflügler kannte man damals noch nicht, der Pastor kam vielleicht einmal im Jahr.

Die Insulanerkultur ist schnell am Absterben. Die Fischerdörfer werden zu Sommerfrischen, die Jugend ist in die Städte abgewandert, die ganzjährige Besiedlung endet mit den letzten Alten. Zurück bleiben wenigstens die Geschichten über das Leben der den Launen des Meeres ausgelieferten Insulaner.

Obwohl das traditionelle Schärenleben schon bald Vergangenheit ist, gehören die idyllischen Dörfer, ihre Häuser und Höfe noch immer zur Landschaft des Schärenmeers. Die strengen Witterungsverhältnisse, die Stürme, der Seegang, die Macht des Eises und der durch die Unebenheit des Felsgrunds verursachte Mangel an anbaugeeignetem Land haben die Lage von Häusern und Höfen diktiert. Daher befindet sich die alte Schärenbauweise in harmonischer Übereinstimmung mit der Natur.

Das Schärenmeer

Vielerorts in den finnischen Küstengewässern kann man drei Gürtel unterscheiden: die Aussen-, die Mittel- und die Innenschären. Im Südwestarchipel ist diese Gürteleinteilung nicht überall so deutlich dreistufig: gleichsam eine Kombination von Aussen- und Mittelschären ist der Seenflächen-Schärengürtel. In diesem Gebiet zwischen den äussersten Klippen und den üppigen Innenschären sind grosse offene Seenflächen von teilweise dichten Schärengruppen eingerahmt, welche manchmal in sich eine eigene Gürteleinteilung erkennen lassen.

Für das Schärenmeer sind Felsufer typisch, aber wo Schäre an Schäre liegt, findet man an geschützten Stellen sogar Uferwiesen und hier und da Schotter- und Sandstrand. Die höchsten Inseln dieser separaten Schärengruppen sind vor so langer Zeit dem Meer entstiegen, dass auf ihnen Wälder Wurzel fassen konnten.

Im Seenflächen-Schärengürtel

The Lush Inner Islands

Die üppigen Innenschären

The Inner Zone is geologically the oldest part of the archipelago. The land is still rising and the innermost islands are gradually becoming a part of the mainland. The high rocks jutting out of arable land in South-West Finland were relatively recently islands and the present sea bottom will be arable land one day.

In the Inner Archipelago, land covers a greater part of the total area than water. There are narrow passages and sheltered bays between the islands. The few areas of open water resemble lakes more than sea. Rocks no longer dominate the shoreline and low meadow shores are a distinctive feature of the scenery.

The sea is nearly saltless in the Inner Archipelago and has been made turbid by the clay brought by small rivers draining the agricultural regions. The flora also reflects the lake-like topography and the low salinity of the sea. Dense stands of common reed stretch for kilometres. Such shallow sea bays are home to a rich variety of birds, thousands of which rest in them during their migrations.

In many places, common reed extends to the forest line, but on pastured shores a strip of meadow intervenes. Common alder grows in large and dense shore woods. In the inner parts of the archipelago, deciduous trees like those in the Åland Islands can be found.

The Inner Archipelago has been most changed by man, since communications are satisfactory, the land is good for cultivation, big islands give shelter from the sea winds, it is easy to build on low land, and dense forests provide abundant wood.

The Inner Archipelago is also the most affected by recreation, but is better able to cope with its impact than the rugged and highly vulnerable outer zone.

Die Innenschären sind der geologisch älteste Teil des Archipels, das zuerst dem Meer entstiegene Gebiet. Auch an hohen Felsen kann man oft noch erkennen, wo die Brandung einst an den vorzeitlichen Ufern genagt hat. Das Land hebt sich auch weiterhin, und die innersten Schären werden allmählich zu Festlandküste. Auch die hohen Felsen der südwestfinnischen Anbaugebiete waren einst Schären: zuerst kleine Aussenklippen, dann Mittelschären und zuletzt Innenschären. Der Meeresboden von heute ist das Anbauland von morgen.

In den Innenschären ist der Flächenanteil des Landes viel grösser als der des Wassers. Zwischen den Schären sind schmale Sunde und geschützte Buchten verblieben. Einige grössere Seenflächen erinnern eher an Binnenseen als an das Meer. Felsen sind nicht mehr dominierend; flache Wiesenufer prägen die Landschaft.

Das Meer der Innenschären ist fast salzfrei und vom Lehm, den die durch Ackerländer fliessenden Flüsse anlanden, getrübt. Die binnenseeartige Landschaft und die Salzarmut des Wassers zeigen sich auch in der Vegetation. Binnenseeschilf wächst stellenweise in quadratmeilengrossen Schilfdickichten. Derart verlandende Buchten sind Brutstätten einer zahl- und artenreichen Vogelwelt.

Die Innenschären haben sich unter der Hand des Menschen am stärksten verändert. Die Verkehrsverbindungen sind zufriedenstellend, die Erde ist gut zum Anbau geeignet, grosse Inseln schützen vor Wellengang, an den flachen Ufern ist der Bau von Häusern problemlos und die Wälder produzieren reichlich Nutzholz.

Die Innenschären ziehen auch die meisten Feriengäste an: sie eignen sich besser für Erholungszwecke als der karge und verletzliche Aussengürtel der Schärenwelt.

The Inner Archipelago is lush, resembling lake scenery. Because of the alluvium brought by the rivers, the water is not as clear as in the outer sea. Bream and pike thrive here, as do numerous bird species from inland waters. The beautiful mute swan, nests in great numbers only in the Åland Islands and southwestern archipelago. Since the 1940s, protection and scarcity of natural enemies have enabled the species to flourish.

Die üppigen Innenschären erinnern eher an eine Binnenseelandschaft. Hier fühlen sich Brachse und Hecht wie auch zahlreiche Binnenseevögel zuhause. Der schöne Höckerschwan, ein Verwandter des sagenumwobenen Singschwans, nistet in Finnland nur auf den Ålandinseln und in der südwestlichen Schärenwelt in grösserer Zahl. Nachdem sie unter Naturschutz gestellt worden war und da sie nur wenige natürliche Feinde hat, konnte sich diese Art seit den vierziger Jahren schnell vermehren.

The Åland Islands
Die Ålandinseln

The bedrock of the Åland Islands is principally coarse-grained granite, so-called Åland "rapakivi", as in this cliff on Eckerö Island (1). The easternmost islands also contain gneiss. The Åland "mainland" is over 50 kilometres long and 40 kilometres wide, crisscrossed by long narrow inlets and isthmuses (2 and 3).

Der Felsgrund der Ålandinseln ist hauptsächlich grobkörniger verwitterter Granit, sog. Åland-Rapakivi, wie hier am Felsufer von Eckerö (1). Auf den östlicheren Inseln findet man auch Gneiss. Die Hauptinsel ist über 50 km lang und 40 km breit, von langen schmalen Buchten und Landengen zergliedert (2 und 3).

The Åland Islands contain two scenically different areas: the Western "mainland" and a labyrinth-like archipelago in the east. The Province of Åland consists of 6,500 islands and countless smaller skerries. The sea is the dominant element. It is visible almost everywhere, as passages and open waters between islands or as bays stretching deep inland. The islands are Finland's only marine province: liberated from the Baltic and still struggling with it. The Åland islanders have always gained a considerable part of their livelihood from the sea.

6,000 years ago only the island's highest point, Orrdalsklint, projected above sea level. The first people arrived there a thousand years later.

A tourist arriving from the Finnish mainland admires the lushness and fertility of the main island. Rare deciduous trees, colourful flower meadows and prosperous-looking farms create a "southern impression".

Die Ålandinseln gliedern sich in zwei landschaftlich verschiedene Teile: im Westen die grosse Hauptinsel und im Osten die labyrinthartige Schärenwelt. Die Provinz besteht aus 6500 Inseln und unzähligen kleineren Klippen. Das dominierende Landschaftselement, das Meer, ist fast überall zu sehen, als Sunde und offene Seenflächen zwischen den Inseln oder als lange, in die Inseln eindringende Buchten. Finnlands einzige Inselprovinz ist eine im Laufe der Jahrtausende der Ostsee entstiegene und immer noch mit ihr ringende Landschaft. Auch heute leben die Åländer zu einem erheblichen Teil vom Meer.

Noch vor 6000 Jahren ragte nur der Orrdalsklint, die höchste Stelle der Ålandinseln, aus dem Meer. Schon tausend Jahre später kamen die ersten Menschen.

Den vom finnischen Festland nach Åland einreisenden Besucher beeindruckt die Üppigkeit und Fruchtbarkeit der Hauptinsel. Edle Laubhölzer, farbenprächtige Blumenwiesen und florierende Bauernhöfe erinnern an das südlichere Europa.

2

3

Meadows and Pastures
Wiesen und Weiden

The maritime location, the number of islands, the favourable climate, the fertile soil and the long coastline are the factors creating the rich flora in the Åland Islands. The sea, bearing seeds from afar, constantly brings new life to the islands.

About 650 plant species have been found in the islands. This is more than in South-West Finland but less than in Sweden at the same latitude. The specialities of the Åland flora are its many orchids, the flowers of the semi-wooded meadows and the yew, which exists nowhere else in Finland.

Rare deciduous trees mostly grow along roads, on slopes and near settlements, which probably accounts for the general image of the island's lushness. However, most of the forests are coniferous.

Die maritime Lage, die Zahl der Inseln, das günstige Klima und die lange Uferlinie sind Faktoren, die zum Entstehen einer artenreichen Vegetation auf den Ålandinseln beigetragen haben. Das Meer führt den Inseln ständig neues Leben zu, bringt teilweise von weither Samen und Sprösslinge.

Auf den Ålandinseln hat man ca. 650 Pflanzenarten gefunden, mehr als in Südwestfinnland, aber weniger als auf gleicher Höhe in Schweden. Zu den Besonderheiten der Vegetation von Åland gehören zahlreiche Orchideen.

Edles Laubholz wächst vor allem am Rande der Strassen, auf Rainen sowie in der Nähe von Ortschaften, so dass man leicht den Eindruck allgemeiner Laubbewaldung erhält. Tatsächlich aber besteht der Wald der Ålandinseln hauptsächlich aus Nadelhölzern.

The Åland Islands have a mild climate. Agriculture and cattle raising are important forms of livelihood. Grazing has produced semi-wooded parklands, but as cattle are no longer pastured in woodlands, this scenic element is disappearing.

Auf den Ålandinseln herrscht ein mildes Klima. Durch das Grasen von Vieh sind lichte baumbestandene Wiesen entstanden, die jedoch allmählich aus dem Landschaftsbild verschwinden, weil die Waldweidung aufhört.

The Arboured Meadows of Åland
Die laubbaumbestandenen Wiesen von Åland

The groves and arboured meadows of the Åland Islands are the northernmost salients of the mixed forests of central Europe. The most densely wooded parts of the main island are its southern districts. The largest deciduous forests grow in the archipelago. The southwest of Föglö island is famous for its lush, foliant woodlands, but the bluish-green of pine forests dominates the Åland scenery.

The arboured meadows of the Åland Islands are the result of pasturage. Grazing animals inhibit forest growth, with the result that trees are scattered sparsely in a parklike landscape. In spring and summer the meadows are adorned with many beautifully flowering plants such as hepatica, wood anemones, cowslips, lilies of the valley and many rare species of orchids. The arboured meadows of Åland, once an essential feature of the scenery, are rapidly having to make way for agriculture and forestry.

Die Haine und laubbaumbestandenen Wiesen der Ålandinseln bilden den nördlichsten Ausläufer der mitteleuropäischen Mischwaldzone. Die am dichtesten belaubten Regionen der Hauptinsel findet man in derem Südteil. Die grössten Laubwälder wachsen auf den Schären. Vor allem der Südosten der Insel Föglö ist für seine Laubwälder bekannt. Im allgemeinen jedoch herrscht auf den Ålandinseln das Blaugrün der Nadelwälder vor.

Die baumbestandenen Wiesen der Ålandinseln sind durch das Grasen des Viehs entstanden. Die grasenden Tiere verhindern das Wachsen von Baumschösslingen, so dass der Baumbestand licht wie in Parks ist. Im Frühling und im Sommer zieren viele Blütenpflanzen die Wiesen, so Leberblümchen, Buschwindröschen, Schlüsselblume und als Besonderheit mehrere seltene Orchideenarten.

Die baumbestandenen Wiesen, einst wesentlicher Bestandteil der åländischen Landschaft, weichen schnell vor Land- und Fortstwirtschaft zurück. Zum anderen wachsen sie wegen abnehmender Viehweidung mit Bäumen dicht.

The flowery splendour of the Åland Islands' lush deciduous forests in spring and summer is without equal in the whole of Finland (1). Primroses (2) burst into bloom towards the end of May. The Åland Islands are particularly rich in orchids. In addition to the more common varieties such as spotted orchids and butterfly orchids, one also finds rarities like fly orchids (3).

Die sommerliche Blumenpracht der üppigen Laubwälder Ålands finden im restlichen Finnland nicht ihresgleichen (1). Die Schlüsselblume blüht Ende Mai (2). Zu den Besonderheiten der Wiesen gehören viele Orchideen, neben häufigeren Arten wie Geflecktes Knabenkraut und Zweiblättriges Breitkölbchen auch Raritäten wie der Fliegen-Ragwurz (3).

Jurmo — An Esker Island

(Deutscher Text: Seite 43)

Most of the islands off the coast of Finland are exposed bedrock. In places, however, the level bed of the Gulf of Bothnia has risen above the surface of the water in the form of sandy islands. The vast quantities of material carried away by the meltwater from the glaciers were washed into the sea, and only the largest terminal moraines were able to form islands.

Continuations of the Salpausselkä esker ridge can be seen in the coastal areas of South-Western Finland and even in the archipelago, as in the case of Jurmo.

Jurmo differs scenically from the rest of the archipelago. About five kilometres long and one wide, it is a ridge which tapers towards both ends and finally disappears into the sea as rocky ledges. Only three small rocky abutments project from the middle of the pebbly island. The eastern side of the island has some small alder groves and stunted pines grow in its central area.

Thus Jurmo is an exceptionally bleak place for people to live. Nevertheless it has been inhabited since earliest times. There is not a single sheltered bay that could serve as a harbour, so the islanders have had to keep an eye on the weather and their boats. Only during the past few years has a proper harbour been built.

On Jurmo, if anywhere, the inhabitants have depended on what nature provided for their means of existence. Their way of life has been harmonised with the cycle of the four seasons. Collecting the eggs of seagulls and eider ducks, seal hunting, hunting long-tailed ducks, gathering eiderdown, herring fishing and a little farming — to each its season. The stony soil of the island has permitted only a limited amount of farming and livestock raising. Potatoes have taken pride of place among the crops, while sheep have been the most important animals.

Emigration has taken a heavy toll of Jurmo's population and in recent years only one man has stubbornly lived there all year.

The heaving of the waves has created steplike ledges of stones that precisely follow the contour of the coastline (1). Jurmo's pretty little chapel was built in 1846 (2).
With year-round habitation almost completely a thing of the past, Jurmo's appearance has changed and dilapidation has set in (3). The third, or innermost, of Finland's Salpausselkä esker ridges is considerably more disjointed than the other two. This ridge intersects the coast near the island of Kemiö. (Pictures on pages 42 and 43).

Jurmo — Insel am Ende des Salpausselkä

Die finnischen Ostseeinseln sind überwiegend Grundfels, aber der ebene Boden des Bottenwieks, des Nordteils des Bottnischen Meerbusens, ist teilweise auch in Form von Sandinseln an die Meeresoberfläche gestiegen. Die vom Inlandeis transportierte Materie wurde ins Meer gespült, und die grössten Randmoränen konnten Inseln bilden. An der Südwestküste und im Schärenmeer sind stellenweise Os-Ketten des Höhenrükkens Salpausselkä erkennbar. Eines dieser Oser ist die weit draussen im Meer gelegene Insel Jurmo.

Jurmo unterscheidet sich landschaftlich deutlich vom Rest des Südwest-Archipels. Jurmo ist ein fünf Kilometer langes und in der Mitte ein Kilometer breites Os, das sich zu beiden Enden hin verjüngt und schliesslich als steinige Sandbank im Meer untergeht. Nur drei kleine Felsbuckel ragen inmitten des steinigen Oses auf. Im Osten der Insel wächst ein Erlenwäldchen, und in der Mitte fristet eine kleine Kiefernpflanzung ihr Dasein.

Jurmo ist also ein äusserst unwirtlicher Fleck Erde. Dennoch haben sich schon früh Menschen auf der Insel niedergelassen. Auf Jurmo existiert keine einzige geschützte Bucht, die als Naturhafen geeignet wäre. Jahrhundertelang mussten die Insulaner das Wetter beobachten und bei Sturm um ihre Boote besorgt sein. Erst kürzlich bekam Jurmo einen richtigen Anleger.

Auf Jurmo wenn überhaupt irgendwo hing die Existenz des Menschen total von den unmittelbaren Gaben des Meeres ab. Die Bewohner hatten ihr Leben dem Rhythmus der Natur angepasst. Das Sammeln von Vogeleiern, der Robbenfang, die Eisentenjagd, das Einsammeln von Eiderentenküken, der Strömlingsfang, der spärliche Ackerbau — für alles gab es eine bestimmte Zeit. Dieses steinige Eiland bietet nur begrenzte Möglichkeiten für Landwirtschaft und Viehzucht. Hauptanbaupflanze war die Kartoffel, wichtigstes Haustier das Schaf.

Jurmo wurde hart von der Abwanderung betroffen; in den letzten Jahren hat nur ein einziger Mann zäh ganzjährig auf der Insel die Stellung gehalten.

2

3

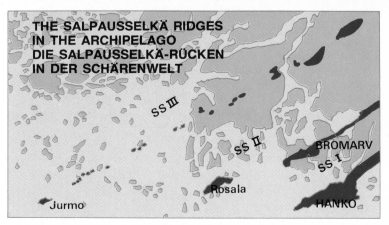

THE SALPAUSSELKÄ RIDGES IN THE ARCHIPELAGO
DIE SALPAUSSELKÄ-RÜCKEN IN DER SCHÄRENWELT

SS III

SS II

SS I

BROMARV

Rosala

Jurmo

HANKO

Der Wellengang hat auf den steinigen Sandbänken parallel zur Uferlinie stufenförmige Wälle angehäuft (1). Die kleine Kapelle von Jurmo wurde 1846 in der Nähe des Inseldorfs errichtet (2). Seitdem die Insel praktisch nicht mehr ganzjährig bewohnt ist, ändert sich das Antlitz Jurmos, und auch der Verfall macht sich breit (3).
Der dritte bzw. innere Salpausselkä ist lückenhafter als die beiden äusseren. Als seine südlichsten Spitzen ragen Jurmo und Utö aus dem Meer. Der dritte Salpausselkä erreicht bei der Insel Kemiö das Festland.

Against the Forces of the Sea

Wind and the currents it causes are the most noticeable and strongest weather factors in the Finnish marine archipelago. However, the dense scattering of islands prevents the emergence of continuous currents such as occur in the oceans. The waves are strongest where the winds are able to blow freely across larger open areas of sea. On rocky shores the waves flush loose material into the sea and gradually abrade the surface of the rock as well. No permanent vegetation can take root on rocks within reach of the waves.

On stony beaches, enough soil is able to accumulate between the loose stones to enable even vascular plants to take root.

The surf on sloping beaches can produce effects even well in from the waterline, but on gently sloping beaches it does not succeed in pounding very hard and shaping the coastline. Land upheaval changes the coastline and prevents the forces of the sea from concentrating their effects in any one place for very long.

DISTRIBUTION OF
SEA BUCKTHORN
DIE VERBREITUNG
DES SANDDORNS

In Finland, sea buckthorn (1) is found only on stony shores around the Gulf of Bothnia. Its berries are rich in vitamins A and C. Some plants take root on stony shores quite soon after the land has risen from the sea (2).
The wind direction fluctuates in the interior of Finland but in sea areas south-westerlies prevail (3).

Sanddorn wächst in Finnland nur an den steinigen Küsten des Bottnischen Meerbusens. Seine Beeren haben einen hohen Gehalt an A- und C-Vitaminen (1). Wenn eine neue Insel dem Meer entstiegen ist, spriessen an ihren Geröllstränden schon bald die ersten Pflanzen (2). Im Binnenland wechselt die Windrichtung ständig, aber auf dem Meer herrschen Südwestwinde vor (3).

Der Kampf gegen das Meer

Der sichtbarste und einflussreichste Wetterfaktor in der südwestlichen Schärenwelt ist der Wind. Der Wind ruft Wellengang hervor, und zusammen mit den Luftdruckänderungen bewirkt er Strömungen. Am stärksten ist der Wellengang dort, wo der Wind ungehindert über grosse Seenflächen hinwegfegen kann. Die Wellen spülen lose Materie ins Meer, und allmählich verwittert auch die Felsoberfläche. Feste Vegetation kann an den vom Wellengang angegriffenen Stellen nicht Wurzel fassen. An Geröllsträenden sammelt sich zwischen den Steinen gerade genug Erde an, damit auch einige Gefässpflanzen sich halten können. Wo Brandung herrscht, reicht die Wirkung der Wellen bis weit über die Uferlinie hinaus. An den flachen Ufern des Bottnischen Meerbusens hingegen haben die Wellen nur begrenzte Möglichkeiten, sich voll auszutoben und die Uferlinie zu formen. Die Landhebung verhindert, dass das Meer über längere Zeit dieselben Stellen angreifen kann.

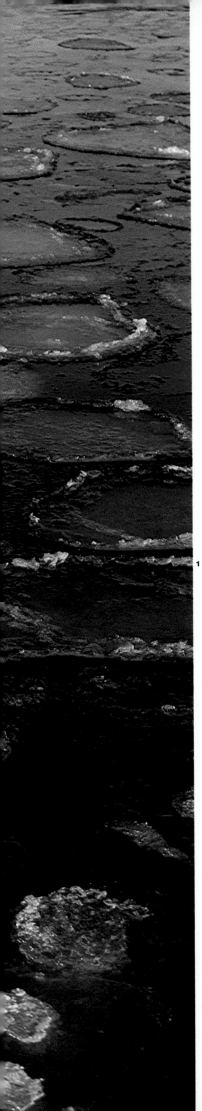

The Sea Freezes

Das Meer vereist

By the beginning of November at Tornio and around Christmas in the Gulf of Finland (in normal years), winter has conquered autumn and the coastal waters are icebound.

The ice is at its most extensive in early March, but by the end of the month open water already extends as far north as the Åland Islands. The Gulf of Finland is ice-free around the end of April, but in the Gulf of Bothnia ice floes can still be encountered in June.

In the open sea, the ice cover is more fragmented than in the archipelago. Here one finds drift ice, which the strong southerly winds push against the mainland. This produces pack ice, which can be several metres thick. The solid ice in the Finnish archipelago is usually about 50 cm thick and up to 70 cm in the Gulfs of Finland and Bothnia.

In normalen Jahren beginnen die Küstengewässer im Bottenwiek Anfang November und im Finnischen Meerbusen um Weihnachten zu vereisen. Ihre grösste Ausdehnung erreicht die Eisdecke Anfang März. Ende März dringt das eisfreie Meer schon wieder bis zu den Ålandinseln vor. Der Finnische Meerbusen befreit sich Ende April von seiner Eisdecke, im Bottenwiek können dagegen noch im Juni Eisschollen treiben.

Auf dem offenen Meer ist die Eisdecke zerrissener als in der Schärenwelt, und hier trifft man auch auf Treibeis, das vom Südwind gegen das Festland gedrückt wird. Hierbei entsteht Packeis, das mehrere Meter dick und zu einem Hindernis für die Schiffahrt werden kann. Das Festeis ist in Schärenfinnland gewöhnlich 50 cm stark, im Finnischen und Bottnischen Meerbusen bis zu 70 cm.

The sea rarely receives its ice coat at the first try. The thin layer of ice formed during a frosty night breaks up into "pancakes", which collide with each other, thickening their edges (1). Changes in water level also move the ice vertically (2). Ice floes are pushed against the shore by the wind (3). Only during the severest winters does the ice cover extend far into the open Baltic. The Gulf of Finland and the Gulf of Bothnia are usually completely frozen.

Selten erhält das Meer seine Eisdecke schon beim ersten Anlauf. Die bei Nachtfrost entstandene dünne Eisschicht bröckelt zu Schollen ab, welche sich hin und her bewegen und aneinanderstossen, wobei ihre Ecken sich abrunden (1). Schwankungen der Wasserhöhe bewegen das Eis auch in der Vertikalen (2). Das abgebröckelte Eis staut sich unter dem Wind am Ufer zu Packeis (3). Nur in strengen Wintern dringt das Eis bis weit in die mittlere Ostsee vor.

1

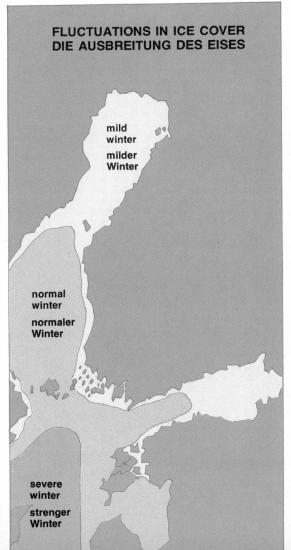

**FLUCTUATIONS IN ICE COVER
DIE AUSBREITUNG DES EISES**

mild winter
milder Winter

normal winter
normaler Winter

severe winter
strenger Winter

2

3

The Finnish Heartland
Kern-Finnland

Proud, Beautiful, Humble, Practical

by/von Päiviö Kangas

What is a landscape?

It is a scene, a milieu created by the Great Stage Setter, in which we all play our parts. It is air, water, and land. It is shapes and their relations, colours and distances. It is nothing else if one considers merely the act of looking at a landscape. Experiencing is something else.

The Finnish Heartland of this book consists of the civilized landscapes of Häme, Kymenlaakso, Satakunta, Uusimaa and Varsinais Suomi. The common denominator is a level, in places mildly undulating quiltwork of fields and forests with the buildings of towns and villages and smoking factory chimneys rising from it.

The Finnish Heartland is a proud phrase.

It is so proud that it could be understood, if one so wished, as underestimating the others and the Finns of other parts would have cause for taking offence. But they are not offended, because they know the Finnish Heartland as sufficient grounds for positive pride.

But the Finnish Heartland is also a word of beauty.

When explaining its landscape, the most common descriptions: rugged, bare, unreachable or untouched, even lush, are unusable. To me the beauty of the Finnish Heartland is realized in the words prosperous, spacious, refined, mild. That's why I believe the famous Finnish writer Aleksis Kivi meant the landscape of his very own, his closest living environment when he wrote of "the friendly mother's face". Isn't there enough beauty in that!

The Finnish Heartland is a humble phrase.

More than any other region in Finland it has allowed itself to be shaped by the hand of man. It has been made bare and then again filled with buildings, its rocks have been broken for numerous passage ways, it has been troubled a thousand years. But it has proved amazingly plastic: the scars left by upheavals have healed over and over again and everything appears whole, although changed.

The Finnish Heartland is a word for practicality.

A lot, material and spiritual, happens in this scenery, people get what they need from the near vicinity. But this sometimes causes severe stress and the longing for rest and silence is enormous. Despite its dense population, the Finnish Heartland has hidden away pockets of original nature in some places. There is the coolness of the lake and the sea, the smell of pitch, fields of star flowers like carpets in the shades of groves, there is the misery of bogs and marshes and finally the windy desolation of rocky skerries.

I'm not actually even trying to imagine what it would be like here if everything was left as nature created it. The landscape would hardly be very grand, rather monotonous: wilderness after wilderness, dense mixed trees growing on the level, flat land to prevent one from seeing far: wilderness, of course, with the organisms belonging to it, but scenically gloomy. However, I would like to return the now subdued rapids to their original state. But of course there are things that are lost. One cannot easily get back with money what once gave money. Perhaps the rivers Kokemäenjoki and Kymijoki miss their salmon and whitefish, perhaps they cry in Pori and Inkeroinen because of their pollution load. The river Vantaa has the same complaint with the advancing pollution of its idyll. Perhaps Lake Pyhäjärvi of Säkylä is afraid of its water flowing to still the thirst and laundries of Turku and Rauma. Will Lake Tuusulanjärvi ever recover from its death throes…

There have been mistakes: maybe there will be more in the future, because what will be will be. But what man has done to the Finnish Heartland has often been necessary and for the most part also right.

One must not understand what I have written above to mean that I would allow anything to happen. Quite the contrary: every thinking person wishes even more profound consideration of everything that changes our living environment. I haven't given up my belief that common sense will finally prevail, because it must.

My landscape thus tells — and it may do so — the results of man's action. Of course, it is a cultural landscape (remember that culture originally meant cultivation). The islets of forests seem dark green, the grove hills have a lighter shade and in autumn they turn a golden colour together with the ripening corn. Lakes and rivers glitter when the fiery rays of the sun bounce from their rippling surface. And they glimmer still blue — although their water may seem horribly dirty on closer examination.

There is one feature in my landscape that I never tire of watching: the changing. I do not mean merely human achievements. The land and the sea themselves are the factors in this changeability. The sea recedes from the land once ground by the ice, and dry gravel soils or muddy marshes come into being. Small details change suddenly, big settings in slow motion.

The Finnish Heartland's long union with the sea is of special importance to me. The coastline stretches from Merikarvia to Vironlahti. The Gulf of Bothnia has hidden submerged reefs and the Gulf of Finland is gentler. In spring, thousands of birds fighting for nesting places shriek around the crags and the surface of the water sways in wide curves, majestically. But wait till the summer is over and the autumn anger erupts! Then the sea lashes its foam-crested billows angrily against stones and smoothworn rocks. Only after the nights of biting frost have begun do the storms cease, they stiffen before a greater might. Soon the ice grinds complainingly and snow hurries onto its surface looking for, but never finding, its final resting place.

Only seldom does one read or hear about "an urban landscape". This is perhaps a sign of the fact that there are no landscapes within a city, only sights, which can nevertheless be charming.

Viewed from further away, a city certainly is a part of a landscape; in the evenings, when fog — do not think of pollution — envelopes it, it is a dominating part. Thousands of colours merge into pastel shades and the cross of a church illuminated by spotlights points upwards. In the countryside, the eye rests with pleasure on the buildings of a well-kept farmhouse, standing amid its fields, often on a hill, they radiate security and homeliness. Nor can one separate medieval churches, which tie the present to the past, from the scenery of the Finnish Heartland. Nor manor houses, in the history of which noble names flash. Their time is gone, but they played their own part by making others work for the development of the Finnish Heartland: sometimes with a very hard hand.

I have attempted to explain what interests me in my landscape; partially also what scares me. From boyhood on I have lived in this kind of environment; I'm used to seeing far without having to climb up to a high place. I know that some people regard these regions as monotonous, but I say they have a superfluous view. The Finnish Heartland is prosperous, open and cultural.

If the land lies low, the vault of the heavens is all the higher.

Stolz, schön, unterwürfig, praktisch

Was ist eine Landschaft?

Sie ist eine vom Grossen Bühnenbildner geschaffene Kulisse, ein Milieu, in welchem jeder von uns seine eigene Rolle spielt. Sie ist Wasser, Luft und Land mit allem, was dazugehört. Landschaft, das sind Formen und ihre gegenseitigen Beziehungen, Farben und Distanzen. Nichts anderes ist die Landschaft, wenn wir nur vom Betrachten sprechen. Das Erleben der Landschaft steht auf einem anderen Blatt.

Das Kern-Finnland dieses Werkes sind die Kulturlandschaften von Häme, Kymital, Satakunta, Uusimaa und Varsinais-Suomi. Ihr gemeinsamer Nenner ist eine ebene, stellenweise sanft hügelige Flickendecke aus Äckern und Wäldern, aus der die Bauten der Städte und Dörfer sowie die qualmenden Fabrikschornsteine herausragen.

Kern-Finnland ist ein stolzes Wort.

Es ist so stolz, das man es, wenn man so wollte, in einem das übrige Finnland abwertenden Sinne gebrauchen könnte, so dass die anderswo Lebenden guten Grund hätten, sich verletzt zu fühlen. Aber sie fühlen sich nicht verletzt, denn sie wissen, dass Kern-Finnland genügend Grund zu positivem Stolz hat.

Aber Kern-Finnland ist auch ein Wort der Schönheit.

Will man Kern-Finnlands Landschaft schildern, sind die für finnische Naturbeschreibungen typischen Wörter wie wild, karg, unnahbar oder unberürt — ja selbst üppig — ungeeignet. Für mich spiegelt sich die Schönheit Kern-Finnlands in den Wörtern wohlhabend, offen, gefühlvoll, warmherzig wider. So glaube ich, dass Aleksis Kivi seine ureigenste, die Landschaft seiner Lebensumwelt meinte, als er vom "freundlichen Muttergesicht" schrieb. Enthält es nicht genügend Schönheit?

Kern-Finnland ist ein unterwürfiges Wort.

Länger als jeder andere Teil Finnlands hat Kern-Finnland sich der Formung durch Menschenhand unterworfen. Es wurde freigerodet und wieder mit Bauten verdeckt, man hat seine Felsen für Verkehrswege durchstossen, es ist tausend Jahre lang geplagt worden. Aber es hat sich als erstaunlich plastisch erwiesen, die Spuren der Gewaltanwendung sind eine nach dem anderen verheilt und alles sieht wieder unversehrt — wenn auch verändert — aus.

Kern-Finnland ist ein praktisches Wort.

In dieser Landschaft ereignet sich vieles, physisch wie auch psychisch, der Mensch bezieht das, was er benötigt, aus seiner näheren Umwelt. Aber hieraus resultiert manchmal ernster Stress, und die Sehnsucht nach Ruhe und Stille wird unermesslich. Trotz seiner dichten Besiedlung hält Kern-Finnland in einigen Ecken die Ursprüglichkeit der Natur verborgen. Da ist die Kühle der Seen und des Meeres, der Duft des Harzes, Felder mit Siebenstern wie Teppiche im Schatten der Haine, da ist das Elend der Moore und schliesslich die stürmische Leere der Klippen.

Eigentlich versuche ich gar nicht erst, mir vorzustellen, wie es hier aussähe, wenn sich alles im Naturzustand befände. Die Landschaft wäre wohl kaum sehr feierlich, eher monoton: Wildnis nach Wildnis, als Bewuchs des gleichmässig ebenen Landes ein dichter Mischholzwald, der die Sicht behinderte; natürlich Wildnis mit ihrer typischen Fauna und Flora, aber düster. Die jetzt gezähmten Stromschnellen hingegen sähe ich gern wieder in ihrem Urzustand. Aber verloren ist eben verloren. Mit Geld bekommt man nicht leicht zurück, was einst Geld gebracht hat. Vieleicht sehnen sich die Flüsse Kokemäenjoki und Kymijoki nach ihren Lachsen und Renken, vielleicht jammert man in Pori und Inkeroinen über die Schmutzfracht der Flüsse; hierüber wie auch über die fortschreitende Zerstörung des landschaftlichen Idylls klagt man in Vantaa; vielleicht hat der Pyhäjärvi-See in Säkylä Angst um sein Wasser, das den Durst der Bewohner von Turku und Rauma stillen, deren Waschküchen füllen soll; wird sich der Tuusulanjärvi-See je von seinen Todeskrämpfen erholen...

Fehler gibt es, wird es auch in Zukunft geben, denn wo gehobelt wird, da fallen auch Späne. Aber was der Mensch mit seiner kern-finnischen Landschaft gemacht hat, war oft unumgänglich und im Prinzip auch richtig.

Das vorangegangene sollte nicht so interpretiert werden, als wenn mir gleichgültig wäre, was geschieht. Natürlich nicht, jeder denkende Mensch hofft, dass alles, was unsere Lebensumwelt verändert, noch sorgfältiger als bisher durchdacht würde. Ich bin überzeugt, dass der Verstand letztlich den Sieg davonträgt, weil dies ein Muss ist.

Meine Landschaft erzählt also — und das darf sie auch — von den Folgen menschlichen Wirkens. Gewiss, ist sie doch eine Kulturlandschaft (es sei daran erinnert, dass Kultur von Kultivieren kommt). Dunkelgrün die Waldinseln im Feldermeer, das hellere Grün der laubbaumbestandenen Hügel, die im Herbst im Wettbewerb mit dem reifenden Getreide golden leuchten. Die Seen und Flüsse sprühen Funken, wenn die feurigen Strahlen der Sonne von ihrer Oberfläche abprallen. Und immer schimmern sie blau — auch wenn ihr Wasser aus der Nähe schmutzigschaurig aussieht.

Ein Merkmal hat meine Landschaft, das zu beobachten ich nie müde werde: ihre Wandelbarkeit. Hiermit meine ich nicht nur die durch den Menschen verursachten Veränderungen. Land und Meer selbst sind Faktoren dieser Wandelbarkeit. Das Meer gibt einst vom Inlandeis überrollten Boden frei, lässt Kiesfelder und schlammige Marschen zurück. Kleine Details ändern sich urplötzlich, grössere Komplexe gemächlich.

Das lange Bündnis Kern-Finnlands mit dem Meer bedeutet mir besonders viel. Die Küste Kern-Finnlands erstreckt sich von Merikarvia bis Virolahti, am Bottnischen Meerbusen birgt sie tückische Klippen, am Finnischen Meerbusen ist sie sanftmütiger. Im Frühjahr zetern über den Klippen Tausende um Nistplätze kämpfende Vögel, und das Meer wiegt sich in weiten Bögen, majestätisch. Aber warte erst, bis der Sommer vorbei ist und die herbstlichen Sturmwogen spritzen. Dann peitscht das Meer mit seinen Schaumkronen zornig auf die Steine und Felsen ein. Erst, wenn die strengen Frostnächte begonnen haben, legt sich die Brandung, erstarrt angesichts stärkerer Mächte. Bald mahlt klagend das Eis, und Graupeln stürmen auf seine Oberfläche ein, suchen ihren eigenen Platz, den sie jedoch niemals finden.

Selten hört oder liest man von der "Stadtlandschaft". Der Grund hierfür ist vielleicht, dass es in den Städten keine Landschaften gibt, sondern nur Ansichten, die allerdings bezaubernd sein können.

Von weitem gesehen ist eine Stadt sicherlich ein Teil der Landschaft; abends, vor allem wenn Nebel — denk nicht an die Verschmutzung! — sie einhüllt, ist die Stadt der dominierende Landschaftsteil. Tausende von Lichtern verschmelzen zu pastellartigen Farben, und das von Scheinwerfern beleuchtete Kreuz der Kirche weist zum Himmel.

Auf dem Lande ruht das Auge gern auf den gepflegten Gebäuden der Bauernhöfe. Inmitten der Felder, oft auf laubbaumbewachsenen Hügeln, strahlen sie Geborgenheit und Gemütlichkeit aus. Und auch die mittelalterlichen Steinkirchen, welche die Gegenwart mit der Vergangenheit verbinden, können nicht aus der kern-finnischen Landschaft weggedacht werden. Ebenso nicht die Gutshöfe, in deren Geschichte adlige Namen aufblitzen. Sie gehören der Vergangenheit an, aber indem die Adligen anderen — oft mit strenger Hand — Arbeit aufgetragen haben, sind auch sie an der Entwicklung Kern-Finnlands Anteil beteiligt gewesen.

Ich habe versucht zu erklären, was mich an meiner Landschaft interessiert, teilweise auch, was mich an ihr schaudert. Von klein auf habe ich in dieser Landschaft gelebt, mich daran gewöhnt, weit zu sehen, ohne hohe Plätze ersteigen zu müssen. Ich weiss, dass manch einer diese Region als monoton empfindet, aber ich behaupte, dass solche Ansichten oberflächlich sind. Kern-Finnland ist wohlhabend, offen und kulturell.

Wenn das Land tief liegt, ist das Himmelsgewölbe umso höher.

Night Frost and First Snow
Nachtfrost und der erste Schnee

The warming effect of the sea means that winter comes to the coastal regions a couple of weeks later than to Northern Finland. Even on the south coast, snow can fall as early as October, but it soon melts away. The permanent blanket of snow does not usually fall until just before Christmas.

Winter can arrive in different ways. Sometimes dry and cold continental air covers Finland for several days. During the nights, as the stars shine clearly, the frost puts its icy seal on lakes and bays. The cooling sun is reflected by plains of ice. The frost penetrates ever deeper into the soil, and the hoary ground crackles beneath one's steps. Sometimes, too, the snow falls on unfrozen ground while the sea is still open. The coastal scenery is then a combination of three colours: the leaden grey of the sky, the jet black of the sea and the snowy white of the land.

About the middle of December the south coast acquires an icy fringe, but further out the waves swell freely deep into winter.

Der wärmende Einfluss des Meeres bewirkt, dass der Winter an der Küste zwei Wochen später eintrifft als weiter landeinwärts. Auch an der Südküste fällt manchmal schon im Oktober Schnee, taut jedoch sogleich. Gewöhnlich bleibt der Schnee erst um Weihnachten liegen.

Der Winter kann auf verschiedene Weise eintreffen. Mal breitet sich zuerst kalte und trockene Kontinentalluft für mehrere Tage in Finnland aus. In sternklaren, windstillen Nächten haucht der Frost eine dünne Eisschicht auf die Seen und Küstenbuchten. Auf den Eisebenen glänzt schimmernd die erkaltete Sonne. Der Frost dringt immer tiefer in den unbedeckten Erdboden ein, und der bereifte, gefrorene Boden knirscht unter den Schritten.

Ein andermal fällt der erste Schnee auf die ungefrorene Erde, während das Meer noch frei wogt.

Mitte Dezember rahmt das Eis die Südküste ein. Das offene Meer bleibt noch bis zum Mittwinter ungefesselt.

Small brooks usually remain ice free throughout the winter. In Southern Finland one can sometimes see a hardy water ouzel diving in the frigid water (1). The thickest coat of ice is found when there is a long continuous snow-free period of frost after the ice has first formed (2). The first snow usually falls when the temperature is around 0°C., and the tree branches bend under their heavy burden (3).

Die kleinen reissenden Bäche bleiben gewöhnlich den ganzen Winter über eisfrei. Auch an den klaren Bächen Südfinnlands kann man im Winter Wasserschmätzer im eisigen Wasser tauchen sehen (1). Am stärksten wird die Eisdecke, wenn auf die Vereisung eine lange, ununterbrochene schneefreie Frostperiode folgt. Dann kann das feste sog. Kristalleis entstehen (2). Der erste Schnee fällt meist bei Temperaturen um Null Grad. Der schwere Schnee biegt die Zweige der Bäume (3).

The Gloom of Deepest Winter

In Finland, the days are at their shortest just before Christmas. Although the winter solstice on December 21st is the darkest time of the year, the severest cold spells do not come until the second week of January.

Thanks the the moist sea air, the coastal areas of Southern Finland do not feel the frost's bite as much as the interior does, but when the temperature drops below —20°C it is much more harshly felt near the sea than inland.

Even the heart of winter has its mild interludes. Severe frost can yield to mild weather in a single night. Sleet sticks to branches and watery lumps plump into the carpet of snow on the ground. The snow drifts soften, icicles hang from the eaves and the roads are covered in slush.

The animals also come to life as the weather grows milder. The magpie squawks on the rubbish heap, flocks of sparrows chatter in the bushes and the greater titmouse gropes for his first spring verses.

Die mittwinterliche Dämmerung

Um Weihnachten sind die Tage am kürzesten. Obwohl das Tageslicht zur Wintersonnenwende, dem 21. Dezember, am spärlichsten scheint, lässt die kälteste Zeit des Jahres noch bis zur zweiten Februarwoche auf sich warten.

Dank der feuchten Meeresluft sind die Fröste an der Südküste nicht so streng wie weiter landeinwärts. Aber wenn es minus 20 Grad und kälter wird, ist dies viel unangenehmer als im Binnenland.

Auch der Mittwinter hat milde Phasen. Ein strenger Frost kann über Nacht in Tauwetter umschlagen. Schneeregen setzt sich im Geäst der Bäume fest. Die Schneewehen lösen sich zu Schneematsch auf, an den Dächern der Häuser bilden sich Eiszapfen und die Strassen weichen auf. Auch die Tiere werden bei warmem Wetter munter. Die scheckige Elster beginnt auf dem Komposthaufen zu schwatzen, Spatzen zwitschern in den Büschen und die Kohlmeise setzt zu ihren ersten Frühlingsstrophen an: die Macht des Winters ist gebrochen.

During the severest days of winter the forests resemble stage settings. The trees stand stiffly and the sun is seldom seen. Even when it shines, its warmth does not penetrate below the surface of the earth. All it can do is illuminate the landscape and cast long shadows.

An Tagen strengen Frosts sehen die Wälder wie Theaterdekorationen mit stocksteif dastehenden Bäumen aus. Die Sonne zeigt sich im Mittwinter nur selten, und ihre Wärme dringt kaum zur Erdoberfläche durch, aber sie beleuchtet wenigstens die Landschaft und lässt lange Schatten fallen.

Winter's Grip Is Broken
Die Macht des Winters ist gebrochen

Tree branches covered with hard crusts of snow look decorative (1). The snow crust easily bears the weight of animals. In the picture, a fox's tracks (2). Coniferous trees are dark in winter since the chlorophyll withdraws from the surface of the needles to their inner parts (3).

Die mit verkrustetem Schnee bedeckten Zweige sind dekorativ (1). Auf dem tragenden Schnee können die Tiere sich mühelos fortbewegen. Im Bild die Spuren eine Fuchses (2). Die Nadelbäume werden im Winter dunkel, da das Blattgrün von der Oberfläche in die Nadelmitte wandert (3).

March in southernmost Finland is no longer really winter, nor is it quite springtime every year, either. The most rapid seasonal change occurs in this month: the transition from February's mid-winter to spring-like April. The 24-hour temperature fluctuates more sharply than at other times. Day and night are nearly the same length. Since March is the month with least rainfall and the sky is thus mostly clear, the warmth accumulated during the day escapes into space at night. The surface of the snow changes from soft to hard, bearing the weight of people — and all within a single day.

The open sea has retreated far to the South-west during the winter. Therefore the climate of the southern coast preserves its continental character for a long time. In the middle of March, however, the snow cover becomes lower each day, the sun melting more than can freeze during the night.

When the snow is glittering, the most courageous birds return. Great mergansers and goldeneyes appear on open water areas. Advance parties of skylarks and starlings arrive, but the main contingents come later. At night the hoot of the owl carries from the forest.

Im März herrscht im südlichsten Finnland kein echter Winter mehr, und oft auch noch kein Frühling. In diesem Monat gehen die schnellsten jahreszeitlichen Veränderungen vor sich: Die täglichen Temperaturschwankungen sind grösser als zu anderen Zeiten. Tag und Nacht sind fast gleich lang. Der von der Sonne beschriebene Bogen ist schon so weit und hoch, dass ihre Wärme die Schneemassen schrumpfen lässt.

Da der März der regenärmste Monat und der Himmel somit die meiste Zeit unbewölkt ist, kann die sich tagsüber ansammelnde Wärme des Nachts in den Weltraum entweichen. Nachgebender Feuchtschnee und tragende harte Schneeflächen wechseln einander mit den Tageszeiten ab.

Mitte März beginnt die Schneedecke endlich zu sinken, und von Tag zu Tag deutlicher schmelzt die Sonne mehr, als die Nacht einfrieren lässt.

Während die schmelzenden Schneeflächen noch in der Sonne glitzern, wagen sich die ersten Zugvögel schon wieder nach Finnland vor. An den eisfreien Stellen der Sunde sind Gänsesäger und Schellente zu sehen. Spähtrupps der Lerchen und Stare treffen ein, aber die Hauptschwärme warten noch, bis das schneefreie Land weiter an Boden gewonnen hat.

Spring Is in the Air
Frühling liegt in der Luft

From the meteorological viewpoint, spring is regarded as having begun when the average temperature for a 24-hour period permanently rises above zero. On this basis, winter ends in Southern Finland in early April.

The snow piles start dimishing around the middle of March, but it is only in early April that a proper thaw gets under way. The fields lose their snow cover around the middle of April, but in the forests the snow remains for a couple of weeks longer.

On the Gulf of Finland coast, the sea swells free at the end of April, but the lakes are still in the grip of ice until after May 1st.

The spring landscape is like a delicate acquarelle: luminous with light colours. The budding deciduous trees grow violet on top. This is delicately complemented by the glowing ochre of the withered autumnal undergrowth.

In the snowfree soil life wakes up and the warming days call back the migrant birds to their nesting regions.

Meteorologisch beginnt der Frühling, wenn die mittlere Tagestemperatur permanent über dem Nullpunkt liegt. Nach dieser Definition beginnt der Winter in der Region Helsinki Anfang April.

Die Schneeflächen schmelzen schon ab Mitte März zusammen, aber erst Anfang April setzt das Tauwetter richtig ein. Die Felder lassen Mitte April ihre Schneedecke versickern, in den Wäldern bleibt der Schnee zwei Wochen länger liegen.

Das Eis wird unter dem Einfluss von Sonnenschein und Regen spröder und dünner. An der Küste des Finnischen Meerbusens löst es sich meist bis Ende April auf, aber die Seen befreien sich erst Anfang Mai von ihrem Eisjoch.

Die frühjährliche Landschaft ist wie ein feines Aquarell: hell und zartfarbig. Die knospentreibenden Laubbäume erhalten an ihren Spitzen einen violetten Anstrich. Diese Farbkomposition wird dezent durch das leuchtende Ocker der im Herbst verwelkten Bodenvegetation abgerundet.

2

3

4

After a frosty night, the ponds are covered with decorative, crystal-like ice (1). The dark-brown, wet soil of the fields is uncovered from the snow (2). The whiny-voiced pewit is one of the first migratory birds (3). The ice on the lake is dark and treacherously brittle in spring (4).

Nach frostigen Nächten überzieht morgens ein kristallähnlicher Eisfilm die Pfützen (1). Die dunkelbraune, feuchte Ackererde kommt wieder unter dem Schnee zum Vorschein (2). Der Gemeine Kiebitz ist einer der ersten Zugvögel des Frühlings (3). Das Eis der Seen ist im Frühling dunkel und trügerisch spröde (4).

The Four Seasons
Die vier Jahreszeiten

Finland has four distinct seasons. A grey sky, dark forest and white snow are the melancholy triad in the winter. But when the sun shines, dazzling brightness and bitter-blue shadows make one screw up one's eyes.

Spring comes early to Southern Finland, but it advances slowly and not abruptly as in the North. When the snow melts the soil is moistened and nurses new life in its bosom. In the spring the buds on the trees and bushes and the withered undergrowth of autumn colour the landscape with delicate

shades found hardly anywhere else. Birds of passage return and give new life to the landscape.

Summer, the period of steady growth, deepens the bright colours. The summer in Uusimaa has blue skies, the dark belt of coniferous and mixed forests, blue lakes and fields turning golden. In the autumn, nature dons her most colourful dress. The rains gradually dim the autumnal colours and the wind denudes the trees of their leaves. Before the sheltering snow falls, nature is grey and melancholy for a couple of weeks.

Finnland gehört zur Klimazone der vier Jahreszeiten. Grauer Himmel, dunkler Wald und weisser Schnee sind der melancholische Dreiklang des Winters. Aber wenn die Sonne scheint, zwicken blendende Helle und scharfblaue Schatten in den Augen.

Der Frühling kommt in Südfinnland früher als im übrigen Lande, aber er schreitet nur langsam voran und trifft nicht schlagartig und tösend ein wie im Norden. Die Erde weicht unter dem schmelzenden Schnee auf und treibt aus ihrem Schosse neues Le-

ben. Mit dem Frühling kehren die Zugvögel zurück und erfüllen die Landschaft mit Leben.

Der Sommer vertieft die hellen Farben. Zum Sommer des südfinnischen Uusimaa gehören blauer Himmel, dunkelgrüne Wälder, blaue Seen und goldschimmernde Felder.

Im Herbst kleidet die Natur sich in ihr buntestes Gewand. Regenfälle lassen allmählich die Herbstfarben verblassen, und der Wind entblösst die Bäume ihres Laubs. Bevor der schützende Schneemantel wieder die Erde bedeckt, ist die

Natur einige Wochen lang trostlos grau und melancholisch.

A V-shaped formation of cranes, harbingers of spring, ploughs slowly through the air over Uusimaa towards the inland marshes greeting the home country with muffled honking.

Boten des Frühlings: Auf seinem Wege zu den Mooren des Binnenlandes durchpflügt ein Kranichzug die Lüfte über Uusimaa und grüsst seine Heimat mit dröhnenden Trompetenstössen.

Shallow Baltic Bays
Die seichten Meeresbuchten

Brightly yellow marsh marigolds decorate the watery coastal meadows at Laajalahti near helsinki in spring (1). Many black-headed gulls and ducks nest on the grassy islets (2).

Hellgelbe Sumpfdotterblumen zieren im Frühling die sumpfigen Uferwiesen der Bucht Laajalahti in Espoo (1). Auf den grassbewachsenen Klippen nisten Lachmöwen und Enten (2).

As the land rises from the sea, the bays become shallower. The rivers carry silt from alluvial regions to the sea, and this combination of abundant nutrients, low salinity and a soft vegetation basis create excellent preconditions for the emergence of dense and extensive aquatic and waterside flora. The shallow bays of Southern Finland are fringed by extensive jungles of common reeds, which sigh green in the summer winds and in winter add an extra touch of straw-yellow colour to the whiteness of the scenery.

These shallow bays provide nesting places for many birds and act as resting and eating places for migratory varieties. The bays near large urban areas, play an important role in recreation.

Indem das Land sich aus dem Meer hebt, werden die Buchten flacher. Die Flüsse führen dem Meer aus lehmigen Gegenden Schlamm zu. Das nährstoffreiche und salzarme Wasser bietet ideale Voraussetzungen für die Entstehung einer dichten und weitläufigen Ufervegetation. Die Ränder der seichten Meeresbuchten sind von ausgedehnten Schilfdickichten gesäumt, deren grüne Rohre im Sommerwind säuseln und die im Winter mit ihrer strohgelben Farbe die Landschaft bereichern.

Derartige seichte Buchten sind Niststätten einer reichen Vogelwelt und Rast- und Futterplätze für die Zugvögel. Da man solche Vogelbuchten auch in der Nähe von Siedlungszentren findet, haben sie einen grossen Erholungswert.

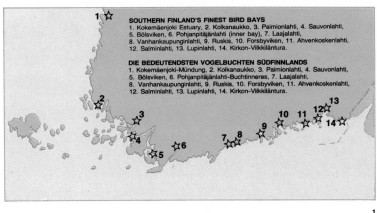

SOUTHERN FINLAND'S FINEST BIRD BAYS
1. Kokemäenjoki Estuary, 2. Kolkanaukko, 3. Paimionlahti, 4. Sauvonlahti, 5. Bölsviken, 6. Pohjanpitäjänlahti (inner bay), 7. Laajalahti, 8. Vanhankaupunginlahti, 9. Ruskis, 10. Forsbyviken, 11. Ahvenkoskenlahti, 12. Salminlahti, 13. Lupinlahti, 14. Kirkon-Vilkkiläntura.

DIE BEDEUTENDSTEN VOGELBUCHTEN SÜDFINNLANDS
1. Kokemäenjoki-Mündung, 2. Kolkanaukko, 3. Paimionlahti, 4. Sauvonlahti, 5. Bölsviken, 6. Pohjanpitäjänlahti-Buchtinneres, 7. Laajalahti, 8. Vanhankaupunginlahti, 9. Ruskis, 10. Forsbyviken, 11. Ahvenkoskenlahti, 12. Salminlahti, 13. Lupinlahti, 14. Kirkon-Vilkkiläntura.

1 2

On the Threshold of Summer
An der Schwelle des Sommers

In May, the birch trees change their shade to bright green (1). When the deciduous trees are budding the farmer is busy with ploughing and sowing (2). Common hepatica (3) decorates the forest soon after the snow has melted and the wood anemones blossom a couple of weeks later (4).

Im Mai färben die Birkenspitzen sich hellgrün (1). Wenn die Birken ausschlagen, haben die Bauern mit der Bestellung ihres Landes alle Hände voll zu tun (2). Das Leberblümchen (3) blüht schon kurz nachdem der Schnee getaut ist, das Buschwindröschen (4) ein bis zwei Wochen später.

As spring advances, the days lengthen so rapidly that one can easily notice it. The weather grows warmer and the actions of nature speed up. However, a lot of thermal energy is consumed in thawing the snow and ice and therefore when the lakes have become ice-free around May Day, a harsh "second winter" can take the wakening nature by surprise.

After the snow has gone and before the trees foliate, the ground in the forests is at its most blossomy. Common hepaticas unfold their petals and wood anemones give the forests a starry border. Marsh marigolds glow by the ditches. The birch blossoms and foliates at about the same time, around the middle of May.

A whole crowd of master singers arrive in May: e.g. the nightingale. Flycatchers and swallows sing together with tomtits, chaffinches and other small birds. Around mid-May one can finally hear the cuckoo and see the swifts with their sickle-shaped wings criss-cross the sky. Summer is at the door.

Mit fortschreitendem Frühling werden die Tage schnell länger. Die Luft wird wärmer und die Vorgänge in der Natur laufen immer rascher ab. Die Schnee- und Eisschmelze bindet jedoch grosse Wärmemengen, und daher kommt es vor, dass die erwachende Natur noch Anfang Mai von einem Nachwinter überrascht wird.

Nachdem der Schnee getaut ist und bevor die Bäume ausschlagen, steht der Waldboden in vollster Blüte. Die Leberblümchen öffnen ihre Kronenblätter, und kurz darauf überziehen Buschwindröschen wie Sterne die Waldränder. An den Bächen glüht die Sumpfdotterblume.

Im Mai trifft eine grosse Schar von Meistersängern ein, so die Nachtigall. In den Höfen singen neben Finken, Meisen und anderen Kleinvögeln auch der Fliegenschnäpper und die Schwalbe. Mitte Mai kann man wieder den Kukkuck vernehmen und die sichelflügelige Mauerschwalbe lauthals kreischend am Himmel kreisen sehen. Der Sommer bricht an.

New Life Unfolds

Tilled fields enrich the landscape. They create open spaces fringed by transitional zones that approximately conform to the terrain. In the forest districts, fields are like islands in a sea of trees and in the agricultural areas there are enclaves of forest among the fields. In the fertile southern part of Finland, the extensive farmlands dominating the landscape begin to turn from black to green towards the end of May. In places, sprouting greenery is seen soon after the snow has disappeared.

Winter corn varieties thrive here and are the first ones to sprout.

Arable land covers less than one tenth of Finland's total area. Most of the cultivated areas are in the coastal regions. In Uusimaa and Southwestern Finland 27—50 % of the land area has been cleared for fields. The fertile alluvial districts near the coast in the same regions are also the largest and most productive farmland areas in the whole country.

In these areas, which have the most suitable climate for farming in Finland, the arable land is cultivated as intensively as possible. Both forest and tilled land must be protected in order to preserve the richness of the scenery. Domestic animals have in the past created distinctive parklands. This valuable landscaping service, a by-product of pasturage, has nowadays been greatly reduced since modern farming favours year-round indoor feeding of animals to prevent fodder from being wasted when animals move about freely.

1

3

2

Aufkeimendes Grün

Felder bereichern die Landschaft Südfinnlands. Sie schaffen offene Räume, die oft erst am Horizont vom Wald abgeschlossen werden. Im nordöstlichen Wald-Finnland sind die Felder Inseln im Waldmeer. Entsprechend ragen in Feld-Finnland inmitten des Feldmeers Waldinseln auf. Die ausgedehnten Anbauflächen, welche die ländliche Natur der südlichen Landesteile beherrschen, beginnen schon Ende Mai, ihre schwarze Farbe gegen Grün einzutauschen.

Ackerland bedeckt ein Zehntel der Fläche Finnlands. Relativ am meisten Fläche wird in der Küstenregion beackert. In der Provinz Uusimaa und in Südwestfinnland sind 27 bis 50 Prozent des Bodens zu Feldern gerodet. In Küstennähe, wo man fruchtbaren Lehmboden findet, liegen auch die grössten und ertragreichsten Anbauflächen.

In diesen klimatisch günstigen Teilen des Landes ist man bestrebt, das anbaufähige Land so gründlich wie möglich zum intensiven Anbau zu nutzen. Die Erhaltung des Reichtums der Ackerlandschaft setzt den Schutz und die Entwicklung der Felder wie auch der Waldinseln voraus. Hier haben die Haustiere, die vor nicht langer Zeit noch die einfriedungsähnlichen eigentümlichen Parklandschaften "scherten", unvergleichliche Dienste geleistet. Diese als Nebenprodukt der Viehweidung erfolgte Form der Landschaftspflege ist in letzter Zeit stark zurückgegangen. Heutzutage zieht die Landwirtschaft ganzjährige Stallfütterung vor.

Finland's Most Fertile Region
Das fruchtbarste Finnland

1   2

A characteristic feature of the cultivated land in Southwestern Finland and of the province of Uusimaa has for centuries been spaciousnesness and an abundance of tilled fields. These cultivated areas gives an impressive picture of prosperity, but on the other hand it is more monotonous than the changing mosaic of forests, fields and water in the Lake District.

The climate is more amenable to agriculture in Southern Finland than further north. Near the coast and in the Lake District the temperatures of the warmest month, July, are more or less the same, but the growing period near the south coast is longer. Here spring sowing can be done earlier and the fields worked longer before their winter rest. Thus in Uusimaa and Southwestern Finland, cereals have a longer time to develop than elsewhere in Finland.

Für die südwestfinnischen Anbaugebiete und für die Landschaft von Uusimaa ist Weite, der Reichtum an Feldern charakteristisch. Die Ausdehnung der Ackerlandschaft zeugt von Wohlstand, ist aber monotoner und nuancenärmer als der ständige Wechsel von Wäldern, Gewässern und Feldern in Seen-Finnland.

Die klimatischen Voraussetzungen für die Landwirtschaft sind in Südfinnland besser als weiter nördlich. Im Juli, dem wärmsten Monat, sind die Temperaturen an der Küste und in Seen-Finnland fast gleich, aber im Süden dauert die Wachstumsperiode länger. Die Felder können im Frühling früher gepflügt und brauchen im Herbst nicht so früh für den Winter aufbereitet werden. So können die Anbaupflanzen im Süden und Südwesten länger wachsen als in den anderen Landesteilen.

In the province of Uusimaa, no less than 40 % of the land area is under cultivation. In areas where one or two plant species are extensively cultivated, the fauna is limited, but in the forests lining the fields songbirds sing their concert in the spring and summer and the preying hawks make their nests (1). Flamingly yellow turnip rape fields blossoming just at the beginning of the summer decorate the southern agricultural regions (2).

In Uusimaa sind vierzig Prozent des Bodens landwirtschaftlich genutzt. Diese Anbaugebiete, auf denen jeweils nur eine oder wenige Pflanzenarten wachsen, haben eine dürftige Fauna, aber aus den angrenzenden Wäldern erschallt im Frühling und Sommer das Konzert der Singvögel. Dort nistet auch der Falke (1), der seine Beute auf den Feldern jagt. Die Anfang Sommer lodernd gelb blühenden Rapsfelder sind eine Zierde des südfinnischen Agrarlandes (2).

The Rivers of the Alluvial Plains
Die Flüsse des Tonlandes

The rivers splitting the alluvial plain of Southwestern Finland have cut their beds deep into the soil. Many rivers flow parallel to each other in a Northeast-to-Southwest direction and their origins are in the lake-abounding watershed of southwestern Häme.

The rivers in the alluvial plain flow sluggishly, but during the spring floods and autumn rains the water often considerably erodes the river bank and its bed gradually widens into a basin with gently sloping sides. The rivers were the channels along which the interior of Finland was populated in the coastal areas and these rivers served as important traffic arteries in summer.

Signs of ancient culture are found everywhere near the rivers. Historians have proved that these regions have been settled nearly as long as Finland has been populated. Signs of more recent times are the mills and old stone bridges which generally no longer serve the main flows of traffic.

Die durch Südwestfinnlands Tonebene fliessenden Flüsse haben ihre Betten tief in das Erdreich eingefurcht. Viele dieser Flüsse entspringen der seenreichen Wasserscheide von Südwest-Häme und strömen in gleicher Richtung von Nordosten nach Südwesten. Die Flüsse des Tonlandes fliessen gemächlich. Aber in der Zeit des Frühjahrshochwassers und der Herbstregen reissen ihre Wässer oft grosse Brocken aus den Uferböschungen, so dass die Flussbetten sich allmählich zu breiten, sanft zur Flussmitte hin abfallenden Tälern erweitern.

Das Vordringen der Besiedelung von der Küste ins Binnenland geschah die Flussläufe entlang, und die Flüsse dienten den Flussanwohnern als Verkehrsadern.

Überall an den Flüssen stösst man auf Spuren alter Kultur. Die Historiker haben nachgewiesen, dass die Flussläufe fast ebensolange bewohnt sind wie in Finnland Menschen leben. Zu den Relikten aus neueren Zeiten gehören Mühlen und Steinbrücken.

The largest alluvial areas in Finland are the Southwestern region and Uusimaa. The Southern cultivated land is split by small rivers, which flow sluggishly in their serpentine courses. Because of the soft growth basins and nutrient-rich water the aquatic flora is abundant.

Die grössten Tongebiete dehnen sich im Südwesten des Landes und in Uusimaa aus. Durch die südlichen Anbaugebiete fliessen in gewundenen Betten kleine trübe Flüsse gemächlich dahin. Aufgrund des weichen Bodens und des nährstoffreichen Wassers ist die Wasservegetation üppig.

The Grove of Karkali
Der Hain von Karkali

Absolutely the finest of the groves in the province of Uusimaa is the Karkali Nature Park. It is located at the end of a narrow promontory in Lake Lohjanjärvi. There is a network of paths at Karkali, along which one can explore the area, but one must not step off them without permission. Karkali has been a nature preserve since 1964.

In spring, when most of the trees and bushes are still leafless, spring plants such as wood anemone, common hepatica, and spring peas blossom. They exploit the brief light period caused by the trees' lack of foliage. The flower display of the grove is at its best in spring.

After the trees have grown their leaves, the low spring plants are overshadowed. In summer, only a little light filters through to the substratum and therefore most of the species have broad leaves and are adapted to shade. In autumn, there is again extra colour in the grove.

The few remaining groves must be protected. With their own special world of flora and fauna, they are valuable components in Finland's nature. Groves account for only one per cent of Southern Finland's forest area. Therefore the disappearance of even a small grove area is a loss.

Der Naturpark Karkali liegt auf einer spitzen Landzunge im Lohjanjärvi-See. Man kann den Hain über ein Netz von Pfaden erreichen, das durch den Naturpark führt. Ohne besondere Genehmigung darf man von von den Pfaden nicht abweichen. Sozusagen in letzter Minute wurde der Hain 1964 unter Naturschutz gestellt.

Im Frühling, wenn die meisten Bäume und Sträucher noch blattlos sind, blühen die Frühjahrspflanzen des Hains, so Anemone und Platterbse. Sie nutzen zum Aufblühen jene kurze Phase, in der das Licht ungehindert bis zum Boden vordringen kann, so dass die Blüte ihren Höhepunkt schon im Frühling erreicht.

Nachdem die Bäume ihr Laub getrieben haben, überdeckt Schatten die niedrigen Frühjahrspflanzen. Im Sommer dringt nur wenig Licht bis zur Bodenvegetation vor, weshalb die meisten Arten breitblättrige Schattenpflanzen sind. Erst der Herbst lässt den Hain wieder in neuer Farbenpracht aufleuchten.

Haine sind eine üppige Ausnahme in der finnischen Natur. — in ihnen lebt eine eigene spezielle Tier- und Pflanzenwelt. Nur ein Prozent der südfinnischen Waldfläche sind Haine.

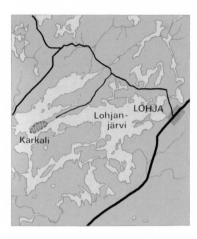

The nature reserve at Karkali is situated 70 km west of Helsinki. The eagle's wing growing to one metre height is Finland's biggest and most handsome fern. In the most verdant groves it covers acres in places (1). During the warm postglacial climatic period hazel trees were more common in Finland than they are now (2).

Der Naturpark Karkali liegt 70 km westlich von Helsinki. Der meterhoch wachsende Straussenfarn ist Finnlands grösste und prächtigste Farnart. In den üppigsten Hainen bildet er stellenweise Hunderte von Quadratmetern grosse Felder (1). In der warmen nacheiszeitlichen Klimaperiode war der Haselstrauch viel häufiger anzutreffen als heute (2).

1   2

The Tammela Heights
Das Hochland von Tammela

The Tammela Heights are a stark contrast to the densely populated agricultural landscape of Varsinais-Suomi and Uusimaa. The Heights are clearly higher than the alluvial coastal areas, the terrain is hilly and sparsely populated. The area is an upland, rugged watershed area. The landscape is characterized by small lakes, ridges, bogs and marshes and extensive uninhabited forests.

The largest lake in the Heights is Lake Pyhäjärvi. The panoramic tower on Kaukolanharju Ridge commands a magnificiently beautiful but little known view over wooded ridges, bogs and chains of lakes. The extensive forests in the Tammela Heights still offer a wilderness atmosphere in places. The district is one of the reserves in which lynx thrive. Torronsuo Bog covers over 1,000 hectares. It is the biggest bog in natural condition in Southern Finland and contains hundreds of small ponds.

Despite its ruggedness, there is plenty of life there: e.g. cranes, the finest representatives of peatland birdlife.

The bog's recreational value is considerably enhanced by the fact that it is located fairly close to the biggest population centres.

Das Hochland von Tammela in der Provinz Häme bildet einen klaren Kontrast zu den dichtbesiedelten Kulturlandschaften von Varsinais-Suomi und Uusimaa. Das Hochland liegt deutlich über der Tonebene der Küstenregion, das Terrain ist hügelig und die Besiedlung dünn. Das Hochland ist ein karges Wasserscheidengebiet. Kleine Seen, Oser, Moore und weitläufige unbewohnte Wälder charakterisieren die Landschaft.

Der grösste See des Hochlands von Tammela ist der Pyhäjärvi. Vom Aussichtsturm auf dem Os Kaukolanharju am Südufer des Sees bietet sich ein grossartiger Ausblick über die bewaldeten Landrücken, Moore und blauen Seen.

Die ausgedehnten Wälder des Hochlandes erinnern stellenweise an die im Urzustand befindliche Wildnis. Diese Gegend ist einer der Zufluchtorte der Luchse von Häme. Hier befindet sich auch das tausend Hektar grosse Torronsuo, Südfinnlands grösstes Moor im Naturzustand. Im Torronsuo stehen Hunderte von kleinen Teichen. Trotz seine Kargheit lebt in ihm eine artenreiche Tierwelt, so der Kranich, der nobelste Verteter der Fauna des Torronsuo.

1

The Tammela Heights contain several natural areas suitable for recreational use. The verdant Saari Nature Park is situated on the land of an old estate (1). Torronsuo bog is the most valuable protected peatland in Southern Finland (2). The beautiful Kaukolanharju Ridge is situated on an isthmus between lakes Kuivajärvi and Pyhäjärvi (3).

Im Hochland vom Tammela findet man mehrere Naturgebiete, die für Erholungszwecke geeignet sind. Der Volkspark Saari liegt auf den Ländereien eines alten Rittguts (1). Torronsuo ist Südfinnlands wertvollstes Moorschutzobjekt (2). Das Os Kaukolanharju auf einer Landzunge zwischen den Seen Kuivajärvi und Pyhäjärvi (3).

2

The Tranquility of the Forests
Die Stille der Wälder

The mixed forest in Southern Finland is a productive and multifarious biological community (1). When gullies get wet and moss-bound the forest changes into a bog. In places water gathers into ponds (2).

Der südfinnische Mischwald ist eine produktive und vielseitige Biozönose (1). In von Torfmoos überwachsenen Niederungen, in denen sich Wasser ansammelt, versumpft der Waldboden. Stellenweise bildet das Wasser kleine Teiche (2).

The mean average daytime temperature in summer is over + 10°C. In the province of Uusimaa, this warm period lasts from the middle of May to mid-September. Because the Gulf of Finland warms up slowly, summer comes to the coastal area a few days after it has arrived several miles further inland.

Nature begins to bloom when the ice has gone. Plants need a lot of water to compensate for heavy evaporation, but often in early summer, when the need is greatest, Finland has long rainless periods. Towards the end of the summer, when it is not so necessary, precipitation is heaviest.

The abundance of flowers found in the bright spring forests is gone by early summer. The overhead foliage creates too much shade and hinders wind-assisted pollination. But modest-looking hays and grasses thrive and the undergrowth starts to bloom. In June, fir blossoms with reddish pistillate flower clusters. The wind blows pollen from staminates and yellowish dust falls everywhere. This is repeated a couple of weeks later when the pines repeat the act.

The fauna are busy in early summer: a new generation must be reared. The male birds sing 24 hours a day, pausing only around noon and during the briefly dark night. The females hatch unseen in their nests. Growth proceeds, summer develops. The oppresive heat of sultry summer days holds life in a similar paralysis to that which grips it during the icy spells of deeperst winter.

In August the waters get cooler and nights longer. After the rains the forest ground is coloured by chanterelles and other mushrooms of the late summer. Colourful mushrooms compensate for the glowing flowers that seem to have fled from forests to meadows at the end of the summer. The heather of dry heaths blossoms however in August when the lingonberries redden. Although Southern Finland is extensively cultivated, forests cover about two-thirds of the land area in the province of Uusimaa, for example. The main species of tree is fir.

2

In Uusimaa liegt die durchschnittliche Tagestemperatur von Ende Mai bis Ende September über zehn Grad. Da der Finnischen Meerbusen sich nur langsam aufwärmt, lässt der Sommer direkt an der Küste einige Tage länger auf sich warten als weiter landeinwärts.

Mit Hilfe der Schmelzwässer beginnt die Natur aufzublühen. Um die Verdunstung zu kompensieren, benötigen die Pflanzen zusätzliches Wasser, aber oft ist gerade der Sommeranfang die regenärmste Zeit. Zum Sommerende, wenn die Natur nicht mehr soviel Wasser benötigt, sind die Regenmengen am grössten.

Einen Blumenreichtum, wie man ihn in den lichtreichen Frühlings-Wäldchen antrifft, findet man zum Sommeranfang nicht mehr. Das Laubdach spendet zuviel Schatten und verhindert die vom Wind getragene Bestäubung. Dafür spriessen umso mehr dürftige Gräser und Kräuter, und die Reiser treiben Blüten.

Der Sommeranfang ist für die Tierwelt eine betriebsame Zeit: eine neue Generation muss aufgezogen werden. Der Gesang der Vögel erschallt Tag und Nacht — nur um Mittag sowie kurz vor und nach Mitternacht schwächt er ab. An Hitzetagen erlahmt das Leben, wie an Tagen strengen Frostes kommt eine Atmosphäre des Stillstands auf.

Im August kühlen sich die Gewässer ab und die Nächte werden länger. Nach den ersten Regenfällen verleihen Pfifferlinge und andere Pilze dem Waldboden einen buntgescheckten Anstrich. Vielfarbige Pilze treten an die Stelle der Blumenpracht, die im Spätsommer aus den Wäldern auf die Wiesen geflohen zu sein scheint. Eine Ausnahme bildet das Heidekraut, das erst im August aufblüht, wenn die Preisselbeere schon rot wird.

Obwohl grosse Teile Südfinnlands landwirtschaftlich genutzt werden, ist etwa Uusimaa zu rund zwei Drittel mit Wald bedeckt.

Salpausselkä

The Salpausselkä ridges are Finland's most striking moraine formations. About 10,000—11,000 years ago, during the final stage of the Pleistocene, the edge of the ice sheet was nearly stationary for a long period, retreating only about 20—30 kilometres in all. Enormous amounts of gravel and sand carried by meltwaters accumulated in front of the continental glacier. This material formed the terminal moraines nowadays known as the Salpausselkä ridges. Inside the ridges, or in the area once covered by the glacier, the most common kind of soil is moraine. It is a glacier-transported unsorted material containing everything from big stones and gravel to the finest of alluvium.

In places the Salpausselkä can be detected in the terrain only as narrow hogbacks. Often the formation broadens to sand plains square-kilometres in area. The Salpausselkä Ridges form a water-damming natural limit in the southern and southeastern Lake District. To the northern side remains the hilly Lake District which is an amazing mosaic of countless lakes. To the South spreads a fairly flat coastal region bounded by the Gulf of Finland.

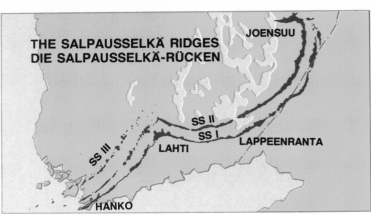

THE SALPAUSSELKÄ RIDGES
DIE SALPAUSSELKÄ-RÜCKEN

JOENSUU

SS II
SS I

SS III

LAHTI

LAPPEENRANTA

HANKO

The Salpausselkä Ridges form a water-damming natural threshold for the Lake District. Alluvial farmlands open up to the South (1). When the ice sheet melted ice blocks were buried under layers of soil. With the climate getting warmer, the ice melted and the layer of soil on top of it sank forming a steep hollow or kettle-hole (2). The heath anemone decorates heathlands (3).

Die Salpausselkä-Höhenrücken bilden eine natürliche Schwelle, welche das Wasser des Seengebiets staut. (1). Als das Inlandeis schmolz, wurden Eisschollen unter den Erdschichten verschüttet. Als dieses Eis schmolz, rutschten die darüberliegenden Erdschichten nach, wobei steilhängige Mulden entstanden (2). Die Frühlingsschelle ist eine Zierde der Os-Landschaft (3).

Die Salpausselkä-Höhenrücken sind Finnlands grösste aus losen Bodenarten bestehende glaziale Formationen. Vor rund 11 000 bis 10 000 Jahren, gegen Ende der Eiszeit, stand der Aussenrand des Inlandeises für längere Zeit fast auf der Stelle. In jener Zeit zog sich das Eis nur 20—30 Kilometer zurück. Vor dem Gletscher sammelten sich gewaltige, vom Schmelzwasser angeschwemmte Kies- und Sandmassen an. Zum grössten Teil aus dieser Materie bestehen der erste und der zweite Salpausselkä, welche die südfinnische Landschaft spalten. Im Inneren dieser Rücken ist die häufigste Erdart die Moräne. Moränen sind vom Eis vorweggeschobene Materiegemische aus vielen Korngrössen — von grossen Steinen bis hin zu feinem Lehm.

Stellenweise setzen sich die Salpausselkä-Höhenrücken vom restlichen Terrain nur als schmale Kämme ab. Oft jedoch erweitern sie sich zu quadratmeilengrossen Sandebenen.

Am Süd- und Südostrand der Seenplatte bilden die Salpausselkä-Höhenrücken eine natürliche Schwelle, welche die Wassermassen staut. Die Höhenrücken trennen zwei verschiedene Landschaftstypen voneinander: im Norden die von unzähligen Seen zersplitterte finnische Seenplatte, im Süden die flache Küstenregion.

Weathered Rock Tells its Tale
Der Rapakivigranit erzählt

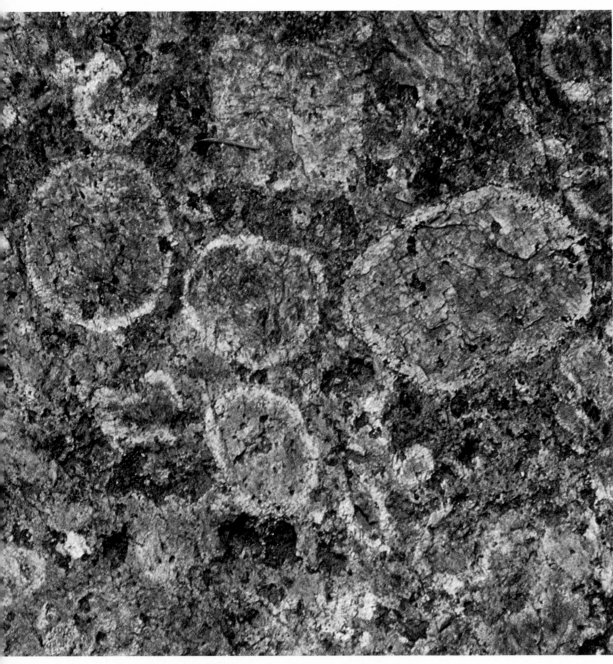

A special, easily-crumbling type of granite called "rapakivi" is found in the valley of the Kymi River, in Southwestern Finland and on the Åland Islands. These weathered granite areas have rounded rock outcroppings thinly covered with pines and the occasional birch. Heather and whortleberry are typical of the undergrowth in the Kymi valley. The rock faces, with their crumbling slopes, are often very steep because of vertical splitting. The flat tops, by contrast, are the result of equally strong horizontal splitting.

Not all types of granite weather in the same way. The process seems to affect the rocks only to a depth of some metres at their summits or on southward-facing slopes. The basic reasons for this weathering are still not well enough known. However, scientists have noticed that the darker coarser-grained varieties crumble more easily. It is possible that the easiest crumbling varieties were affected by slight movement's of the earth's crust shortly after they had crystallized.

Den für seine ungewöhnlichen Verwitterungseigenschaften bekannten Rapakivigranit trifft man vor allem im Kymital, in Südwestfinnland sowie auf den Ålandinseln an. Die Rapakivigebiete charakterisieren flachkuppige Felsen, auf denen ein lichter Kiefernbestand und vereinzelt Birken wachsen. Die typische Bodenvegetation des Rapakivigebiets im Kymital ist Heide und die vor allem auf Verwitterungsgrus wachsende Gemeine Bärentraube. Die Felswände mit ihren Verwitterungsgrushängen sind wegen der Zersplitterung in vertikaler Richtung steil und oft pfeilerähnlich. Die flachen Kuppen wiederum sind durch ebenso starke horizontale Zersplitterung entstanden.

Nicht alle Rapakivigesteine verwittern, ebenso nicht alle Teile gleichartiger Rapakivifelsen. Die Verwitterung ist offenbar ein Oberflächenphänomen, das sich auf eine höchstens mehrere Meter dicke Schicht auf der Felskuppe oder generell an den der Sonne zugewandten Wänden beschränkt.

THE RAPAKIVI AREAS IN FINLAND
FINNLANDS RAPAKIVIGEBIETE

PORI

KOUVOLA
KOTKA

The most typical types of granite consist of potassium feldspar spheres several centimetres in diameter, which are surrounded by a thin shell of plagioclase (1). The rock is called "rapakivi" because of the ease with which it crumbles into granules.

Einige der typischsten Rapakiviarten bestehen aus mehrere Zentimeter dicken Kalifeldspatkugeln mit ringförmigen Pagioklashüllen (1). Mehrere Rapakiviarten verwittern leicht zu Grus (2).

In the Kymi Archipelago
Die Schären im Kymital

The islands in the Kymi Archipelago are well spaced, and in places one can see wide open sea stretching right to the horizon (1). During cold weather, optical illusions can be produced on the sea. The lower layer of air is cooler than that above it. Rays of light are "bent" downwards and the islands appear to float in the air (2). This "rapakivi" shore near Kotka is worn smooth (3).

Die Inselwelt des Kymitals ist licht, und stellenweise kann man bis zum Horizont blicken (1). Bei kühler Luft entstehen über dem Meer manchmal Kimmungen. Die untere Luftschicht ist kälter als die darüberliegende, und das Licht wird nach unten gebrochen, so dass die Inseln in der Luft zu schweben scheinen (2). Rapakivifelsen auf einer Insel vor Kotka (3).

The island belt in the Gulf of Finland varies considerably in width. In places the three different archipelago zones — inner, intermediate and outer — can be clearly distinguished, but around Kotka an observer standing on the mainland often has an unobstructed view all the way to the horizon. Further to the east, the archipelago stretching southwards from the Kymi Valley is again broader, although the individual islands are so sparse as to seem sprinkled in the sea.

Most of the islands in the Kymi Archipelago are rocky, but some, such as Kaunissaari, are gravel ridges that have risen from the sea because of a phenomenon known as isostatic recovery.

Here, too, one finds several idyllic island communities, where beautiful old, dwellings and boathouses cluster tightly around little harbours. Unfortunately, these too are becoming deserted.

Die Breite des Schärengürtels im Finnischen Meerbusen variiert erheblich. Stellenweise trifft man alle drei Schärengürtel an: Aussen-, Mittel- und Innenschären. Um Kotka hingegen hat man vielerorts vom Festland freie Sicht bis hin zum fernen Horizont. Im Ostteil des Kymitals, vor Hamina und den Buchten Vehkalahti und Vironlahti, ist der Schärengürtel wieder breit, wenn auch die einzelnen Inseln und Klippen dünn verteilt sind, so als hätte man sie ins Meer gestreut.

Die Inseln des Kymitals sind gewöhnlich felsig. Zu den Ausnahmen gehört Kaunissaari, eine dem Meer entstiegene Os-Formation.

Im Kymital gibt es auch einige idyllische Schärenkolonien, deren schöne alte Wohnhäuser und Bootsschuppen sich dicht um die Häfen gruppieren. Leider veröden auch diese Fischerkolonien allmählich.

As an ice sheet advances, the stones embedded in its base gouge the rock beneath, carving longitudinal grooves.

Die vom Inlandeis mitgeschleppten Steinmassen schliffen die Felsoberfläche, wobei Rundhöcker mit längsgerichteten Furchen entstanden.

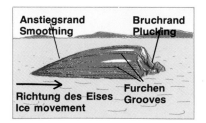

Anstiegsrand
Smoothing

Bruchrand
Plucking

Richtung des Eises
Ice movement

Furchen
Grooves

3

The Fields Settle down to Rest
Die Felder begeben sich zur Ruhe

Work in the fields has always culminated in the autumn harvest. The yellow, swaying waves of corn change their expression in a few weeks. In the old days shocks and sheaves of corn appeared in the fields and on clear autumn days the roar of the threshing mills could be heard from the farmyards. Nowadays the combine harvesters advance across the fields with much less commotion.

The farmer is still busy during the harvest. His rush is even more merciless than before, even if it does not last so long. And of course the farmer is still subject to the caprices of the weather.

Stubble burning spreads an acrid smell, and the fire burns black patterns on the fields. Burning is the easiest way to get rid of stubble, but experts say that ploughing it into the ground would be the best thing for the soil.

Ploughing changes the colour of the fields to an autumnal grey. The fields planted with winter wheat later stand out in sharp contrast to those ploughed.

Seit je erreicht die Arbeit auf den Feldern zur herbstlichen Erntezeit ihren Höhepunkt. Die gelb wogenden Getreidefelder verändern innerhalb weniger Wochen ihr Antlitz. Früher erschienen zu diesem Zeitpunkt auf ihnen Stiegen und Getreidereuter. An klaren Herbsttagen erscholl aus den Dreschscheunen der Lärm der Dreschmaschinen. Die modernen Mähdrescher von heute arbeiten sich unauffälliger durch die Felderlandschaften vor.

Das Abbrennen von Stroh und Stoppelgräsern verursacht einen stechenden Geruch. Das Feuer zeichnet im Stoppelfeld schwarze Muster. Das Abbrennen ist das einfachste Mittel, das Stroh und die Getreidestoppel, die sonst das Pflügen behindern würden, loszuwerden. Allerdings wären das Roden der Stoppelfelder und das Unterpflügen des Strohs für die Bodenstruktur vorteilhafter.

Wenn schliesslich das Pflügen beginnt, halten die herbstlichen Grautöne Einzug in die Felderlandschaft.

The Colours of Autumn
Die Farben des Herbstes

The rainiest part of the year is not autumn; it is summery August. August rains fall in short but intense showers, whereas autumnal rains, falling as drizzle, last longer. The skies are full of grey clouds, puddles gather and the roads become muddy. Gloom prevails.

However, the troughs of low pressure disappear before long. The sun no longer has the heat of summer, but is bright enough to illuminate the colourful splendour of nature's autumn costume. The deep green of summer is replaced by a myriad of golds and flaming reds.

When nature's extravagent display of colour has ended, the cold showers of autumn begin to lash the landscape. The last migratory birds have departed, the sun sinks from view and the days get darker and darker. The deciduous trees stretch their wet, dark limbs towards the leaden sky. Autumn has stripped them of their leaves, hoar frost coats the land and a thin layer of ice the ponds.

Nicht einer der Herbstmonate ist der regenreichste Monat des Jahres, sondern der sommerliche August. Im August fallen kurze heftige Güsse, im Herbst hingegen regnet es zwar länger, aber tröpfelnd. Graue Wolkenmassen verhängen den Himmel, und aus ihnen nieselt es gemächlich. Es bilden sich Pfützen, und die Wege werden morastig. Die Stimmung ist niederdrückend.

Schon bald jedoch weichen die Tiefdruckgebiete. Die Sonne scheint nicht mehr so wärmend wie im Sommer, beleuchtet jedoch die herbstliche Farbenpracht. Das dunkle Grün des Sommers hat goldenen und glühend roten Farben Platz gemacht.

Wenn das flammende Feuerwerk der Natur erloschen ist, beginnen die kalten Herbsttage das Land zu plagen. Die letzten Zugvögel haben ihre Reise angetreten. Die Sonne entzieht sich den Blikken. Die Tage werden dunkler. Die Laubbäume recken ihre dunklen nassen Äste zum bleigrauen Himmel. Die Bäume werden kahl, die Erde weicht auf, ein dünner Eisfilm überzieht die Teiche.

The Plains of Ostrobothnia
Die Tiefebene von Österbotten

The Sky Is High Above the Plains

by/von Venny Kontturi

I have a poet friend who calls the plains of Ostrobothnia the landscape of his soul. I can agree with him, no matter how many times I have heard disparaging remarks about flat scenery. Some person without understanding, a newcomer who had just drifted in has said: "It's not scenery!" Perhaps such people, after their first hurried glimpse of the plains of Ostrobothnia, believe that their secret will be revealed at first sight, that one needs look no deeper.

However, I would say that these plains are real scenery; their innermost being, their delectableness must be sought, and may take long to find. The plains will hardly ever reveal themselves to those who approach them in an overbearing or indifferent manner, only to the person who approaches them in a receptive frame of mind.

It is not difficult to get to know the plains. There are no gloomy, tangled forests, no inaccessible hills, no broad expanses of water that have to be crossed. There are only sluggish rivers, nearly all of which have been harnessed to serve the energy needs of man.

I love Ostrobothnia and the plains, but still I ask myself: am I the right person to talk about the plains? After all, I am a child of the sea shore. My earliest childhood experiences are linked with the coast of the Gulf of Bothnia, the sea! It was there that my world unfolded and I experienced the eternally tedious longings of my youth, the presentiments of the future. It was there that I experienced perhaps the same longing stemming from the adventuresomeness and vigour that gave my people the assurance they needed to depart and made pioneers of some of them.

I would also assert that everybody who has grown up on the plains regards the sea as his own. And it could not be otherwise. The sea wraps the shores of the plains in its bosom and salty sea winds blow deep inland across the unobstructing plains. Every town on the plains has been built beside a river flowing into the sea, where the river contributes its water to the sea and the sea in turn gradually withdraws and, centimetre-by-centimetre, doles out more land... The water recedes and the earth rises; this phenomenon I have experienced — in my own lifetime.

In the course of the years I have discovered more and more in the plains and my attachment to these landscapes has steadily strengthened. It is here that I find what I like to call characteristic of the plains, that liberating something that has made me love them.

On the plains I can enjoy the tranquility and peace and the glimmering space curving unobstructedly above it. I can be contented on the banks of placid rivers, when they are placid. In spring they often grow wild, and the unregulated ones lose control and burst beyond their banks. Then the river waters encroach on agricultural land, rock barns, gurgle across farmyards and sever roads — the calm river shows the proud people its surprising ferocity.

I admit that I do not want to encounter a hillock or a waterbody at every step; nor do I feel any particular urge to climb to the top of a hill to see the landscape around me. On the contrary, I enjoy the fact that there is no hill nor mound rising up suddenly to obstruct my view, that nothing will echo my shout — and that's just how the plains are. I also believe that the forests are different on the plains; they have their gloomy and shadowy spots, their fragrance of resin and mossy patches. But nothing threatens in my forest, it is not the same forest as the one inhabited by the bogeymen and goblins of my childhood fairy tales. The further north one travels in the Ostrobothnian plains, even as far as the valley of the Tornio River, the more gaunt the spruce trees become, the more sparse their branches. Nor do the leaves in northerly birch groves grow bigger than one's hand. There is enough light in my forest!

My forest often ends at the edge of a bog, which extends farther than the eye can see into the distance. Not all of these bogs have yet been drained by the ditching machines, nor have all of them caught the eyes of the peat harvesters. There one catches the fragrance of wild rosemary

and, resting on their hummocks, cloudberries grow and wait to be picked. Of course I have sometimes been moved almost to tears when captivated by the charm of a mountain view, on seeing the proud sweep of a ridge. But my admiration has always been blended with an odd sense of fear and strangeness — since I can identify only with the gentle closeness of the plains. I feel secure on the plains, the plains receive me like a mother when I return from a trip astray to some strange place.

On the plains one has good visibility in every direction: forwards, backwards and sideways, and the magnificence of the high, clear sky is always in front of one. Sky and earth, on the plains they cannot be separated from each other, since on some horizon or other they always merge into the same hemisphere.

In the opinion of the plains people, rightly or wrongly, the sky is higher here than anywhere else. Here people stare at the sky until their eyes are sore. And then to rest their eyes they direct their gazes to the edge of some distant grove; one of the many that girdle the plains with their green border.

The cries of the gulls above the plains announce that the time of growth and reproduction has come. The willows shed their catkins and the chokecherry trees burst into bloom beside the rivers and on the edges of the fields. The farmer follows his plough and the tarred road, the main thoroughfare in Ostrobothnia, is repaired, made free of potholes for those who want to get to know the plains better.

People say to me: oh, dear, you have no hills here at all! And this is said in a voice containing a slight note of sympathy. I always answer that indeed we do have some rather fine hills. And then I list the names of some of them: Lauhavuori, the highest hill in Western Finland — 231 metres — Pyhävuori and Simpsiö.

To this I sometimes add that if we didn't have all the hills we needed here on the plains, then this people would make them themselves. Although on the other hand I have also noticed that if any kind of projection of the earth tries to soar too high above the rest of the terrain, it will not be tolerated for long. If necessary, a fanatic of this kind is levelled, its feeling of almightiness stripped away.

I admit that it bothers more than pleases me that in hilly settings I am not able to encompass all the scenery in a single gaze. All of a sudden I am confronted with a hill, which I have to go round. But on the plains, here everything is clear and honest. A landscape that does not resort to tricks gives everything that it promised at the outset. The plains are not deceitful, they do not say: when you reach the other side of that rise, when you pass this hillock, when you manage to reach the other side of that lake, the seven wonders await you there somewhere!

My plains do not do that, they are open and honest.

Über der Tiefebene ist der Himmel hoch

Ich habe einen Freund, einen Dichter, der Österbotten "Landschaft seiner Seele" nennt — ich kann mich ihm da anschliessen, dasselbe sagen, obwohl ich häufig abfällige Bemerkungen über die Landschaft der Tiefebene gehört habe. Ein Verständnisloser, ein gerade Angekommener, hat "Unlandschaft" gesagt. Nachdem sie nur einen flüchtigen Blick auf das Tiefland von Österbotten geworfen haben, glauben solche Ignoranten wahrscheinlich, dass die Ebene ihre Geheimnisse schon auf den ersten Blick verrät, dass sich ein näheres Kennenlernen erübrigt.

Ich hingegen würde sagen, dass diese Ebene überhaupt erst eine richtige Landschaft ist; ihr innerstes Wesen, ihre Sensibilität, muss gesucht werden, und es kann lange dauern, bis man es entdeckt. Wer ihr unfreundlich oder gleichgültig gegenübertritt, dem dürfte das Wesen des Tieflands wohl für immer verborgen bleiben. Dem erschliesst sich die Landschaft, der aufgeschlossenen Geistes in die Tiefebene kommt.

Ich kann versichern, dass es nicht schwer ist, mit der Tiefebene Bekanntschaft zu schliessen: hier stösst man nicht auf finsteres Dickicht, auf schwer begehbare Berge, auf ausgedehnte Gewässer, die überquert werden wollen. Die Gewässer von Österbotten, das sind gemächlich dahinfliessende Flüsse, deren unwirtlichste Stellen, die Stromschnellen, fast ausnahmslos dem Menschen zu Dienste gebändigt sind.

Ich liebe Österbotten und seine Tiefebene, aber dennoch frage ich mich, ob ich die richtige Person bin, über die Ebene zu sprechen. Bin ich doch an der Küste aufgewachsen. Meine frühesten Kindheiterinnerungen sind mit dem Bottnischen Meerbusen verbunden, mit dem Meer! Dort hat sich mir die Welt eröffnet, und beim Starren auf das Meer habe ich die Sehnsüchte meiner Jugend, den Drang in die Ferne erlebt und Zukunftsahnungen in mir gespürt. Dort habe ich vielleicht die gleiche Sehnsucht verspürt, welche einem Teil meiner Leute die zum Aufbruch nach Westen benötigte Zuversicht verliehen hat.

Ich würde auch sagen, dass jeder, der in der Tiefebene von Österbotten aufgewachsen ist, sich auch am Meer zu Hause fühlt. Anders könnte es überhaupt nicht sein, das Meer schliesst die Tiefebene in seinen Schoss, salzige Meereswinde wehen bis weit in die Tiefebene hinein. Die Städte der Tiefebene wurden sämtlich am Ufer eines der ins Meer mündenden Flüsse gebaut, dort, wo der Fluss sein Wasser an das Meer abgibt und von wo das Meer sich allmählich zurückzieht und Zentimeter für Zentimeter seines Bodens freigibt... Das Wasser flieht und das Land hebt sich — dieses Phänomen habe ich mit eigenen Augen verfolgen können.

Im Laufe der Jahre habe ich die Tiefebene immer mehr und mehr entdeckt, und ich fühle, wie ich sie immer tiefer ins Herz schliesse. Hier finde ich das, was ich als charakteristisch für die Tiefebene bezeichnen möchte, das befreiende Etwas, das mich die Tiefebene lieben lässt. Hier kann ich Ruhe und Frieden und den unbehindert schimmernden Himmel geniessen, der sich über der Tiefebene wölbt. Ich fühle mich an den Läufen der stillen Flüsse wohl, solange sie wirklich still sind. Im Frühling, wenn sie sich von ihrer Eisdecke befreien, geraten sie oft ausser Rand und Band. Die unregulierten Flüsse werden des ewig gleichen Trottes überdrüssig und treten über ihre Ufer. Dann greifen sie nach dem Ackerland, lassen Scheunen wanken, plätschern auf den Höfen und schneiden die Strassen ab — dann geben sich die ruhigen Flüsse überraschend wild.

Ich muss zugeben, dass ich nicht mit jedem Schritt eine Anhöhe oder ein Gewässer erleben will, ich verspüre keinen sonderlichen Drang, Hügel zu besteigen, um die umliegende Landschaft zu sehen. Ganz im Gegenteil, ich geniesse es, dass kein Berg und kein Hügel mir die Sicht versperren, dass kein Hinderniss meinen Ruf als Echo zurückwirft — daher fühle ich mich gerade in der Tiefebene so wohl.

Ich meine, dass auch die Wälder in der Tiefebene anders sind; sie haben natürlich auch ihr Dämmerlicht und ihre Schatten, ihren Harzduft und ihre Mooshöcker. Aber in meinem Wald lauern keine Gefahren, er ist nicht der Urwald, in dem die Gespenster und Kobolde der Kindermärchen hausen. Je weiter man in der Tiefebene nach Norden kommt — und sie reicht weit, bis hin zum Tornionjokital — desto schmäler werden die Fichten, desto dünner ihr Astwerk, und die Blätter der Birken wachsen nicht mehr handtellergross. In meinem Wald herrscht kein Mangel an Licht!

Meine Wälder enden oft an einem Moor, das sich so weit erstreckt, wie das Auge reicht. Nicht alle Moore der Tiefebene sind von Baggern dräniert worden, noch sind viele der Aufmerksamkeit der Torfgräber entgangen. In solchen Mooren duftet der Sumpfporst, und auf Bülten ruhend wachsen die Moltebeeren und warten darauf, aufgelesen zu werden.

Natürlich war ich manchmal begeistert, zu Tränen gerührt, wenn Berglandschaft mich in ihren Bann gezogen, wenn ich die wildromantische Schönheit von Bergkämmen gesehen hatte. Aber meine Begeisterung haben immer eine seltsame Angst und das Gefühl des Fremdseins gebremst, denn nur in der Tiefebene fühle ich mich zu Hause. In ihr fühle ich mich geborgen, die Tiefebene nimmt mich wie eine Mutter in ihren Schoss zurück, wenn ich von einer Irrfahrt durch irgendeine fremde Landschaft zurückkehre.

In der Tiefebene von Österbotten hat man in alle Richtungen gute Sicht, nach vorn, nach hinten und zu den Seiten, und über einem wölbt sich immer der grossartige hohe, klare Himmel. Der Himmel und die Erde, in der Tiefebene kann man beide nicht voneinander trennen, denn stets vereinen sie sich irgendwo am fernen Horizont zur selben Hemisphäre.

Die Tieflandbewohner behaupten — vielleicht zu Recht, vielleicht auch nicht — dass der Himmel hier höher ist als anderswo. Hier sieht der Mensch sich am Himmel krank. Bis er, wenn sie ermüdet sind, seine Augen wieder irgendwo in der Ferne auf dem Rande eines Waldes ruhen lässt, einem jener Wälder, welche als grüne Bänder die Ebene einrahmen.

Der Schrei der Möwen über der Tiefebene tut kund, dass wieder Zeit des Wachstums und der Fruchtbildung ist. Die Weiden treiben ihre Kätzchen und der Ahlbaum lodert an den Ufern der Flüsse und den Rainen der Felder auf. Der Bauer tritt in die Ackerfurchen, und die Schlaglöcher der Teerstrassen, Österbottens Hauptverkehrswege, werden gefüllt, um so jenen einen freundlichen Empfang zu bereiten, die nähere Bekanntschaft mit der Tiefebene schliessen wollen.

Manchmal bekomme ich zu hören: Ach je, hier gibt es ja überhaupt keine Hügel, und dies wird mit leicht mitleidigem Unterton gesagt. Darauf antworte ich: Aber ja, natürlich gibt es hier Hügel, sogar recht beachtliche. Und ich zähle ein paar mit Namen auf: der Lauhavuori, mit 231 Metern Westfinnlands höchste Erhebung, der Pyhävuori und der Simpsiö.

Vielleicht füge ich noch hinzu, dass, wenn wir nicht genügend Hügel für den Eigenbedarf hätten, wenn wir uns nach mehr sehnten, die Leute hier selbst welche schaffen würden. Obwohl ich andererseits bemerkt habe, dass, falls in der Tiefebene irgendein Hügel versucht, sich zu weit über die Ebene zu erheben, dieser Zustand nicht lange geduldet wird. Ein solcher Brausekopf wird eingeebnet, ihm wird seine Grossmannssucht ausgetrieben.

Ich muss gestehen, dass es mich mehr stört als befriedigt, wenn ich in einer Hügellandschaft nicht das ganze Land mit einem Blick erfassen kann. Plötzlich ragt vor mir ein Hügel auf, der umgangen sein will. Aber in der Tiefebene... — hier ist alles deutlich und aufrichtig. Ohne Sperenzchen erfüllt die Landschaft all das, was sie schon von weitem verspricht. Die Tiefebene betrügt nicht, sie sagt nicht: Wenn du erst diesen Hügel umgehst, diese Kuppe überwindest, wenn du diesen See überquerst, dann erwarten dich sieben Wunder!

Nein, das tut meine Tiefebene nicht, sie ist offen und fair.

The High Points of Ostrobothnia
Die Erhebungen von Österbotten

Ostrobothnia is generally regarded as a flat region. Its surface features are not so broken as those of other parts of Finland. Before the last ice age, the region was covered by horizontal layers of shale, which protected it from weathering. This was later broken up into sand and gravel, which accumulated in valleys or formed esker ridges.

In some places, however, higher points have been preserved, either because of a harder type of rock or for some other reason. Lauhavuori (231 m), the highest point in Ostrobothnia, contains sandstone. These high points are called "relict mountains" and can be compared to knots in a well-worn wooden floor. Most of them still rise to the same level at which the weathering process began.

In places where the water level has remained constant for some time, cliffs and ridges have been formed. The traces of ancient shorelines can still be seen on the flanks of the hills, in the form of weathered strata several metres thick. The highest ancient beaches in Ostrobothnia are those made by the Yoldia Sea and the largest were caused by fluctuations in the levels of the Yoldia Sea and Ancylus Lake. The best cliffs can be seen at Parravuori and at Pyhävuori. Although these rocks rise to heights of 70—80 metres, they do not appear very high, because of their gentle slopes.

The hill slopes support many species of plants that do not thrive on the plain or that have been eliminated there by farmland clearance.

Österbotten ist als ebene Landschaft bekannt, deren Bodengestalt nicht so uneinheitlich ist wie im restlichen Finnland. Vor der Eiszeit bedeckte eine horizontal abgelagerte Schieferschicht die Oberfläche dieser Gegend und schützte vor Verwitterung. Später löste sich diese Schicht auf: sie wurde zu Sand- und Kiesmassen zermahlen, die sich in den Talsohlen ansammelten oder Os-Formationen bildeten.

An einigen Stellen haben jedoch Bodenerhebungen die Eiszeit überstanden, dank ihrer widerstandsfähigeren Gesteinsstruktur oder aus anderen Gründen. Der Sandstein des Bergs Lauhavuori (231 m), der höchsten Erhebung der österbottnischen Küste, ist immer noch fester Fels. Derartige Erhebungen nennt man Restberge. Sie sind wie Aststellen auf abgenutzten Holzfussböden. Die meisten von ihnen ragen zu ungefähr jener Höhe auf, in der die Erosion einst eingesetzt hat.

In Perioden, in denen das Sinken des Meeresspiegels bzw. die Landhebung für einige Zeit verlangsamt vor sich ging, kam es stellenweise zur Bildung von Ufergeröll und -wällen. An den Berghängen kann man immer noch die vorzeitlichen Ufer erkennen, mehrere Meter breite blossgespülte Geröllfelder.

Die besterhaltenen Ufergeröllfelder findet man am Parravuori in Teuva sowie am Pyhävuori in Lappväärtti. Obwohl die Restberge Süd-Österbottens 70—80 Meter über ihre Umgebung hinausragen, wirken sie nicht allzu hoch, da ihre Hänge sehr sanft abfallen.

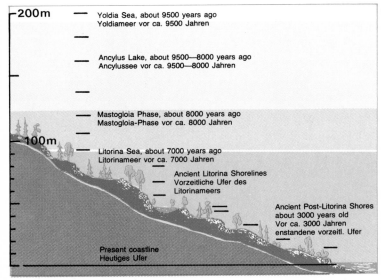

200m	Yoldia Sea, about 9500 years ago / Yoldiameer vor ca. 9500 Jahren
	Ancylus Lake, about 9500—8000 years ago / Ancylussee vor ca. 9500—8000 Jahren
	Mastogloia Phase, about 8000 years ago / Mastogloia-Phase vor ca. 8000 Jahren
100m	Litorina Sea, about 7000 years ago / Litorinameer vor ca. 7000 Jahren
	Ancient Litorina Shorelines / Vorzeitliche Ufer des Litorinameers
	Ancient Post-Litorina Shores about 3000 years old / Vor ca. 3000 Jahren enstandene vorzeitl. Ufer
	Present coastline / Heutiges Ufer

Most of Ostrobothnia is a subacquatic district; in other words, even after the ice sheet had receded the land here was still covered by water for a long time. Only the occasional hilltop protruded as an island above the water at first. As the land rose because of a phenomenon called "isostatic recovery", the islands grew bigger and the region gradually evolved into dry land.
The development of the Baltic area since the departure of the Pleistocene glaciers involved the four successive phases shown in the diagram. The shorelines in successive periods are recorded on cliffs at various heights. These traces can be seen in the form of rocky beach strata and sandy bulwarks. Beach traces have been left everywhere that conditions permitted the elements to do their work effectively.

The picture on the left shows rocks that once formed part of the shore of the Gulf of Bothnia at Parravuori Hill, Teuva.

Österbotten ist grösstenteils subaquatisches Gebiet; mit anderen Worten war das Land nach der Eiszeit von Wasser bedeckt. Nur einige höhere Gipfel haben gleich, nachdem das Land vom Inlandeis befreit war, als Inseln aus dem Wasser geragt. Im Zuge der Landhebung ist das ganze Gebiet allmählich zu trockenem Festland geworden. Nach der Eiszeit hat die Ostsee die im grafischen Schema dargestellten Entwicklungsphasen durchlaufen, in deren Verlaufe die an den Ufern wirkenden Naturkräfte an den Hängen der Bodenerhebungen in verschiedener Höhe Ufermarkierungen abgetragen oder akkumuliert haben. Ufermarkierungen sind an solchen Stellen entstanden, wo der Untergrund und die Geländegestalt dem Wasser das Formen der Erdoberfläche ermöglicht haben.

Im Bild links das Geröll einer vorzeitlichen Uferlinie des Bottnischen Meerbusens am Berg Parravuori in Teuva.

The Plains

Die Tiefebene

The main reason for Ostrobothnia's flatness is the fact that the surface of the plains survived the tumult of the ice age rather intact. The edge of the ice sheet did not stop long here, so few terminal moraines came into being. The area was also under water for a relatively long period. Fine material was detached from ancient shores by the waves and more was carried down by the rivers and deposited on the ancient seabed. Finer material was also carried furthest from the various shorelines and deposited in the deepest places. All this made the topography fairly flat.

The plain was created by the peasants of Ostrobothnia during centuries of assiduous toil. They cleared fields, giving it its most typical expression. The most fertile land, usually along the rivers, has been cleared for agricultural use.

The most extensive stretches of cleared agricultural land are along the Kyrö and Lapua rivers, with salients extending to Seinäjoki and Kauhava. The northern part of Ostrobothnia, around Liminka, is another impressive, continuous stretch of farmland. In the southern part of the region, the farmland zone is rather clearly limited to the belts along the rivers.

Habitation and the road network mostly lie along the rivers, but not right beside their banks. The farmhouses have been built several hundred metres from the river banks and from five to ten metres above the normal water level, so flood precautions have been taken.

Die Hauptursache für die Flachheit von Österbotten liegt darin, dass die Oberfläche der Tiefebene den Ansturm der Eiszeit relativ unbeschadet überstanden hat. Bei seinem Rückzug hat der abschmelzende Rand des Inlandeises in dieser Gegend nicht sehr lange Halt gemacht, so dass keine Endmoränen entstehen konnten. Weiterhin hat dieses Gebiet relativ lange unter Wasser gestanden. Feine Materie, die von den Flüssen mitgeführt und vom Meer aus den früheren Ufern ausgespült wurde, lagerte sich schichtweise auf dem Boden des einstigen Meeres ab. Die feinste Materie wie beispielsweise Ton trieb am weitesten ins Meer hinaus und setzte sich in den tiefsten Niederungen ab.

Die Ebenheit entstand nicht zuletzt auch durch den Menschen. Charakteristisch für diese Landschaft sind ausgedehnte Feldermeere: die fruchtbarsten Ländereien, zumeist an den Flussläufen, sind zu Äckern gerodet worden.

Die ausgedehntesten Feldflächen erstrecken sich über die Flusslandschaften am Kyrönjoki und Lapuanjoki. Ein weiteres einheitliches, in seiner Ebenheit noch eindrucksvolleres Gebiet breitet sich in der Gegend um Liminka aus. In Süd-Österbotten beschränken sich die offenen Feldflächen zumeist auf die Flussläufe.

Besiedlung und Wegenetz folgen gewöhnlich den Flussläufen. Die Häuser stehen jedoch nicht direkt an den Ufern. Vor allem an den Unterläufen befinden sie sich 5—10 Meter über dem normalen Wasserspiegel, oft Hunderte Meter von den Flussbetten entfernt.

1

2

In a typical Ostrobothnian landscape, villages and roads are on both banks of the river (1). Cornstacks are nowadays quite an unusual sight (2).

A decline in rye cultivation and greater emphasis on seed purity has made the cornflower a rare species in this part of the world (3).

The corncrake has been becoming rarer as a species since the turn of the century. However, in the past decade or so its homely call has again been heard more frequently on the Ostrobothnian plains (4).

In der typischen Landschaft Österbottens liegen Dörfer und Strassen beidseitig der Flussläufe (1). Getreidegarben sind ein seltener Anblick geworden (2). Die Kornblume trifft man nicht mehr so häufig an wie früher, da der Roggenanbau zurückgegangen ist und das Saatgetreide gründlicher gereinigt wird (3). Der Wiesenschnarren ist seit der Jahrhundertwende seltener geworden. In den letzten Jahrzehnten ist das trauliche Knarren dieses Vogels jedoch wieder etwas häufiger von den Feldern und Wiesen zu hören (4).

3

4

The Suupohja Coast
Die Suupohja-Küste

The southernmost part of Ostrobothnia is called Suupohja. The coast of the open area of sea north of the Åland Islands is relatively unindented and has few islands. The even, little-changing features of the terrain are copied on the sea bottom.

Fishing has meant a lot to the Suupohja area. Abundant catches, mostly herrings, have been hauled in with seine nets just offshore. There are plenty of idyllic small jetties and boathouses just short distances from each other. One can see fishermen clearing their nets or freezing the fish by the sheltered side of the boathouse. In the future, most fish landings will be in Kaskinen and some other better-equipped fishing harbours, but smaller jetties will remain in the fishermen's home harbours and for recreational use.

Until now no large-scale industry has visible influenced the environment. This is, however, changing. The district's industrial potential has now been noticed. In particular the forests of Suupohja have caught the eye of industrial interests and a major wood-processing complex is now in operation at Kaskinen.

Agriculture is still the most important form of production in this region. The area has specialised in greenhouse-centred market-garden cultivation and this manifests itself in the landscape. In Närpiö, one of the principal towns in the area, there are so many greenhouses they nearly touch each other. The area is almost a glittering sea of glass. This tendency to specialise has spread from the Swedish-speaking districts along the coast to the Finnish-speaking areas only to a limited extent.

Als Suupohja bezeichnet man den südlichsten Teil Süd-Österbottens. Die Küste des mittleren Bottnischen Meerbusens südlich des sogenannten Meerquarks ist offen und inselarm. Die ebene, nur wenig variierende Oberflächengestalt des Terrains setzt sich gleichmässig auch auf dem Meeresboden fort.

Der Fischfang ist für die Suupohja-Bewohner von grosser Bedeutung. Vor allem Strömlinge gehen vor der Küste in grösseren Mengen ins Netz. An der Küste stehen in geringen Abständen zahllose kleine Bootsschuppen mit Stegen. Im Schutze der Schuppen arbeiten häufig Fischer beim Entwirren ihrer Netze oder beim Sortieren des Fangs. In Zukunft wird sich die Fangannahme immer mehr auf Kaskinen und einige andere gut ausgestattete Fischereihäfen konzentrieren.

Grosse, die Landschaft prägende Industrie gibt es im Suupohja-Bereich noch nicht. Dies dürfte sich jedoch bald ändern. Die Möglichkeiten, welche diese Gegend der industriellen Produktion bietet, sind inzwischen entdeckt worden. Vor allem die Wälder dieser Region haben das Interesse der Industrie geweckt.

Die Moore der österbottnischen Küste sind geologisch noch jung und haben daher nur eine flache Torfschicht, so dass ihre Entwicklung Gegenstand besonderen Interesses ist. Zwar kann man den Fabriken strenge Auflagen zur Abwasserreinigung machen, aber dennoch beschleichen Zweifel die Naturfreunde: wird man in Zukunft im Suupohja-Gebiet noch Edelfische fangen?

Die wichtigste Produktionsform ist hier auch weiterhin die Landwirtschaft. In dieser Gegend hat man sich auf den Treibhausanbau spezialisiert, und dementsprechend ist auch das Landschaftsbild. In Närpiö steht praktisch Treibhaus neben Treibhaus. Diese Gegend ist geradezu ein glitzerndes Glasmeer.

There are two types of alders in Finland, the common alder and the speckled alder. For some reason, the latter seems to avoid Southern Finnish seashores as far north as Kokkola. From there northwards, speckled alder is very common even on the coast (1). In the picture, a dense growth of common alder by the sea.

An old fishing port at Kaskinen (2).

In Finnland gedeihen zwei Erlenarten, die Rot- und die Grau-Erle. Aus irgendeinem Grunde meidet die Grau-Erle die Küste des Bottnischen Meerbusens bis hinauf nach Kokkola. Erst weiter nördlich ist sie auch an der Küste verbreitet. Im Bild dichte Rot-Erlenbewaldung an der Küste (1).

Der alte Fischerhafen in Kaskinen (2).

1

2

An Ever-Changing Coastline
Die Küste verändert sich

An examination of maps drawn in different years gives a very good idea of the extent to which the land is rising. The diagram below was prepared on the basis of maps drawn in 1906 and 1963. In 57 years, over 60 hectares of seabed had been exposed, and a part of it had already been placed under crops (1). What was once seabed is now a marshy coastal meadow (2).

Beim Vergleichen von Landkarten verschiedenen Alters erhält man einen Begriff von den Auswirkungen der Landhebung. Die untenstehende Zeichnung basiert auf Landkarten aus den Jahren 1906 und 1963. Innerhalb von 57 Jahren hat das Meer hier 60 Hektar Land freigegeben, das zum Teil schon landwirtschaftlich genutzt wird. (1) Der einstige Meeresboden ist heute nasse Uferwiese (2).

The land area of Finland is increasing by about 10 km² per year. With the exception of Lapland, the whole country is rising, most of all along the Gulf of Bothnia coast between Kokkola and Raahe. The annual rate of rise is 7—8 mm in the Northernmost parts of the Gulf, 5 mm around Turku and even at Helsinki about 4 mm. It manifests itself most perceptibly on shallow shores, such as those north of Vaasa and south of Oulu.

One explanation that has been presented for this phenomenon is that it results from isostatic recovery after the withdrawal of the massive ice sheet that covered Finland during the Pleistocene. However, it is also connected with the continuous movement of the earth's crust, which never rests in its efforts to achieve equilibrium with itself.

Land upheaval also affects the lives of the coastal inhabitants. In the course of the years, whole maritime towns have had to be moved nearer to the sea.

Who owns this new bottom land? According to the law, the land belongs to the riparian owner, but one may not begin cultivating it until an official land distribution has been carried out.

Different species of plants establish themselves on newly emerged islands in accordance with a very rigid pattern. Thus on the basis of the flora it contains, it is possible to determine when and in the course of what period

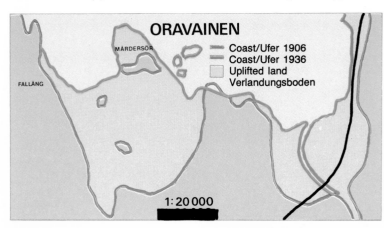

ORAVAINEN

MÄRDERSÖR

FALLÄNG

— Coast/Ufer 1906
— Coast/Ufer 1936
▢ Uplifted land
Verlandungsboden

1:20 000

1

2

an island or its various parts have risen from the sea.

Three pioneer species, reed canary grass, Bothnian hairgrass and spike rush can establish themselves on islands that have risen only about 10 cm above the sea. Next come narrow small reed and creeping fescue. Other plants that appear on an island at quite an early stage are a variety of field milk-thistle, tufted vetch and purple loose strife. Sea buckthorn is also common.

Botanists have found that 22 plant species established themselves on the islands of the Kvarken Strait during their first century of existence as dry land. Within another century, the number of species had grown to seventy.

Das finnische Festland wächst alle hundert Jahre um rund zehn Quadratkilometer. Mit Ausnahme Lapplands hebt sich das Land überall in Finnland, am meisten an der Küste zwischen Kokkola und Raahe. Die jährliche Landhebung beträgt maximal 9 Millimeter, im Norden des Bottnischen Meerbusens liegen die Werte bei 7—8, um Turku bei 5 und selbst in Helsinki noch bei 4 Millimetern.

Als Erklärung für die Landhebung haben die Geologen das Einsinken der Erdoberfläche unter dem Inlandeis und ihren elastischen Wiederanstieg nach Verschwinden dieser Belastung angeführt. Gleichzeitig bestehen jedoch auch Zusammenhänge mit anderen permanenten Bewegungen der Erdkruste. Die Massen der Erdkruste streben einen Zustand des Gleichgewichts an.

Das Phänomen der Landhebung beeinflusst auch das Leben der Küstenbewohner. Im Laufe der Zeiten sind ganze Städte an die neuen Küsten verlegt worden, da die alten Zentren weit im Binnenland zurückgeblieben waren.

Wem gehört das vom Meer freigegebene Land? Dem Gesetz nach dem Besitzer des Wassergebiets. Dennoch darf es nicht gewerblich genutzt werden, bevor die Landteilung offiziell besiegelt ist.

Die Pflanzenarten halten in recht exakter Reihenfolge Einzug auf den neuen Inseln. Daher kann man aus der Zusammensetzung der Flora Rückschlüsse auf das Alter der Inseln und ihrer einzelnen Teile ziehen.

Die Pionierarten, Bottnische Schmiele, Glanzgras und Nadelbinse, fassen auf Inseln Fuss, die erst zehn Zentimeter über den Meeresspiegel hinausragen. Als nächste erobern Moor-Reitgras und Rot-Schwingel die Insel. Weiterhin werden im Frühstadium die Küstenart der Acker-Gänsedistel, Vogelwicke, Gemeiner Blutwenderich und Sanddorn ansässig.

Auf den Inseln im Mittelteil des Bottnischen Meerbusens wurden 22 Pflanzenarten gezählt, die innerhalb der ersten hundert Jahre der Existenz der Inseln auf diesen Fuss fassen konnten. Im folgenden Jahrhundert erreichte der Pflanzenbestand schon 70 Arten.

A Land of Rivers

Land der Flüsse

Ostrobothnia is a region of few waterbodies. In Southern Ostrobothnia water covers less than one per cent of the total area. The terrain is flat and even the higher ridges are aligned in the same direction as the rivers, so no large water basins have been able to form. Of the few lakes that once existed, many have been drained and partially reclaimed for agricultural use. The lakes that remain are mostly in the rivers' source areas, in the Suomenselkä watershed.

The Ostrobothnian rivers of today flow in valleys several kilometres wide, which were carved out by mighty rivers before the last Ice Age. For the most part they flow sluggishly. Only as one approaches the Suomenselkä Ridge do they flow through deep canyons, sometimes forming small rapids. Here and there in their lower reaches the rivers fall over shallow ledges. Since the land is rising faster at the coast than upstream, the rate of fall of the rivers is constantly declining.

Österbotten ist eine wasserarme Region. Weniger als ein Prozent Süd-Österbottens ist Wasser. Das Terrain ist eben, und auch die höheren Erdrücken verlaufen parallel zu den Flüssen, so dass keine grösseren Wasserbecken entstehen konnten. Etliche der wenigen Seen, die hier einst existiert haben, sind ausgetrocknet. Seen findet man in erster Linie an den Oberläufen der Flüsse im Wasserscheidengebiet des Suomenselkä.

Die Flüsse von Österbotten haben in die alten, vor der Eiszeit entstandenen Flussbetten zurückgefunden. Nur so sind die mehrere Kilometer breiten Flusstäler zu erklären. Die meisten Flüsse fliessen langsam. Nur an ihren Oberläufen strömen sie durch tiefe Cañontäler und bilden örtlich kleine Stromschnellen. Hier und da müssen sie auch an den Unterläufen flachere Schwellen überwinden.

Da das Land sich in den Mündungsgebieten schneller hebt als an den Oberläufen, flachen die Fussgefälle auch weiterhin ab.

1

Ostrobothnia has numerous sluggish rivers which flood in spring (1).

Ostrobothnia is an agricultural region. Plant exuberance in the waterbodies is caused by the rich nutrients leached from the fields (2).

The shallow shore of Evijärvi Lake (3).

In Österbotten gibt es zahlreiche langsam fliessende Flüsse, die während der Schneeschmelze im Frühjahr über ihre Ufer treten (1).

Österbotten ist eine Agrarlandschaft. Aus den Feldern sickern grosse Nährstoffmengen in die Flüsse, und die Wasservegetation eutrophiert (2).

Das flache Ufer des Evijärvi-Sees (3).

THE RIVERS OF OSTROBOTHNIA
DIE FLÜSSE VON ÖSTERBOTTEN

Lappajärvi

Lake Lappajärvi has been called the "Pearl of Ostrobothnia". It richly deserves this name, since its broad expanse of open water makes a truly exceptional impression amid the rivers of the plains and the bleakness of the Suomenselkä Ridge.

The blue waters of Lake Lappajärvi are one of the largest single expanses of inland waters in Finland. There are few islands, and most of them are small, so there is an unobstructed view from one shore to the other. Viewed longitudinally, the opposite shore is not visible at all in some places. From North to South the lake is 25 km in length, its greatest width is 13 km and its area 160 km². The bed of the lake contain two valleys extending along its full length and reaching depths of 38 and 36 metres. A few islands lie in the shallow central zone. The largest of these, Kärnänsaari, is in the northern part of the lake.

Dacite-type rocks which are classified as an igneous variety have been found on the island of Kärnänsaari and named "kärnäite". It was earlier supposed that the island was on the site of a volcanic crater which had filled with lava. However, the most recent studies have indicated that the crater was in fact caused by a meteor. The geologic changes in evidence were produced by an explosion of such violence that a volcano could not have caused them. The nickel and cobalt traces in the minerals also correspond to those found in meteorites.

Kärnäite is found in the bedrock of the northern part of Kärnänsaari as well as on two other smaller islands nearby.

The water of Lake Lappajärvi is very clear — quite suitable for drinking. The shores are mostly either rocky or grassy, but a few sandy beaches can also be found.

The eastern shore of the lake is shallow; in the bays one can wade out quite a distance before reaching swimming depth. The western shore slopes much more steeply. Because its western side is rising faster than elsewhere, the lake is constantly expanding, but this growth is now being artificially regulated to suit the requirements of the Hanhikoski hydroelectric plant.

Man nennt den Lappajärvi-See "Perle Österbottens". Nicht ohne Grund: seine offene Seenfläche zwischen den Flussläufen des Flachlands und dem kargen trocknen Waldboden des Suomenselkä bietet wirklich einen unerwartet schönen Anblick.

Die blau schimmernde offene Seenfläche gehört zu den grössten offenen Gewässern Finnlands. Inseln gibt es nur wenige, und die meisten von ihnen sind klein. Die Länge des Sees beträgt in Nord—Süd-Richtung 25 Kilometer, seine grösste Breite 13 Kilometer und seine Fläche 160 Quadratkilometer. Auf dem Boden des Lappajärvi-Sees verlaufen in Längsrichtung zwei Täler, deren tiefste Senkungen 38 und 36 Meter messen. In der flacheren Seemitte gibt es einige Inseln, deren grösste, Kärnänsaari, nur durch einen schmalen Sund vom Kirchdorf Lappajärvi getrennt ist.

Auf Kärnänsaari wurde eine zu den Lavagesteinen gehörende dacitähnliche Gesteinsart gefunden, die man Kärnäit benannt hat. Früher nahm man an, dass sich an der Stelle der Insel einst ein Krater befunden hatte, der sich mit Lava gefüllt hat. Neuere Untersuchungen haben jedoch ergeben, dass der fragliche Krater durch Meteoriteneinschlag entstanden ist. Die Veränderungen in den Gesteinen wurden durch eine Explosion derartiger Intensität verursacht, dass vulkanische Tätigkeit als Erklärung ausscheidet. Weiterhin entspricht der Nickel- und Kobaltgehalt der Steinminerale den Werten anderenorts gefundener Meteoriten. Kärnäit ist im festen Felsgrund im Nordteil von Kärnänsaari sowie auf den Inseln Lokkisaari und Vartiasaari anzutreffen.

Das Wasser des Lappajärvi-Sees ist sehr klar und gut zum Trinken geeignet. Das Ufer ist grösstenteils steinig und grasreich, aber stellenweise findet man auch Sandstrand.

Das Ostufer des Sees ist flach, und man muss weit waten, um Schwimmtiefe zu erreichen. Das Westufer fällt erheblich steiler ab, und die Landhebung vergrössert diesen Unterschied. Die Fläche des Sees wächst langsam aber stetig, da das Land sich bei den Abflüssen schneller hebt als in den anderen Teilen des Sees.

Lappajärvi Lake is in a part of Ostrobothnia otherwise poor in water bodies. It is no wonder that such an exceptional feature of the region is called a "pearl". The largest island in the lake, Kärnänsaari, is located in its northern part. This island has become famous for a type of rock found there and called kärnäite. This rock was once believed to be volcanic in origin. In reality, however, the Kärnänsaari crater is not volcanic, but was caused by the impact of a meteorite long before the dawn of history.

Der Lappajärvi-See liegt in der Provinz Vaasa inmitten des sonst seenarmen Österbotten. Kein Wunder, dass man diese landschaftliche Ausnahme "Perle Österbottens" nennt. Die grösste Insel des Sees, Kärnänsaari, ist durch eine besondere Gesteinsart, das Kärnäit, bekannt geworden, von der man lange annahm, sie sei vulkanischen Ursprungs. Tatsächlich gibt es auf Kärnänsaari keine Vulkankrater, sondern vermutlich handelt es sich um einen durch Einschlag und Explosion eines Meteoriten verursachten Krater.

Street Villages and a "Haybarn Archipelago"

Strassendörfer und Scheunenmeer

The farms of Ostrobothnia are most typically located in long queues on both sides of the roads. This is because the roads run parallel to the rivers and the most advantageous site for a farmhouse is as close as possible to both road and river. There are few cluster-type villages such as one finds in central Europe. Instead, they are long, narrow street villages, often merging into each other.

The most typical farmhouses are long, two-storey types and the best village units are to be found in the communities along the Lapuanjoki River.

The abundance of haybarns is a striking feature of Southern Ostrobothnia. In the days before mechanised farming it was easier to store hay where it was mown and then transport it by sled in winter.

Die in Österbotten am weitesten verbreitete Siedlungsform ist das Strassendorf. Die Strassen folgen den Flussläufen, und die Häuser stehen am Rande der Strassen. Da der Bau eines Hauses in Strassen- und Flussnähe die meisten Lage-vorteile bietet, sind die Dörfer langgezogen und teilweise zusam-mengewachsen.

Auch die Landteilung hat zum Entstehen der Strassendörfer in Österbotten beigetragen. Die best-erhaltenen Dorfkomplexe findet man in Kauhava, Lapua und Kuor-tane.

Auffallend in Süd-Österbotten ist der Scheunenreichtum. Früher musste das Heu von Hand in die Scheunen getragen werden. Daher wurden dicht an dicht Scheunen gebaut, aus denen man das Heu erst im Winter auf Schlitten zu den Viehställen transportierte.

The Lapua—Kauhava—Ylihärmä "haybarn archipelago" has been estimated to contain as many as 20,000 haybarns. The picture below is a view of the Kauhava district.

Die für Österbotten typischen Landhäuser sind langgestreckt und teilweise zweistöckig. Man hat im "Scheunenmeer" der Gegend Lapua—Kauhava—Ylihärmä mehr als 20 000 Scheunen gezählt. Im Bild die Scheunenlandschaft bei Kauhava.

Suomenselkä

3

The Suomenselkä Ridge is a watershed zone separating the waters of the lakes in the Finnish interior from those draining into the Gulf of Bothnia. The ridge varies from 100 to 200 metres in height, with Lauhavuori Hill rising to 231 metres in the South-West. The district to the east of it is a fairly level upland.

In central Ostrobothnia the ridge is more level. After this it veers eastwards into the Kainuu region, where it also reaches its greatest height.

Also where climate is concerned, the Suomenselkä Ridge is at a disadvantage compared with its neighbouring regions. The Haapamäki — Myllymäki districts are covered in snow when Oulu, quite a bit further north, is still snowfree.

The soil is also poor. Because of this, the range of flora is less extensive than that in Ostrobothnia or the Lake District. Sedges and dwarf birch are common, but a number of sub-species typical of northern regions are also found.

White ptarmigan, cranes and several other bird species rare in Southern Finland are common here, while clearly northern species have also been found.

Because of the unfavourable climate and soil, agriculture is not very profitable. The marshy fields are sensitive to frost and not all grain varieties thrive in the district. Farms are small and livestock raising the most important source of livelihood.

More than half the total land area is covered by peat bogs. In the Suomenselkä Ridge these are mainly aapa bogs of Nordic type, but in the districts flanking the ridge one can also find raised mires or combinations of both bog types.

2

Der Landrücken Suomenselkä ist ein Wasserscheidengürtel, der die innerfinnische Seenplatte von jenen Flüssen trennt, die in den Bottnischen Meerbusen münden. Der Suomenselkä, der sich inmitten flacheren Terrains erhebt, ist 100—200 Meter hoch.

Durch Mittel-Österbotten verläuft der Suomenselkä als ebeneres Hochland. Nachdem er nach Osten abgeknickt ist, erreicht er in Kainuu seine höchste Stelle.

Der Suomenselkä unterscheidet sich klimatisch nachteilig von seiner Umgebung. So kann es geschehen, dass man im Herbst auf seiner Bahnreise von Süden nach Norden zwischen Haapamäki und Myllymäki durch verschneite Wälder fährt und einige Stunden weiter nördlich wieder schwarze Landschaft um sich hat.

Auch ist der Erdboden steinig. Daher ist die Vegetation artenärmer als in Österbotten und in der Seenplatte. Riedgras und Zwergbirke sind auf dem Suomenselkä weit verbreitet, aber auch nördlichere Pflanzenarten wachsen hier. Entsprechend die Vogelwelt: Moorschneehuhn und Kranich, sonst in Südfinnland selten anzutreffen, wie auch eindeutig lappländische Arten sind hier heimisch.

Des ungünstigen Klimas und Bodens wegen ist die Landwirtschaft nicht sehr ertragreich. Die oft moorigen Felder sind frostempfindlich. Nicht alle Anbaupflanzen gedeihen auf dem Suomenselkä. Die Höfe sind klein, und Viehzucht ist die Haupteinkommensquelle der Bevölkerung.

Mehr als die Hälfte des Bodens ist Moorland. Der häufigste Moortypus ist das nordische Aapamoor, aber daneben existieren auch Hochmoore und Mischformen aus Aapa- und Hochmoor.

The farms in the Suomenselkä region are mostly small. Agricultural yields are low and cattle raising is the most important source of livelihood (1). The region is dominated by bogs and forests (2). An old bridge at Reisjärvi (3).

Die Bauernhöfe des Suomenselkä sind klein und die Felder nicht sehr ertragreich. Die wichtigste Erwerbsform ist die Viehzucht (1). Im Bild Aussicht vom Hügel Suokonmäki in Lehtimäki (2). Alte Holzbrücke in Reisjärvi (3).

The Dunes of Kalajoki
Die Dünen von Kalajoki

The coast of the northern part of the Gulf of Bothnia is mostly flat and without islands. Only now and then does one find an island far out to sea, such as those of the Kallat group. Because the wind can blow unimpeded across those sandy beaches, areas of drifting sand ridges have formed in several places. The Dunes of Kalajoki are among the best examples of these.

An even more extensive area of shifting dunes can be found at Lohtaja south of Kalajoki, while there are smaller areas at Siikajoki, Haukipudas and Hailuoto.

Dunes are created through the action of wind and, to a lesser extent, water. The swell of the waves "sifts" the sand and casts the finer particles up on the shore. After it has dried, this sand is carried further inland by the wind. Uplifting along the coast of the Gulf of Bothnia further assists this process. The sand continues to drift until it meets resitance, usually vegetation. The gradual accumulation of sand leads to the formation of a dune. The side facing the wind slopes gently, while the sheltered side is steeper. Sand is carried up the gentle slope and dropped down the other side; this is how the dunes advance.

The dunes at Kalajoki can be as high as 10 metres and kilometres long. There can be several ridges behind each other. The land between the dunes is hard and coarse-grained. A dune "dies" when vegetation covers it completely.

Die Küste des Bottenwieks ist zumeist eben und insellos. Nur weit draussen auf dem Meer hier und da eine Insel. Da der Wind ungehindert über die sandigen Strände fegen kann, konnten sich Flugsandfelder wie die bekannten Sandbänke von Kalajoki bilden.

Dünen entstehen durch die Tätigkeit des Windes und teilweise auch des Wassers. Die Wellen "sortieren" den Sand und werfen die feineren Körner am weitesten über die Uferlinie hinaus aufs

Dunes are created where the wind is free to blow and pile up sand.
They are forever moving and growing inland. Plants anchor the sand and slow down the rate of advance. Lyme grass is one such anchoring plant (1).

The coast of the northern part of the Gulf of Bothnia is flat and mostly islandless (2).

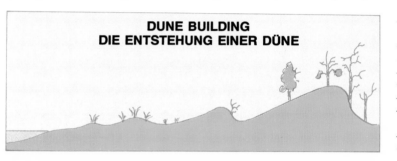

DUNE BUILDING
DIE ENTSTEHUNG EINER DÜNE

Dünenstrände entstehen dort, wo der Wind ungehindert wehen und Sand anhäufen kann. Die Dünen wachsen und bewegen sich landeinwärts. Pflanzen binden den Sand und erschweren so die Fortbewegung der Dünen. Eine dieser dünenbindenden Pflanzen ist der Strandhafer (1).

Die Küste der Bottenwiek ist flach und vorwiegend insellos (2).

1

Land. Wenn der Sand getrocknet ist, greift der Wind zu und weht ihn weiter. Am Ufer des Bottnischen Meerbusens trägt auch die Landhebung zur Freilegung des Sandes bei. Der Wind transportiert den Sand landeinwärts, bis dieser an irgendeinem Hindernis wie beispielsweise Pflanzen hängenbleibt. Hier beginnt sich daraufhin immer mehr Sand anzuhäufen, und eine Düne entsteht. Ihre dem Wind zugewandte Seite steigt sanft an, die windgeschützte fällt steil ab. Der Wind weht den Sand die sanft ansteigende Seite hinauf und lässt ihn auf der geschützten Seite jäh fallen. Auf diese Weise wandern die Dünen.

Die grössten Dünen von Kalajoki sind zehn Meter hoch und viele Kilometer lang. Örtlich ragen mehrere Dünenketten hintereinander auf. Wenn sich Vegetation ihrer bemächtigt und den Einfluss des Windes vollständig unterbindet, bleiben die Dünen stehen und "sterben".

Die Dünen wandern langsam, aber es kommt vor, dass sie bis zum Waldrand vordringen und diesen unter sich begraben. Dies ist auch in Kalajoki geschehen: Die Dünen haben den Wald verschüttet und getötet.

Hailuoto

Hailuoto is a lonely and bleak island in the northern part of the Gulf of Bothnia. It is partly wooded and now has an area of 195 km². At the beginning of its recorded history, it was three separate islands, which have grown together because of the land uplifting going on in the area. The highest point of the island is now a good 32 metres above sea level.

The sea around the island is quite shallow, and since the land continues to rise the coastline is constantly changing. In just a few centuries there will be only a narrow channel between Hailuoto and Oulu, now nine kilometres away.

The shores of Hailuoto vary in type; in places they are grassy or reedy, even boggy, while elsewhere they are gravelly. Where the ridges running across the island reach the sea there are sand dunes.

The shallow, herbaceous bays are ideal for water fowl, especially waders. Hailuoto is an important resting place for birds of passage at migration time. It is one of Finland's most important duck-shooting centres.

The sea gives the inhabitants of Hailuoto "silver", but it is the heathy pine forests that yield "gold". The sandy soil of the heaths is excellent for growing a type of lichen called Iceland moss. Immediately after it rains, the collectors rush to fill their boxes with the lichen, which must be picked while wet to avoid crumbling. It is exported mainly to central Europe, where it is used for pharmaceutical and decorative purposes. It earns more for the islanders than fishing and farming together.

Hailuoto ist eine einsame und karge, bewaldete Insel in der Bottenwiek, dem Nordteil des Bottnischen Meerbusens. Zu Beginn ihrer überlieferten Geschichte bestand Hailuoto aus drei einzelnen Inseln, die später im Zuge der Landhebung zusammengewachsen sind. Die höchste Erhebung der heute 195 Quadratkilometer grossen Insel liegt 32 Meter über dem Meeresspiegel.

Die Uferlinie von Hailuoto ändert sich ständig. Das umliegende Meer ist sehr flach. In einigen hundert Jahren wird nur noch eine schmale Rinne Hailuoto von Oulu trennen. Heute liegen zwischen Hailuoto und Oulu noch neun Kilometer Wasser.

Das Ufer von Hailuoto ist teilweise gras- und schilfbewachsen, örtlich sogar sumpfig. Anderswo dominieren Kiesfelder. Wo die quer über Hailuoto verlaufenden Oser die Uferlinie schneiden, dehnen sich Sandfelder aus.

Die flachen, grasbewachsenen Buchten sind gute Niststätten für die Wasservögel, besonders für die Stelzvögel. Während der Zugzeit ist Hailuoto ein bevorzugter Rastplatz der Zugvögel. Der Wasservogelbestand ist sehr gross.

Auf den sandigen Waldböden von Hailuoto gedeiht das Rentiermoos. Nach Regenfällen stürmen die Moossammler mit ihren Kisten in die Wälder. Zum Sammeln muss das Rentiermoos feucht sein, sonst zerbröckelt es. Das Moos wird als Rohstoff für die pharmazeutische Industrie oder als Dekorationsmaterial exportiert. Es ist für die Insulaner eine wichtigere Einkommensquelle als Landwirtschaft und Fischfang zusammen.

2

Creeping fescue is one of the first plants to establish themselves on land just emerged from the sea (1). The sea goose, which nests on Hailuoto, is the largest of Finland's sea birds (2). Hailuoto is a sandy island. The bedrock is 30 m below the surface (3).

Als eines der ersten Gräser hält der Rot-Schwingel auf dem vom Meer freigegebenen Land Einzug (1). Auch die grosse und prächtige Graugans nistet auf Hailuoto (2). Hailuoto ist eine Sandinsel. Der Felsgrund beginnt erst in dreissig Meter Tiefe (3).

3

Rokua

Rokua National Park contains broad expanses of pine heath carpeted with Iceland moss. Many small basins have grown into peat mires.

Die Kiefernwaldböden des Nationalparks sind mit Flechten bewachsen. In den Os-Mulden haben sich kleine Teiche gebildet, die zugewachsen sind. Die Darstellung zeigt das Verwachsen eines Teichs.

Northern Ostrobothnia is mostly flat; fields, meadows and peat bogs. However, the Rokua district west of Lake Oulujärvi is an exception to this rule. Rokuanvaara Hill is not a moraine hill with a rock core like the arctic hills of Eastern Finland. It is, in fact an esker ridge, which has been broken up by kettle-holes and further scarred by wind and water. The largest and most open of these glacial pits is a lake called Pitkäjärvi.

Stagnant water favours peat formation. Sphagnum moss and other plants can begin growing in a pond or lake, either along the bottom or on the surface. Growth along the surface occurs in ponds poor in nutrients. That is what has happened at Rokua. A "raft" of sphagnum and other water plants has begun growing out from the banks, forming a treacherous

The diagram shows how a basin is transformed into a tertiary mire system. A peat layer grows across the surface, while vegetable debris accumulates on the bottom.

Das Torffloss wächst vom Ufer zur Teichmitte hin. Gleichzeitig sammeln sich auf dem Teichboden Pflanzenreste an.

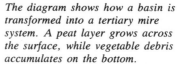

PALUDIFICATION
DAS VERWACHSEN EINES TEICHS

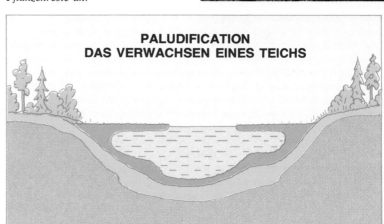

quagmire. In time, the whole pond will be filled with vegetation, but a soft hole can remain in the middle for a very long period.

Only after the entire water volume has been filled with peat will the upper layers begin to grow. Trees may also grow on the surface.

Since 1956, there has been a 420-hectare national park around Rokuavaara Hill and to the South stretch the drained peatlands of Pelso.

Der Norden von Österbotten ist grösstenteils Flachland: Felder, Wiesen, Moore. Eine Ausnahme bildet hier das Rokua-Gebiet im Gebiet der Gemeinde Vaala am Westufer der Oulujärvi-Sees. Der Rokuanvaara ist ein von Os-Mulden zersplittertes Os-Gebiet. Hinzu kommt, dass einst Wind und Wasser seiner Oberfläche hart mitgespielt haben. Die grösste und offenste Os-Mulde des Rokua ist der Pitkäjärvi-See.

Stehende Gewässer bieten gün-stige Voraussetzungen für die Ver-sumpfung. Ein Teich kann über die Oberfläche oder den Grund mit Torfmoos und anderen Sumpf-pflanzen verwachsen. Nährstoffar-me und saure Teiche verwachsen über die Oberfläche. So auch am Rokuanvaara. Vom Ufer her be-ginnen Torfmoos- und Bitterklee-flösse die Teichoberfläche zu über-wachsen, wobei sich ein trügeri-scher Sumpfboden bildet. Im Laufe der Zeit verwächst der ganze Teich, aber in seiner Mitte kann noch lange Zeit eine Blänke aus-gespart bleiben. Erst nachdem die Wasseroberfläche vollständig zu-gewachsen ist, beginnt die Bildung der oberen Moorschichten. Oben-auf können auch Bäume wachsen; dann ist das Endresultat ein Reiser-moor.

Der Rokuanvaara wurde 1956 zum Nationalpark erklärt und misst insgesamt 420 Hektar. Süd-lich von ihm dehnt sich die weit-läufige trockengelegte Moorebene von Pelso aus.

The Aapa Bogs of Peräpohjola
Die Aapamoore von Peräpohjola

Martimo Bog is one of Finland's most valuable bird bogs (1). The red-throated loon is still numerous at Martimo Bog (2). The crane is the king of the bog (3).

Das Martimoaapa ist ein wertvolles Vogelmoor (1). Der Sterntaucherbestand des Moores ist ungewöhnlich gross (2). Der Kranich ist der König der Moorvögel (3).

1 The most common mire complexes found in Peräpohjola, the northernmost part of Ostrobothnia, are called aapa bogs. Aapa bogs are deepest around the edges and shallowest in the middle. The geographical differences in the distribution of these two types are the result of climatic conditions. Aapa bogs develop in colder and drier climates and thus one finds them in Lapland.

The peat is deeper at the edge of an aapa bog because growth conditions are better there than in the centre. The surface of the peat is closer to mineral-bearing soil at the edge. The surface topography of this kind of bog also means that the water flows towards the middle. The narrow strips of peat on which the sphagnum moss grow align themselves with the direction of water flow. Between them are marshy zones growing sedge peat. The centre of an aapa bog sometimes contains a small pond with the sphagnum strips arranged in a helical pattern around it.

Der in Peräpohjola, dem nördlichsten Teil von Österbotten, am weitesten verbreitete Moortyp ist das Aapamoor. Während das im Süden überwiegende Hochmoor zur Mitte hin ansteigt, ist das Aapamoor an den Ränder am höchsten und fällt zur Mitte hin ab. Aapamoore entstehen in kälterem und tröckenerem Klima, so dass man sie in Nordfinnland einschliesslich Österbotten und Kainuu antrifft.

Dass die Ränder des Aapamoors höher liegen als der Mittelteil rührt daher, dass sie bessere Wachstumsbedingungen bieten. An den Rändern liegt der Mineralboden näher an der Oberfläche. Aufgrund der Oberflächengestalt fliesst das Wasser von den Rändern auf die Mitte zu. Schmale weisstorfbildende Stränge wachsen vertikal zur Strömungsrichtung. Zwischen diesen Strängen wächst torfbildendes Ried. Das feuchte und nachgebende Ried überwiegt gegenüber den festeren Strängen. In der Mitte können Teiche stehen. Oft umlaufen die Stränge wie ein Spinnennetz die Aapamoormitte.

2

3

Oulujärvi

Lake Oulujärvi is the main component of a large water system. Its area, usually about 900 km² fluctuates from 778 km² to 944 km² because of artificial regulation. There is a difference of 2.7 m between the maximum and minimum water levels and since the lake's shores slope gently large areas are regularly covered and uncovered as if the lake were tidal.

In common with most other Finnish water bodies, Lake Oulujärvi is quite shallow. The deepest point is 34.5 m, but the depth is usually less than 14 m. The island of Manamasalo divides the lake into two areas of relatively open water.

The river draining the lake flows out of its western side, where land upheaval is greatest. As the lake basin gradually tilts its eastern parts are deeping, leading to shore erosion and steep banks. Water level regulation has altered conditions in Oulujärvi Lake, but nothing can change the slow, but steady process of land upheaval.

Der Oulujärvi-See ist das Zentralgewässer des Oulujoki-Flussgebiets. Seine Fläche beträgt rund 900 Quadratkilometer, aber da der See reguliert wird, variiert sie stark (778—944 qkm). Das Ufer des Oulujärvi ist seicht, so dass die Regulierdifferenz von 2,7 Metern grosse Uferteile freilegt oder bedeckt.

Wie die meisten finnischen Seen ist der Oulujärvi relativ flach. Die tiefste Stelle misst 34,5 Meter, aber zumeist bleibt die Tiefe unter 14 Metern. Die schöne Sandstrandinsel Manamansalo teilt den Oulujärvi in zwei Teile.

Der Oulujärvi fliesst an der gleichen Stelle ab, an der auch die Landhebung am schnellsten vorangeht. Weil das Seenbecken somit kippt, steigt am Ostufer allmählich der Wasserspiegel. Die Folge ist eine Erosion des Ufers und das Entstehen steiler Uferböschungen. Die Regulierung hat den See verändert, die durch die Landhebung verursachte Entwicklung hingegen kann vom Menschen nicht aufgehalten werden.

The shores of Lake Oulujärvi slope gently and water level regulation causes enormous fluctuations in its area. Fishing and boating are also affected.

Das Ufer des Oulujärvi ist seicht, und die Regulierung der Wasserhöhe ändert stark die Uferlinie. Die Regulierung erschwert auch Bootssport und Fischfang.

1 2

The Finnish Lakeland

Seen-Finnland

When The Lakes Are Smiling

by/von Elina Karjalainen

With summer giving way to autumn, I returned home from a long journey. As the evening was growing dim, I reached the heart of the Finnish Lake District, between Jyväskylä and Kuopio, where the road runs alongside great stretches of water for long distances. The scenery already gave a hint of the coming colours of autumn: the rowan branches, reddened by the cold nights, dropped towards the water from the banks and in the green of the forest the aspen glowed like a flame.

At a parking place situated in the most beautiful spot along this lake-embracing road, I stopped to rest. From the top of a high hill a lakescape opened out before me. The setting sun had nearly reached the dark, serrated edge of the forest. Slender, dark night clouds like long, greedy tongues cast their shadows on the waters and the colour display of autumn made the scenery all the more striking.

As I sat and rested, my mind still retained the images gained during several months in Europe. I remembered an evening strolling by Lake Geneva with a friend, when I had remarked that the scenery, beautiful as it was, seemed strangely exhausted and worn.

"Do you believe that a landscape can grow tired if too many eyes view it?", asked my friend. I laughed increduously, but he went on: "This lake has been spread all over the world as pretty postcards, and it has been brought home as pictures on boxes of chocolates. In addition, because through the years it has been a place of refuge for exiles, the eyes that have beheld it would have preferred to see the scenery of their own, lost homelands, deeply rooted in their hearts."

I remembered this poetic claim as I smilingly sat in the darkening evening viewing a Finnish lakescape. It bore a unique expression: at that moment, those colours and those shadows, lights, patterns on the surface of the water and the fiery farewell of the setting sun were meant for me and me alone.

My home district is in Northern Savo, in the middle of the Finnish Lake District. It is surrounded by lakes with names like Kallavesi, Juurusvesi, Ruokovesi and Suvasvesi. Almost as though this wealth of water were not enough, small, detached patches of lake dot the landscape here and there. Sometimes in her acts of creation nature can perform deeds of amazing extravagance, and this is what has happened to the inhabitants of the Lake District; they certainly need not complain of a shortage of water.

People came to these districts along the water routes, and their lives are still oriented towards the lakes. The windows look towards the shore, garden paths lead down towards the lake and saunas stand mopingly by the waterline. These saunas and their Saturday fragrance are part of my lakeland atmosphere. They are the culmination of a humdrum and hard working week. They suck the people exhausted by work and toil into their dark wombs. Cares and stress fade away with the angry hissing of the water on the hot stones and the cleansing lake is always waiting.

Rowing across the lake on Saturday evenings in summer, I have seen a human figure, reddened by the steam, sitting by the smoke shrouded sauna. He reclined in the pleasant afterglow of the steam and the water, limbs relaxed, his thoughts indolently surging and moving across the surface of the water, which buoys them up like water lilies. Time flows past, tension and haste are gone.

There is a different atmosphere during the day. A tractor sputters in a shoreside meadow and cocks of hay stand like portly old ladies standing along the road leading to the church. Further away, where the gleaming blade of the mowing machine is cutting down the beauty of summer; bluebells, oxeye daisies, buttercups and the strawberries drooping along the drains, one hears the grunts of people hard at work and haywads cleave the air on the ends of their forks.

Like the natives, another lakeshore population that is growing rapidly, the summer residents, have turned their lifestyle around water. However, these residences are surrounded by a different kind of atmosphere than that in which land owned by the same family for several generations is steeped. The summer residents have done their work in winter; now

their main task in life is to be leisurely. They are entitled to their sweet leisure; to sprawl in a deckchair with the house-pennant streaming at the end of a pole or to take off in a speedy, high-powered boat to picknicks on island promontories.

The natives watch this commotion, leaning on hayforks or resting against the bench of a mowing machine, but soon turn their attention back to work. For them, the winter of the Lake District is the time when the work lets its doer take a break and lie long hours on the bench under the window, an old worn fur hat under one's head and a coat as a bedcover, or steep one's limbs in the warmth of the fire. In their annual rhythm they are much closer to nature than the holiday residents.

The Finnish Lake District is at its best in the sunny days of summer. And when I think of my childhood, I feel the sun always shone, but this isn't at all true. In autumn, when it was time to soak flax in the black waters of the pond, it mostly rained. It was hard to yield to autumn and to give up summer. So we went to do this work barefoot and ones legs were covered with dried and cracked soil that stung. My wet skirt beat against my calves and the cold made me shiver to the heart. Or we went to the mill. The horse plodded along the road by the lake shore pulling the load of corn. The surface of the water was full of widening circles caused by the falling raindrops. Grey fog wafted by the shores, the horse's hair gleamed wetly and the wheels of the cart jerked in the rain-made ruts in the sandy road. The forest smelled of decay and mushrooms, sweet melancholy lived in the mind of the miller.

Winter. Across my home lake goes a staked road. In the white plain the stakes look like hands, appeals for help.

An icy lid has covered the lake and I imagine that the billows under the ice have also frozen just as they lapped. The chilly moonlight of midwinter comes, when millions of diamonds sparkle on the snow. After midwinter, time proceeds until the Tengmalm's owls make their appearance. Bright bubbling echoes on the shores. In the daytime men fishing through a hole drilled in the ice move about on the lake and their footmarks are visible on the snow. The ice melts away, there's a strong wind from the South. The ice lid breaks to pieces and the wind brings ice cubes to the shore, tinkling and ringing when they hit the rocks. The people in the Lake District are like the landscape. The lakes smile and the people, too, smile easily in these parts. The shoreline is capricious, but there are also caprices in the human mind; they find expression in the flexible turn of speech and hilarious metaphors of the dialect. I believe that those who dwell by the shores have got a little of the glimmer of the lakes into their lives.

People have left these shores for distant stone villages in the South and West. Like an echo of the depression caused by this exodus, the alarm signals of nature protection ring for our polluting lakes. A human being becomes very keen-eared and easily notices the warning signs in his own landscape. Prophesy, predicting doom is the burden of the shoreline dweller, but alas: the landscape breathes calmly and tranquilly in harmony with time, and as long as it breathes like this from summer to winter and from winter to summer, the shore dwellers remain optimistic.

Wenn die Seen lächeln

Am Wendepunkt zwischen Sommer und Herbst kehrte ich von einer langen Reise zurück. Der Abend brach schon an, als ich endlich im Herzen des finnischen Seengebiets ankam, in der Landschaft zwischen Jyväskylä und Kuopio, wo die Landstrassen auf langen Strecken den Seen folgen. In der Landschaft lag schon eine Ahnung der Farben des Herbstes: Auf dem Uferhügel neigte sich die von der nächtlichen Kälte gerötete Eberesche dem Wasser zu, und im Grün des Waldes loderte die Espe wie eine Flamme.

Auf einem Parkplatz an der schönsten Stelle dieser seenfreudigen Strasse legte ich eine Rast ein. Von einem hohen Hügel sah ich hinab auf den See. Die Sonne war am Untergehen und hatte schon fast den dunklen Sägeblattrand des Waldes erreicht. Schmale schwarze Nachtwolken warfen wie lange gierige Zungen ihre Schatten auf das Wasser, und die herbstlichen Farben wurden betont.

Während ich dort sass und mich ausruhte, lebten in meiner Erinnerung die europäischen Eindrücke meiner vielwöchigen Reise auf. Ich entsann mich eines Abends, an dem ich mit einem Freund am Ufer des Genfer Sees spazierengegangen war und festgestellt hatte, dass die Landschaft, so schön sie auch ist, auf seltsame Weise erschöpft und abgenutzt aussieht.

"Glaubst du mir, dass eine Landschaft ermüden kann, wenn sie von zuvielen Augen angesehen wird?", fragte mein Freund. Ungläubig lachte ich auf, aber er fuhr fort: "Dieser See ist auf dekorativen Ansichtskarten in alle Welt verbreitet worden, er hat auf dem Deckel von Pralinenschachteln auf unzähligen Wohnzimmertischen gelegen. Hinzu kommt, dass er im Laufe der Zeit Heimstatt vieler Flüchtlinge gewesen ist, dass ihn Menschen betrachtet haben, die an seiner Statt lieber die eigene Heimaterde gesehen hätten, diejenige, in der die Seele dieser Menschen verwurzelt war."

An diese poetische Behauptung erinnerte ich mich lächelnd, als ich an jenem schon dunkelwerdenden Abend dasass und auf die finnische Seenlandschaft schaute. Sie zeigt sich dem Betrachter als etwas Einmaliges: in diesem Augenblick für mich und einzig für mich, diese Farben und diese Schatten, diese Lichter und Spiegelungen der Wasserhaut, dieser feurige Abschiedsgruss der untergehenden Sonne.

Ich bin im Herzen des finnischen Seengebiets in Nord-Savo zu Hause. Um mich die Seen Kallavesi, Juurusvesi, Ruokovesi und Suvasvesi. Als reichte diese Wasserfülle noch nicht, schimmern hier und da kleine, von den grossen Wasserrouten unabhängige Seenflecken. Wenn sie beginnt, die Kreaturen der Schöpfung zu verwöhnen, kann es geschehen, dass die Natur zum masslosen Verschwender wird, und so ist es auch den Menschen des Seengebiets ergangen: sie haben wirklich keine Veranlassung, über Mangel an Wasser zu klagen.

Die Menschen sind über das Wasser in diese Gegend gekommen, und daher ist das Leben der Uferbewohner auch heute noch zum Wasser hin ausgerichtet. Die Fensteraugen der Häuser blicken auf das Ufer, von den Höfen führen Pfade zum See, und am Wasser hocken die Saunas. Diese Saunas mit ihren samstäglichen Gerüchen sind Bestandteil meiner Seenlandschaft. Die Sauna ist die Endstation der grauen und schweren Arbeitswoche. Durch ihren schwarzen Schoss saugt sie die von Arbeit und Plackerei erschöpften Menschen in sich auf. Mit ihren gereizt zischenden Ofensteinen wischen sie die Bürden des Alltags weg, und nebenan steht immer Wasser zum Abkühlen und Reinigen bereit.

An sommerlichen Samstagen mit dem Ruderboot auf dem See unterwegs habe ich oft eine menschliche Gestalt beobachtet, die gegen die Wand einer in blauen Rauch gehüllten Sauna gelehnt sass. Völlig entspannt ruhte sie unbeweglich in der Nachatmosphäre der Hitze und des Wassers, die Gedanken träge quellend und die Wasseroberfläche entlang schweifend, von dieser getragen wie auf Seerosenblättern. Die Zeit fliesst vorüber, Anstrengung und Eile sind wie weggeblasen.

Tagsüber ist die Atmosphäre anders. Der Traktor knattert auf der Uferwiese, und Heureuter stehen Spalier, als wären sie auf dem Wege zur Kirche stehengeblieben; mollige alte Frauen. Weiter entfernt, wo die blitzende Klinge der Mähmaschine die Schönheit des Sommers fällt, Glockenblumen, Margeriten, Ranunkeln und an Grabenrändern Erdbeeren; dort hört man die ächzenden Geräusche der Arbeit, und auf den Spitzen der Heugabeln durchpflügen Heubüschel die Luft.

Wie die Einheimischen haben auch die Sommergäste, diese an den Seenufern sich heftig vermehrende Rasse, ihren Lebensrhythmus zum Wasser hin ausgerichtet. Aber in der Umgebung ihrer Behausungen herrscht eine andere Atmosphäre als dort, wo das Land schon seit vielen Generationen im Besitz derselben Familie ist. Die Ferienhausbewohner haben ihre Arbeit im Winter geleistet, jetzt ist Müssiggang ihre Hauptbeschäftigung. Sie haben ein Recht auf süsses Nichtstun, ihnen ist es vergönnt, unter der am Fahnenmast wehenden Flagge im Liegestuhl zu sitzen oder mit steilem Bug zu den Inseln zu rasen.

Auf Heugabeln gestützt oder vom Sitz der Mähmaschine sehen die Einheimischen zu, um sich dann wieder ihrer Arbeit zuzuwenden und das Gesehene zu vergessen. Für sie ist der Winter die Zeit, die dem Schaffenden erlaubt, zu verschnaufen und sich nach dem Essen auf der Bank beim Fenster zu rekeln — unter dem Kopf die Pelzmütze, als Decke ein Mantel — oder seine Füsse am Ofen zu wärmen. In seinem Jahresrhythmus ist er der Natur näher als der Sommergast.

An wolkenlosen Sommertagen zeigt Seen-Finnland sich von seiner besten Seite. Wenn ich an meine Kindheit zurückdenke, scheint es mir, als hätte die Sonne immer geschienen, was natürlich nicht stimmt. Im Herbst, wenn es an der Zeit war, das Leinen im schwarzen Wasser des Teichs zu tränken, regnete es meistens. Es war schwer, sich dem Herbst zu unterwerfen und den Sommer aufzugeben. Daher machten wir uns barfuss an die Arbeit. Der nasse Rock klatschte gegen die Knie, und die Kälte liess einen bis aufs Herz frösteln. Oder wir gingen zur Mühle. Das Pferd stolperte seine Kornlast schleppend die Uferwege entlang. Die Wasseroberfläche war übersät mit immer grösser werdenden Ringen, ausgelöst durch die aufprallenden Regentropfen. Ein grauer Nebel waberte am Ufer, das Fell des Pferdes glänzte nass und die Räder des Pritschenwagens holperten über den vom Regen durchlöcherten Sandweg. Der Wald roch nach Vermoderung und Pilzen, im Herzen des Müllers wohnte eine entzückende Melancholie.

Winter. Über meinen See führt ein mit Pricken markierter Eisweg. In der weissen Ebene ragen die Prickenquaste wie Hände, Hilferufe auf.

Ein Deckel aus Eis schliesst den See ab, und ich stelle mir vor, dass auch die Wellen unter dem Eisdeckel im eigenen Geplätscher erstarrt sind. Die eisigen Mondnächte des Mittwinters beginnen, auf den Schneehängen glitzern Millionen von Diamanten. Der Mittwinter bleibt zurück, die Zeit der Falkeneulen bricht an. Ihr helles Gluckern erschallt von den Ufern. Tagsüber sieht man immer häufiger Eisangler auf dem Eis. Das Eis schmilzt, aus dem Süden weht ein heftiger Wind. Die Eisdecke zersplittert und der Wind treibt Eiswürfel ans Ufer, die beim Aufprallen auf die grauen Felsen klingen und klirren.

Die Menschen des Seengebiets ähneln der Landschaft. Die Seen lächeln, und locker sitzt auch das Lächeln der Menschen. Die Uferlinie ist launisch, und Launen hat auch der menschliche Geist, der sich mit den geschmeidigen Wortwendungen und den herrlichen Sprachbildern seines Dialekts äussert. Ich bin zu dem Ergebnis gekommen, dass das Funkeln der Seen auf den Alltag der Uferbewohner abgefärbt hat.

Von den Ufern sind Menschen zu fernen Steindörfern im Süden und im Westen aufgebrochen. Wie ein Echo auf diese durch den Aufbruch verursachte Lähmung erschallen zur Warnung vor der Verschmutzung unserer Seen die Notfanfaren des Naturschutzes. Der Mensch wird immer hellhöriger und bemerkt die Notsignale in seiner Landschaft. Die Prophetie, die Vorhersage der Vernichtung, liegt schwer auf den Uferbewohnern, aber dennoch: die Landschaft atmet ruhig, und solange sie von Sommer bis Winter und von Winter bis Sommer so atmet, bewahren sich die Menschen an den Ufern ihren Optimismus.

Thousands of Lakes
Tausende von Seen

The Lake District covers nearly one third of the total area of Finland and contains thousands of water bodies of all shapes and sizes. From one-tenth to half of any given district is covered by water. Although the Finnish lakes contain a relatively small volume of water, the sheer size of the area they cover makes them an inseparable component of the scenery.

The lakes of Finland are typically arranged in long chains. In places they narrow to sounds, in which the flow of water from one open area to another is barely perceptible. The lakes are shallow, abound in islands and do not usually have very extensive areas of open water.

Seen-Finnland bestreitet fast ein Drittel der Landesfläche. Auf dieses Gebiet konzentrieren sich Abertausende von Seen verschiedener Grösse und Form. Der Anteil des Wassers an der Landschaft variiert zwischen einem Zehntel und der Hälfte.

Die finnischen Seen haben zwar ein geringes Volumen, dafür aber

ist ihre Fläche umso grösser. Sie bilden lange Ketten, die durch Bäche oder Flüsse miteinander verbunden sind. Stellenweise verengen sie sich zu schmalen Sunden, in denen die Strömung von einem See in den anderen kaum erkennbar ist. Die Seen sind zerlappt, inselreich und haben gewöhnlich keine sehr langen und weitläufigen offenen Seenflächen.

The typical scenery of the Finnish interior is dominated by the dark green of pine forests and the blue of the lakes (1). Bright lakeside groves of birch and alder are also very common, especially in the eastern parts of the Lake District (2).

In der urtypischen finnischen Landschaft wechseln das dunkle Grün der Nadelwälder und das Blau der Seen einander ab (1). Auch hellgrüne Birken- und Erlen-Uferwaldungen sind in Seen-Finnland und besonders in seinen Ostteilen weit verbreitet (2).

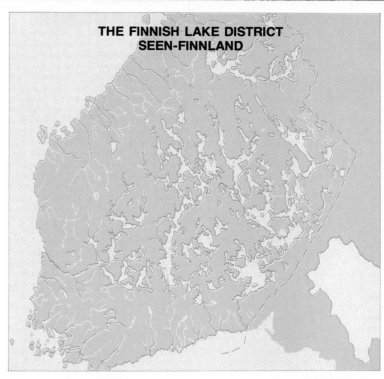

THE FINNISH LAKE DISTRICT
SEEN-FINNLAND

Late-Summer Thunderstorms
Spätsommerliche Gewitter

The amount of precipitation in Finland imposes no constraints on agriculture, but it is badly distributed throughout the year. In late spring/early summer, when the crops could use some rain, little falls, but in late summer, when the grain crops are ripening and the hay drying, there is sometimes too much. However, the Finnish farmer's problems are still slight compared with those of his counterparts in less fortunate countries, although the amount of rainfall and its timing will of course affect the size of his crop.

A large part of the late summer rainfall comes in the form of violent thunderstorms. Sometimes, too, these are linked with hail-

storms, which can badly lodge corn crops and seriously reduce yields.

Thunderstorms are usually preceded by clear omens. Those familiar with such signs are able to predict a thunderstorm before the first dark cloud is seen. Others merely suffer from the oppressive heat.

Die Niederschlagsmengen legen der finnischen Landwirtschaft keine nennenswerten Beschränkungen auf, aber ihre monatliche Verteilung ist ungünstig. Im Frühling, wenn die Pflanzen Feuchtigkeit benötigen, regnet es relativ wenig. Im Spätsommer hingegen, wenn das Getreide zur Reife gelangen und das Heu trocknen soll, fallen manchmal unangenehm grosse Niederschläge. Dennoch sind die Probleme des finnischen Bauern relativ geringfügig, wenn man sie beispielsweise mit der Wetterabhängigkeit des indischen Bauern vergleicht.

Ein grosser Teil des spätsommerlichen Regens fällt in heftigen Gewittergüssen, und die hierbei mitunter auftretenden Hagelschauer können im Getreide erhebliche Schäden anrichten.

Den Gewittern gehen gewöhnlich deutliche Vorzeichen voraus. Wer mit diesen vertraut ist, kann mit relativ grosser Sicherheit das Kommen eines Gewitters voraussagen, bevor die ersten Gewitterwolken am Himmel aufziehen.

Rain Fills the Lake Basins
Der Regen füllt die Seen auf

There is a distinct seasonal rhythm in the volume of water in Finland's lakes. In winter, when precipitation is in the form of snow, the water level is usually at its lowest. When the snow melts in spring, the amount of water increases in the upper reaches of the rivers. Rainfall and the depth of the permafrost also play a decisive role.

If there is a lot of rain while the snow is melting and the water is not absorbed by the frozen ground, there will also be a rapid rise in the water level in the lakes themselves, although the maximum is not usually reached until later in the summer. Because of a high evaporation rate, the volume of water gradually declines by autumn, when the

rains following a drop in this evaporation again cause a peak.

Annual precipitation in the Saimaa lake district totals 650—750 mm. An average of 40% of this finds its way into the watercourses, while the rest evaporates. The natural fluctuation in the level of Lake Saimaa is over three metres, quite a problem for many people.

Der Wasserstand der Seen folgt deutlich dem jahreszeitlichen Rhythmus. Im Winter, wenn die Niederschläge als Schnee fallen, sind die Wassermengen gewöhnlich am geringsten. Wenn im Frühling der Schnee schmilzt, steigt der Wasserspiegel an den äusseren Zipfeln der Gewässer. Entscheidend für das Ansteigen des

Wasserspiegels sind die Niederschlagsmengen sowie die Dicke der gefrorenen Bodenschichten. Wenn während der Schneeschmelze grosse Regenmengen fallen und das Wasser nicht im Boden versickern kann, steigt der Wasserspiegel auch in den mittleren Teilen der Seengebiete schnell, wenn auch die Wasser-

höhe ihren Höhepunkt gewöhnlich erst später im Sommer erreicht.

Die jährliche Niederschlagsmenge beträgt im Seengebiet Saimaa 650—750 Millimeter. Rund 40 Prozent hiervon füllen die Gewässer auf und 60 Prozent verdunsten. Die natürlichen Höhenschwankungen des Saimaa sind gross, mehr als drei Meter.

1

2

3

What Water Plants Reveal
Die Wasserpflanzen erzählen

Man has changed his environment in many ways. Water levels have been raised and lowered, rapids tamed, dams and hydro-electric plants built, and even completely new lakes have been created. A significant part of Finland's water bodies have also been altered by discharges of wastewaters. These contain nitrogen and phosphate compounds, which are important plant nutrients. They can also contain downright toxic substances or heavy metals.

A vigorous increase in plant growth is usually the first indication of the phenomenon known as exuberance. Microscopically small algae obscure the water. Reed patches along the lakeshores spread

and cattails conquer new territory. The free water surface is soon covered by yellow water lilies and certain species of pondweed proliferate beneath the surface. Thus is the ecological balance upset.

The vegetation in a lake gives a rough idea of its condition. This white species of bartrachium is a sign of clean water.

Der Mensch hat die Natur auf vielerlei Weise verändert. Seenspiegel wurden erhöht und gesenkt, Stromschnellen gebändigt, Staudämme und Kraftwerke gebaut, selbst völlig neue Seen hat der Mensch geschaffen. Viele der finnischen Gewässer haben sich auch durch Abwasserzufluss verändert. Die Abwässer enthalten Stick-stoff- und Phosphorverbindungen, welche wichtige Pflanzennährstoffe sind, und manchmal sogar Giftstoffe und Schwermetalle.

Die Eutrophierung geschieht gewöhnlich in Form starken Wachstums der Wasservegetation. Mikroskopisch kleine Algen trüben das Wasser. Die Schilfgürtel an den Ufern werden breiter.

Die vormals freie Wasseroberfläche ist bald von Seerosenblättern bedeckt, und unter der Oberfläche vermehren sich bestimmte Laichkrautarten.

Schon aus der Seevegetation kann man Rückschlüsse auf den Zustand des Gewässers ziehen, da in sauberem Wasser andere Arten gedeihen als in eutrophierten.

2

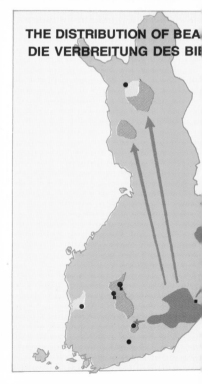

A Beaver Dam

Biberteich

The last indigenous Finnish beaver was shot in 1868. In 1930, some European beavers were introduced from Norway and American beavers from the United States. These have adapted well and even managed to expand their range of habitation.

The presence of beavers in a district cannot be overlooked, since they keep the water level in their pond constant by damming the stream or small river flowing out of it.

A beaver dam is very carefully constructed with logs gathered from a large area. The beavers fell the trees by gnawing them with their chisel-like front teeth. The felled trunks are floated to the dam and used as building material. Trees are also gathered as food, since beavers are very partial to the bark of deciduous varieties. Upstream from the dam a largish beaver pond forms, criss-crossed by their log-floating channels. A conical lodge up to five metres in diameter stands beside the dammed pond. This nest provides excellent protection. Enemies are not able to penetrate its tough dome and the beaver can steal silently along the underwater passage leading to its home. Beavers can live in the same artificial pond for decades.

A beaver's nest is either a large lodge or a hollow dug into the river bank (1). A beaver dam causes flooding and some damage (2 and 4). American beavers live in the brown areas on the map, European beavers in the pink areas and both species in the purple areas. The dots indicate where European beavers were set loose, and the squares where American beavers were introduced. The arrows show how the American beavers have migrated.

Finnlands letzter urwüchsiger Biber wurde 1868 erlegt. In den dreissiger Jahren hat man aus Norwegen eine europäische Rasse und aus den Vereinigten Staaten den Amerikanischen Biber nach Finnland geholt und in der Natur ausgesetzt. Beide haben sich gut anpassen und ihr Verbreitungsgebiet ausdehnen können.

Wenn irgendwo ein Biber ansässig wird, ist dies kaum zu übersehen. Indem er den Abfluss eindämmt, hält er den Wasserspiegel seines Heimteiches auf konstanter Höhe.

Das Holz für seinen sorgfältig konstruierten Damm beschafft er aus weitem Umkreis. Mit seinen groben, meisselförmigen Vorderzähnen nagt er die Bäume durch. Die gefällten Stämme transportiert er über das Wasser zur Dammbaustelle. Indem der Dammbau voranschreitet, bildet sich ein grösserer Stausee, über den vom Biber freigeräumte Flösswege führen. Am Ufer des Stausees befindet sich der kegelförmige Biberbau, der bis zu fünf Meter Durchmesser haben kann. Der Bau bietet hervorragenden Schutz, denn die Feinde können nicht in den harten Kegel eindringen. Mit dem Freien ist der Bau durch einen Unterwassergang verbunden.

Als Biberbau dient ein grosser Kegel oder eine in die Uferböschung gegrabene Höhle (1). In der Umgebung des Bibersees (3) tritt das Wasser über die Ufer und richtet Schäden an (2 und 4). Karte: Vorkommen des Amerikanischen Bibers (braun), des Europäischen B. (hellviolett), gemischte Vorkommen (dunkelviolett). Aussetzungsgebiete des Europäischen B. (Punkt), des Amerikanischen B. (Viereck). Pfeile: Wanderrichtung des Amerikanischen Bibers.

Toriseva — a Lake in a Gorge
Der Schluchtsee Toriseva

The bedrock of Finland is shattered by fracture lines. These were caused by shifts and movements in the earth's crust millions of years ago.

These movements were accompanied by violent earthquakes. The relief formations thrown up at the same time have been largely weathered away. However, along the fracture lines, where the bedrock has split or great sheets of rock ground against each other, the rock is fractured and crumbled. Fracture lines manifest themselves in the topography as straight valleys, lake basins and, in marine archipelagoes and lake districts, as bays and sounds.

Toriseva near Virrat, Helvetinkolu near Ruovesi and Julma-Ölkky at Kuusamo are typical examples of straight, narrow fracture valleys. Lakes have formed anywhere that the ice sheet gouged out deeper than usual grooves in valley beds or where its meltwaters were dammed by moraine formations across the fold valleys.

Finnlands Felsgrund ist durchweg von Bruchlinien zersplittert, Folgen der vor Jahrmillionen geschehenen Verwerfungen der Erdrinde.

Die durch die Verwerfungen verursachten Profiländerungen haben sich im Laufe der Zeit grösstenteils geglättet. In Bruchlinien hingegen, welche entlang der Fels gebrochen ist oder in denen die Steinmassen sich im Verhältnis zueinander verschoben haben, ist die Steinmaterie zersplittert und zerrieben. Die Bruchlinien sind in der heutigen Landschaft als gradlinige Täler, Seenbecken sowie in den Schären und in der Seenplatte als Buchten und Sunde erkennbar.

Der aus drei Teilseen bestehende Toriseva in Virrat ist ein typisches gradliniges und schmales Bruchtal. Ihm ähnlich sind auch der Helvetinkolu in Ruovesi und der Julma-Ölkky in Kuusamo. Solche Seen sind an Stellen entstanden, wo das Inlandeis die Täler tiefer als gewöhnlich ausfurchen konnte oder wo der Gletscher oder seine Schmelzwässer Erdformationen angehäuft hat, die als Dämme fungieren.

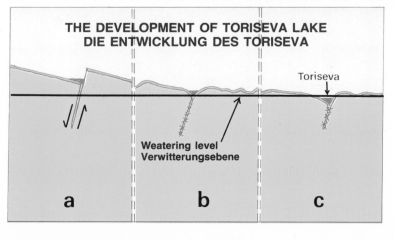

THE DEVELOPMENT OF TORISEVA LAKE
DIE ENTWICKLUNG DES TORISEVA

Toriseva

Weatering level
Verwitterungsebene

a   b   c

Toriseva Gorge probably formed along an old fault line, where the rock is more fragmented than usual (a). The weathering forces of nature have gouged this cleft deeper into the surrounding terrain (b and c), making the walls of the lake basin steeper.

Der Toriseva ist möglicherweise in einer alten Bruchlinie entstanden, in welcher das Gestein zersplitterter war als gewöhnlich (a). Offenbar haben die Erosionskräfte daher diese Bruchzone erheblich tiefer eingekerbt als die Umgebung (b und c) und so ein steilwändiges Seenbecken entstehen lassen.

The Rapids of Central Finland
Mittelfinnlands Stromschnellen

The special characteristics of Finland's bedrock and soil also leave their mark on the country's water bodies. The lakes are often situated in bedrock fracture zones, and are linked into chains by shortish rivers. Especially in the lake district, the rivers do not flow evenly; there are numerous rapids, but no major waterfalls.

This wealth of rapids is particularly pronounced in the waterways of Central Finland. This stems from the fact that the bedrock is very fractured and there are no deep clay layers to even out topographical depressions such as there are in Southern Finland.

The waterways of Finland were undergoing a process of transformation long before man arrived on the scene to regulate them. After isostatic recovery following the withdrawal of the ice sheet had caused the Päijänne area to rise from the sea about 8,000 years ago, the waters of the lake discharged into the Gulf of Bothnia, but as the land continued to rise and tilt eastwards, a new course leading southwards to the River Kymijoki was carved out about 6,000 years ago. It was about then that the lakes and rivers of Central Finland began to develop into their present form. However, the phenomenon of land upheaval continues, altering both lake shorelines and river courses.

Die speziellen Charakteristiken des finnischen Felsgrunds und Bodens prägen auch die Gewässer. Die Seen liegen häufig in Bruchzonen des Felsgrunds, und über kürzere Flüsse sind sie zu Seensystemen verbunden. Die Flüsse — vor allem die der Seenplatte — verlaufen nicht gleichmässig, sondern sie bilden vielerorts Stromschnellen. Bedeutende Wasserfälle hingegen findet man nirgendwo.

Gerade für die mittelfinnischen Gewässer ist der Stromschnellenreichtum charakteristisch. Dies liegt einerseits daran, dass der Felsgrund in dieser Gegend sehr uneinheitlich ist, und andererseits daran, dass hier, anders als in Südfinnland, keine Tonschichten die Bodenvertiefungen ausgefüllt haben.

Nachdem das Päijänne-Seengebiet vor rund 8000 Jahren von der Ostsee abgeschnürt wurde, floss es anfänglich nach Nordwesten zum Bottnischen Meerbusen ab. Die Landhebung kippte das Gebiet jedoch derart, dass aus dem Päijänne vor etwa 6000 Jahren ein neuer Abfluss zum Kymijoki-Fluss ausbrach. Danach begann die Entwicklung der mittelfinnischen Gewässer zu ihrer heutigen Gestalt. Die Landkippung hat jedoch auch noch in späteren Jahrtausenden die Umrisse der Seen wie auch die Strömung der Flüsse geändert, und dieser Prozess dauert auch weiterhin an.

Water wheels are no longer used as a source of energy, but as cultural monuments they will be preserved and maintained in working order (1). At the Viitasaari route (2).

Die Wassermühlen sind heute nicht mehr in Betrieb, werden aber als Kulturdenkmäler gepflegt (1). Der Kärnäjoki, eine stromschnellenreiche Flussroute in Viitasaari (2).

In the Heart of the Finnish Lake District
Im Herzen von Seen-Finnland

The best overall view of the Finnish Lake District is obtained from the air. Travelling on the surface, one notices forests and cultivated land and catches glimpses of lakes and ponds between the trees, but one does not form a conception of the total pattern of lakes and rivers, rapids and groups of small water bodies. A map of the Finnish Lake District reveals an amazingly fragmented picture. A more careful examination shows that the lakes follow the main fracture lines, but these lines are so interwoven as to produce a richly varying mosaic. The relief picture is also characterised by great variety. It is difficult to find any large areas of flat country, although the overall height differences are not so great.

The Finnish Lake District is not a forest wilderness in which natural scenery clearly dominates, but on the other hand the population is not so dense nor the impact on the environment so great as on the south coast. Forests cover 80 % of the land area. They are typically cultivated forests, but have remained in a natural state to a greater extent than elsewhere in Finland.

The forests of the Finnish Lake District are also rich in wildlife. Elks, hares, foxes and squirrels are the most common mammals. There are also predators: the lynx, which adorns the coat-of-arms of the province of Häme, has now returned to the area and can be found even in its southwestern parts. Birds like ptarmigen and grouse, which need quiet nesting places, have become rarer in the Finnish Lake District and the loss of suitable mating grounds has proved fateful for the capercailie or large wood grouse. By contrast, elk and deer thrive in even the youngest of forests and close to human habitation.

Because of the changing relief picture of the eastern parts of Finland, only a comparatively small part of the Lake District is covered by peat bogs, most of which are small. The Salpausselkä Ridge, through which only two rivers emerge from the Lake District, can be regarded as its southern limit.

The village of Evo is situated near Lammi in central Häme. The district between Evo and Padasjoki is one of the most extensive forest areas in Southern Finland. The scenery is characterised by old pine forests and beautiful lakes with narrow isthmuses (4). Evo is also the site of a forestry institute and game research centre.

Das Dorf Evo und der Park Valtionpuisto liegen inmitten von Häme im Nordteil der Gemeinde Lammi. Das Gebiet zwischen Evo und Padasjoki ist eine der weitläufigsten Waldlandschaften Südfinnlands. Örtlich charakterisieren alte Nadelwaldungen und schöne Seen mit schmalen Landzungen die Landschaft (4). In Evo gibt es eine Forstlehr- und eine Fischzucht- sowie eine Wildforschungsanstalt.

Elk are numerous (1). The pine marten, beaver and lynx are among the mammal species found. The capercailie still mates in tangled backwoods clearings (2). The smoky-gilled wood lover, which grows beside softwood tree stumps, is an excellent edible fungus (3).

Der Elchbestand ist gross (1). Marder, Biber und Luchs sind hier heimisch. In vielen Walddickichten balzt noch das Auerhuhn (3). Der an Nadelbaumstämmen wachsende Rauchgraublättrige Schwefelkopf ist ein ausgezeichneter Speisepilz (3).

Das beste Gesamtbild von Seen-Finnland erhält man aus der Luft. Wer zu Lande durch diese Landschaft kommt, sieht Wald und Felder sowie durch die Bäume schimmernde Seen, nicht jedoch die ganzen Seenkomplexe, die Systeme oder die kleinen Seengruppen. Das Kartenbild Seen-Finnlands weist eine grosse Zerrissenheit auf. Eine genauere Betrachtung lässt im Terrain die Hauptlinien der Felsgrundbrüche erkennen, aber da diese kreuz und quer verlaufen und von grosser Zahl sind,

bleibt als Gesamteindruck dennoch nur das Bild eines wechselhaften Mosaiks.

Seen-Finnland ist keine Waldwildnis, in welcher die Naturlandschaft dominierte, aber andererseits ist es auch nicht so dicht besiedelt wie Südfinnland. Rund achzig Prozent der Oberfläche sind Wälder. Sie sind typische Nutzwälder, haben ihre Naturwüchsigkeit aber besser bewahrt als die vieler anderer Teile Finnlands.

Die Fauna der seen-finnischen

Wälder ist vielseitig. Die wichtigsten Wildsäuger sind Elch, Hase, Feldhase, Fuchs und Eichhörnchen. Von den grösseren Raubtieren ist der Luchs zurückgekehrt, und zwar bis hin in die Südwestteile des Seengebiets. Die Moorschneehühner, die eine ruhige Nistumgebung benötigen, haben in Seen-Finnland zahlenmässig abgenommen. Die Vernichtung geeigneter Balzplätze ist dem Auerhuhn zum Schicksal geworden. Hingegen fühlen sich Elch und Wildrentier auch in jüngeren

Forsten und in der Nähe menschlicher Siedlungen wohl.

Wegen des unregelmässigen Profils der östlichen Gegenden ist nur ein relativ kleiner Teil der Wälder versumpft. Die meisten Moore sind klein.

Als Südgrenze Seen-Finnlands kann man den Salpausselkä ansehen. Dieser ist nur an zwei Stellen von Gewässern durchbrochen, welche über den Kymijoki zum Finnischen Meerbusen und über den Vuoksi zum Ladogasee abfliessen.

Päijänne

Päijänne is quite an exception where Finland's large lakes are concerned. It is deep (104 metres) and has large island-free stretches. Nearly 150 kilometres long, Päijänne runs through quite many different types of scenery. Steep banks are a typical feature.

As recently as 7,000 years ago, Päijänne discharged its water into the Gulf of Bothnia, but as the land tilted upwards this gradually changed and a new channel leading into the Gulf of Finland through the Kymenlaakso Valley was created about 6,000 years ago.

There is a major difference between the view from the eastern and western shores of Päijänne. In the east, the rather rugged scenery soars steeply from the lakeshore, while in the west it is more sedate and bears more signs of the influence of man.

Der Päijänne ist fast eine Ausnahme unter den grossen finnischen Seen. Er ist tief (104 Meter) und hat grosse insellose Seenflächen. Der fast 150 Kilometer lange Päijänne erstreckt sich über sehr abwechslungsreiche Landschaften.

Noch vor 7000 Jahren hat der Päijänne seine Wässer über den Fluss Kalajoki zum Bottnischen Meerbusen entlassen. Da die Landhebung im nordwestlichen Suomenselkä doppelt so schnell vor sich ging wie im Südteil des Päijänne, flachte die Abflussrinne ab, und das Wasser fand einen neuen Abfluss durch den Salpausselkä. Seit etwa 6000 Jahren fliesst er über den Fluss Kymijoki zum Finnischen Meerbusen ab.

Zwischen den beiden Ufern bestehen grosse landschaftliche Unterschiede. Im Osten ragt das Ufer steil auf, im Westen steigt die Landschaft allmählich an und trägt mehr Spuren menschlicher Hand.

Päijänne's shores are often rocky and resemble those in the marine archipelago. The wooded shores elsewhere are typical of a Finnish lakescape.

Die Ufer des Päijänne sind stellenweise felsig, schärenähnlich. Dann wieder bewaldete Ufer, eine typische finnische Seenlandschaft.

The Devil's Trench

Die Teufels- gruft

Hitonhauta is Finnish for the "Devil's Trench" and is the name of a remarkable gorge about half a kilometre long and 20 metres deep, which is one of the most distinctive natural features of Central Finland. The gorge is only a few metres wide at its north-western end, but soon widens to 30—40 metres. Its walls are sheer and rugged rock.

The gorge runs from North-West to South-East — the same direction as that in which the massive ice sheet advanced across Finland long ago. The advancing ice was able to scoop out the fragmented rocks along a fault line and deepen the valley that already existed.

Die Teufelsgruft — Hitonhauta — liegt im Nordwestteil der Gemeinde Laukaa. Sie ist eine rund 500 Meter lange und fast 20 Meter tiefe Schlucht, eines der ungewöhnlichsten Naturdenkmäler Finnlands. An ihrem Nordwestende ist die Teufelsgruft nur wenige Meter breit. Zum Mittelteil erweitert sich dieser Felsriss auf 30 bis 40 Meter. Das Tal ist von steil abfallenden schroffen Felswänden umgeben.

Die Teufelsgruft verläuft von Nordwest nach Südost, also in gleicher Richtung wie der vordringende eiszeitliche Gletscher. Daher konnte das Inlandeis diese gebrochene Felsstelle bearbeiten und das Bruchtal vertiefen.

The Hitonhauta gorge has sheer, rugged walls. Its floor is rocky because the smaller particles were washed away by the floods from the melting glaciers (1).

Caves are quite rare in Finland and are often associated with horrifying folk myths (2).

Zu beiden Seiten der Schlucht ragen steile Felswände auf. Der Talgrund ist steinig, da die Schmelzwässer des Inlandeises den losen Boden grösstenteils fortgespült haben (1).

Höhlen sind wirkliche Seltenheiten in der finnischen Natur. Mit ihnen sind oft schaurige Mythen und Erzählungen verbunden (2).

1   2

Primeval Forests
Urwald

Genuinely virgin forests can be found in only a few areas in Finland. Most of them are in existing or proposed nature reserves. Around the middle of the last century the lumber trade boosted the forests' value and soon they had to yield to the woodsman's axe.

Old pines with rugged, shield bark and silver-flanked deadwood

trees are the proud emblems of an ancient primeval forest. Here and there among the gloomy undergrowth old trunks rot, while in the light clearings created by the fall of large old trees young seedlings thrive. The flanks of the oldest trees bear the scars left by forest fires.

Primeval forests are by no means cases of arrested development. Old trees gradually make way for young ones, although the rate of change — barring major natural catastrophes such as forest fires and great storms — is so slow that the overall impression of age is retained. Biologically, too, these forests are much more diverse than tended stands of trees.

Nur an wenigen Orten Finnlands wächst noch echter Urwald. Die letzten Wildniswälder liegen zumeist in Naturschutzgebieten. Der Holzhandel liess den Wert der Bäume ab Mitte letzten Jahrhunderts steigen, und die alten Wälder fielen dem Einschlag zum Opfer.

Plattenborkenkiefern und silberfarbene ausgedörrte Föhren sind die stolzen Symbole des Urwalds. Während auf den dämmrigen Waldböden hier und da moosüberwachsene morsche Stämme liegen, sieht man auf durch gefallene Baumgreise entstandenen Lichtungen junge Sprösslinge. An den Kiefern erkennt man noch die Spuren der Waldbrände, die zu Lebzeiten der Baumgreise gewütet haben.

Aber der Urwald ist in seiner Entwicklung durchaus nicht stehengeblieben. Die alten Bäume machen allmählich den jüngeren Platz, wenn auch dieser Wandel sehr langsam vor sich geht. Der Urwald ist biologisch erheblich vielseitiger als gepflegte Holzanpflanzungen.

Nature has been allowed to evolve on her own terms in the Pyhä-Häkki National Park (1). The Seitseminen district in Northern Häme is characterised by primeval forests and watery marshes (2). In this district one can still see a pine marten cub (3) climbing its home tree or a pygmy owl (4) peeping from the hollow where it has made its nest.

Im Nationalpark Pyhä-Häkki hat sich die Natur ungestört entwickeln können (1). Charakteristisch für das Gebiet Seitseminen im Norden der Provinz Häme sind alte Urwälder und Sümpfe (2). Hier kann man noch Marderjunge am Stamm des Heimbaums klettern (3) und die Sperlingseule (4) aus ihrem Baumloch glotzen sehen.

The Farmlands of Häme
Die Äcker von Häme

When the first human inhabitants of the region now called Häme arrived the stoneless and fertile clay fields were cleared for cultivation. Before the arrival of man, these clay fields had probably been covered by mostly deciduous forests and were easy to clear, for example by slash-and-burn methods. As much farmland as possible was usually cleared. On one side was the lake and on the other poorer moraine soils. In many of Häme's municipalities, the land nearest the lake is cultivated and settled, while those areas further from the water are sparsely inhabited. a Typical piece of Häme scenery consists of a belt of gently rolling farmland hugging the lakeshore and surrounded in its turn by forests on

slightly higher ground.

The elevation differences in Häme are greater than along the coast, which gives the terrain a richer and more varied appearance. The farmland scenery is further enriched in places by small patches of forest, while the last remnants of partially wooded pastures are situated close to the fields. Stone churches and fine manor houses tell a tale of old and prosperous economic endeavour in this region.

The lakes in the middle of the clay fields are rich in plants and their waters obscure. Nutrients are leached from the fields and into the lakes, which suffer from plant exuberance as a result. In the worst cases lakes can become completely

choked by plants and weeds. In other places, efforts have been made to increase the arable area by draining lakes or lowering their water level. The latter measure has frequently led to rapid plant exuberance and, unfortunately, has by no means always produced the desired result.

In many places good farmland has been sacrified to meet the demands of expanding urban centres, new roads and industry. The old villages are undergoing rapid expansion as migration brings people into communities located near the large centres of population. It is becoming increasingly common to see fields being tilled and tended in the shade of modern apartment blocks.

Als der Mensch nach Häme kam, wandelte er zuerst die steinlosen und fruchtbaren Tongebiete in Anbauland um. Gewöhnlich wurde das Ackerland so weit wie möglich ausgedehnt, am einen Ende bis zum nächsten See, am anderen bis zum steinigen Moränenland. In vielen Gemeinden der Provinz ist das an den See grenzende Land kultiviert und bewohnt. Die weiterab vom See gelegenen kargeren Wasserscheidengebiete hingegen sind dünn besiedelt. Dies sind auch die Grundelemente der typischen Häme-Landschaft: die dicht an dicht gelegenen Seen sind von leicht hügeligen offenen Feldern und diese wiederum von höher gelegenen Wäldern eingeschlossen.

Die Höhenunterschiede sind in Häme grösser als an der Küste, so dass das Geländeprofil wechselhafter und vielseitiger ist. Die Ackerlandschaft wird vielerorts von kleinen Waldoasen bereichert. In der Nähe der Äcker stehen auch die Überreste der letzten Haine. Steinkirchen und Gutshöfe erzählen von alter und hochentwickelter Landwirtschaft.

Die Seen inmitten der Tongebiete sind üppig und trübe. Von den direkt ans Wasser grenzenden Äckern werden Nährstoffe in die Seen gespült. Diese Belastung erkennt man oft am Wuchern der Wasservegetation. In den schlimmsten Fällen füllt die Wasservegetation das ganze Seenbekken. Hin und wieder ist versucht

worden, die Ackerflächen durch völlige Austrocknung flacher Seen oder durch ein Senken des Wasserspiegels auszudehnen. In solchen Fällen hat in den Seen schnell eine Eutrophierung eingesetzt. Derartige Massnahmen haben bei weitem nicht immer zum gewünschten Ergebnis geführt.

Vielerorts ist auch in Häme gutes Ackerland der expandierenden Besiedlung, neuen Strassen oder der Industrie geopfert worden. Da es die Menschen heute in die Landgemeinden nahe den Städten zieht, wachsen die Kirchdörfer schnell. Es ist kein ungewöhnlicher Anblick mehr, wenn direkt neben vor Neuheit blitzenden Etagenhäusern Äcker gepflügt und bestellt werden.

Eskers
Oser

Central Finland is one of the country's largest lake districts, with hills, knolls and ridges adding to the countless shallow lakes to enrich the scenery.

The esker ridges of Central Finland are over 9,000 years old. As the ice sheet melted, its edge gradually retreated from the southern part of Finland towards Northern Sweden between 9,000 and 11,000 years ago. The debris carried and piled up by the floodwaters from this melting ice sheet formed the eskers. The material, washed and sifted by the floods, always piled up near the edge of the ice sheet. As the ice retreated, so did the outlets of the rivers flowing under and through it, forming long, slightly crooked ridges. The eskers that formed in ice tunnels have steep sides because the ice supported the material forming them. Wherever the succesive layers of sand and gravel formed outside the ice, however, the ridge is flatter and broader across the base.

Mittelfinnland gehört zur ausgedehnten finnischen Seenplatte. Neben zerlappten Seen bereichern zahlreiche Anhöhen, Hügel und Landrücken die Landschaft.

Die mittelfinnischen Oser sind vor mehr als 9000 Jahren aus der vom Schmelzwasser des Inlandeises transportierten und akkumulierten Materie entstanden. Die vom Wasser gespülte und sortierte Materie sammelte sich jeweils in der Nähe des Gletscherrandes an. Indem sich der Gletscherrand zurückzog, wanderte auch das Mündungsgebiet der Schmelzströme. So wurden aus den Osern längliche, leicht gewundene Landrücken. Teilweise sind die Oser in Tunnels entstanden, welche sich im Gletscher nahe dem schmelzenden Rand gebildet hatten. Die auf diese Weise entstandenen Oser sind steilhängig, da die Eiswände die sich ansammelnden Sandschichten stützten. Wo der Os-Kies und der Os-Sand sich vor dem Gletscherrand aufschichteten, erhielt der Oser eine flachere Form und dehnte sich gleichzeitig über eine breitere Fläche aus.

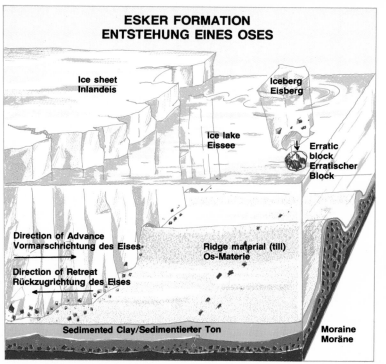

ESKER FORMATION
ENTSTEHUNG EINES OSES

Ice sheet
Inlandeis

Iceberg
Eisberg

Ice lake
Eissee

Erratic block
Erratischer Block

Direction of Advance
Vormarschrichtung des Eises

Direction of Retreat
Rückzugrichtung des Eises

Ridge material (till)
Os-Materie

Sedimented Clay/Sedimentierter Ton

Moraine
Moräne

The belt of stones along the base of the ridge is an ancient shoreline and shows how high the water once was before the process of land upheaval began (1). Eskers are characteristically long, narrow ridges. The most typical form of vegetation is sparse pine forest (2). Esker ridges were formed from the material carried by glaciers and deposited when they melted.

Der Steingürtel auf der Os-Kuppe ist ein vorzeitliches Ufer der Ostsee (1). Charakteristisch für ein Os ist sein schmaler länglicher Rucken. Lichtreiche Kiefernwälder sind die typischste Os-Vegetation. Im Bild das Joutsniemi-Os in Leivonmäki (2). Längs-Oser sind aus der vom Inlandeis und dessen Schmelzströmen transportierten und akkumulierten Materie entstanden.

Paludification
Ein Waldteich versumpft

There are about 55,000 lakes in Finland. In arriving at this total, only lakes more than 200 metres in diameter were counted, so there are also countless more thousands of smaller forest lakes and ponds.

The shores of forest ponds are usually paludified. Waterside vegetation can grow undisturbed, because the wind is seldom able to blow strongly in these sheltered nooks and waves are rarely high. A soggy "raft" of moss gradually grows around the shore in the course of the centuries. In small ponds, a swampy belt of moss often completely encircles the water area and debris accumulates on its bed.

In the course of time the area of open water gradually declines as the moss belt spreads towards the centre and makes the pond more circular in form. This process of growth ultimately transforms the pond into a mire. Many of the small, almost circular peat bogs in Finland were tranquil forest ponds many centuries or millenia ago.

In Finnland gibt es insgesamt etwa 55 000 Seen mit einem Durchmesser von mehr als 200 Metern. Hinzu kommen unzählige kleinere Waldteiche.

Die Ufer der Waldteiche sind zumeist versumpft. Die Ufervegetation kann sich ungestört entwickeln, da der Wind nur äusserst selten mit grosser Stärke bis zur Teichoberfläche vordringen kann. Nennenswerter Wellengang tritt praktisch nie auf. Im Laufe der Jahrhunderte entwickelt sich in Ufernähe allmählich eine wabbelige Moosdecke. In kleinen Teichen läuft die nachgebende Moosdecke ringförmig um das ganze Ufer.

Mit der Zeit verringert sich die freie Wasserfläche langsam zur Teichmitte hin, und die vordringende Moosdecke rundet die Teichform ab. Ergebnis dieses Zuwachsens über die Oberfläche hinweg ist, dass der Teich endgültig zum Sumpf wird. Viele der kleinen finnischen Moore sind in früheren Jahrhunderten und -tausenden derartige friedliche Teiche gewesen.

A sedge-fringed peat layer advances towards the middle of the pond, gradually transforming it into a peat bog (1). Wild rosemary blooms near a forest pond (2).

Die am Rande mit Riedgras bewachsene Moosdecke breitet sich zur Teichmitte hin aus, und der Teich versumpft (1). Blühender Sumpf-Porst im Uferwald eines Waldteichs (2).

Saimaa — Finland's Largest Lake

Der Saimaa — Finnlands grösster See

Lake Saimaa, and the entire Vuoksi system to which it belongs, were created during the most recent phase of the Finnish lakes' development. After the Ice Age, about 10,000 years ago, the waters of what were to become lakes Päijänne and Saimaa discharged into the Gulf of Bothnia. Land uplift led to Päijänne's waters being diverted southwards to the Gulf of Finland and Saimaa's eastwards. And when Greater Saimaa became separated from Päijänne and its waters broke through the Salpausselkä Ridge ,about 5,000 years ago, the eastwards-flowing Vuoksi watercourse was created. The principal lake in this system is 1,490 square kilometres in area; its shoreline — without the islands — is 900 kilometres in length and the greatest depth 82 metres.

The numerous lakes in the Greater Saimaa system are connected by sounds. The water in these lakes is 76 metres above sea level. The system extends from Lappeenranta and Mikkeli to Joensuu and Varkaus and covers a total of 4,400 square kilometres, making it the fourth-biggest lake in Europe. The many islands have a combined area of about 1,700 square kilometres and the average depth is 17 metres. The lakes forming the system are: South Saimaa (or Saimaa Proper), Pihlajavesi south of Savonlinna and Haukivesi to its North, Puruvesi and Orivesi, which lie further East, and Pyhäselkä, which extends as far as Joensuu.

As a scenic lake system, Greater Saimaa is without parallel in the world. In it, the best features of Finnish lakescapes are combined: broken shorelines, a labyrinthine mosaic of land and water, an abundance of islands and winding water routes.

Wie auch die anderen Gewässer des Vuoksi-Seensystems ist der Saimaa in der letzten Phase der Entwicklung der finnischen Seen entstanden. Nach dem Ende der Eiszeit, vor rund 10 000 Jahren, floss das Wasser der späteren Seen Päijänne und Saimaa in den Bottnischen Meerbusen ab. Als Folge der Landhebung schufen sich der Alt-Päijänne und das Vuoksi-Seensystem einen neuen Abfluss, den Kymijoki. Als der Gross-Saimaa sich vom Päijänne abschnürte und seine Wässer vor 5000 Jahren den Salpausselkä-Höhenrücken durchbrachen, entstand der Fluss Vuoksi. Der Eigentliche Saimaa — Varsinainen Saimaa — ist das Zentralgewässer des Vuoksi-Seensystems und misst 1490 Quadratkilometer; die Länge seiner Uferlinie ohne Inseln beträgt 900 Kilometer und seine grösste Tiefe 82 Meter.

Der Gross-Saimaa ist eine Seengruppe, deren zahlreiche Seenbecken durch Sunde miteinander verbunden sind. Seine Oberfläche liegt 76 Meter über dem Meeresspiegel. Er erstreckt sich von Lappeenranta bis Mikkeli, Varkaus und Joensuu. Wenn man ihn als ein einziges grosses Seengebiet betrachtet, ist er mit 4400 Quadratkilometern Europas viertgrösster See. Zum Gross-Saimaa gehören Inseln mit einer Gesamtfläche von 1700 Quadratkilometern und, wenn man die Inseln mit einbezieht, 13 700 Kilometern Uferlinie; seine mittlere Tiefe beträgt 17 Meter.

Der Gross-Saimaa ist ein auf der ganzen Welt einzigartiger Seenlandschaftskomplex. In ihm vereinigen sich in grossartiger Weise die typischsten Charakteristiken der finnischen Seen: Zerlapptheit, Labyrinthartigkeit, Inselreichtum und verschlungene Seensysteme.

A Lakeshore in Savo

Seeufer in Savo

The Saimaa shoreline is long: 13,700 kilometres when the islands are counted. On the other hand, trees grow right to the water's edge in many places, so the actual shore strip dividing land and water is blurred. There are also shallow shores with extensive growths of long-stemmed water plants such as bulrushes and lake reeds.

The numerous bleak sandy beaches, smooth-worn rocks and heathy lakeside tracts are excellent for recreational purposes. Because of this, many officially supervised camping areas and holiday settlements have been established in the region.

Holiday residences should be located sufficiently far from the water and in carefully selected places in order to maintain the untouched nature of the sandy beaches and rocky cliffs. From the viewpoint of recreational use it is also important to ensure that there are enough free beaches and shoreline near towns and villages. The water must also be kept unpolluted.

Die Uferlinie des Saimaa ist lang, mit den Inseln 13 700 Kilometer. Andererseits wachsen die Bäume oft direkt an der Wassergrenze, so dass die eigentliche Uferlinie, an der das Wasser zum Land übergeht, sich verwischt. Man findet auch flache Ufer, vor denen eine üppige hochspriessende Wasservegetation wächst.

Die vielen unbewachsenen Sandstrände, Rundhöcker und waldbodenähnlichen Ufer eignen sich gut für Erholungszwecke. Daher sind an den Ufern zahlreiche offizielle und überwachte Campingplätze sowie Feriendörfer eingerichtet worden.

Die Ferienhäuser sollten weit genug von der Uferlinie errichtet und die landschaftlich wichtigen Stellen wie Sandstrände und Felsenhänge unbebaut belassen werden. Weiterhin wäre es zu Erholungszwecken wichtig, in der Nähe der Siedlungszentren genügend freie Ufer und gute Badestrände auszusparen. Aus demselben Grunde sollte auch das Wasser reingehalten werden.

Man in a Lake Setting
Der Mensch in der Seenlandschaft

The establishment and growth of the communities in the Saimaa region of Eastern Finland were closely linked with fur trapping. The oldest relics of the past are cave drawings found at Yövesi near the village of Ristiina. On the basis of the water level and arrowheads found there, these drawings are estimated to be 3,000 or 4,000 years old.

The straggling lakes, with their innumerable waterways connecting every shore with everywhere else, naturally attracted and facilitated habitation. Waterborne travel has been developed with the aid of the many canals and deep channels. Log floating is the most important type of water traffic in terms of volume transported. The development of other forms of inland shipping has failed to reach the goals set for it, partially owing to a lack of suitable vessels. Passenger services on Lake Saimaa are important, but also this industry is suffering from shortage of capital.

About 400,000 people live in the Saimaa Lake District, which is about as big as the Netherlands and Belgium combined. About one quarter of these are on the southern shore of Saimaa Proper, the largest water sheet, where most of the wood-processing industry is located. Agriculture and forestry are thriving thanks to the favourable climate and rich soil, while the natural beauty of the region and the bourgeoning tourist industry resulting from this are leading to a rapid expansion of the service sector.

Die Besiedlung des Saimaa-Gebiets ist eng mit dem Pelztierfang verbunden gewesen. Die ältesten Andenken an die Vorzeit sind auf dem Gebiet von Ristiina am Ufer des Yövesi gefundene Höhlenmalereien, deren Alter anhand der Ufermarkierungen und der am selben Ort gefundenen Pfeilspitzen auf 3000 bis 4000 Jahre geschätzt wird. Die zerlappten Seen mit ihren unzähligen Wasserrouten von und nach allen Ufern förderten und erleichterten natürlich den inneren Verkehr des Saimaa-Ge-

Water connects people. It serves as a communications channel, as fishing grounds and as a recreational amenity. Some of Finland's greatest artists have also derived their inspiration from lakescapes (1). Pike and bream spawn in the rushy and reedy inlets (2). At least a million people in Finland are estimated to practise recreational fishing (3).

Das Wasser ist ein Faktor, der die Menschen miteinander verbindet: es ist ein Verkehrsweg. Die Schönheit der Seenlandschaft hat auch die grossen finnischen Künstler inspiriert (1). Die binsen- und schilfbewachsenen Buchten sind Laichplätze von Brachse und Hecht (2). In Finnland gibt es mindestens eine Million mehr oder minder aktive Freizeitangler (3).

biets. Nachdem die Besiedlung feste Formen angenommen hatte, begann man, den Binnenseeverkehr mittels vieler Kanäle und Fahrrinnen auszubauen. Gemessen am Transportvolumen ist die Flösserei die wichtigste Wasserverkehrsform. Die Entwicklung des sonstigen Binnensee-Frachtverkehrs ist hinter den gesteckten Zielen zurückgeblieben, dies unter anderem wegen Mangels an geeigneten Fahrzeugen. Der Passagierverkehr auf dem Saimaa ist zwar bedeutend, aber auch er leidet unter Kapitalmangel.

Im Seengebiet Saimaa leben rund 400 000 Menschen. Ein Viertel hiervon wohnt am Südufer des Eigentlichen Saimaa, wo sich auch die meisten Holzveredlungsbetriebe dieser Region niedergelassen haben. Dank dem günstigen Klima und Boden werden Land- und Forstwirtschaft in grossem Umfang betrieben. Das Dienstleistungsgewerbe hat expandiert, da der Saimaa wegen seiner Naturschönheit eine der attraktivsten finnischen Ferienlandschaften ist. **3**

Evening Clouds
Abendwolken

The skies in Finland are clearest in the months of June and July and cloudiest in November and December. The number of cloud shapes is infinite, but certain recurring types have been classified and given names, which can be translated into English as "downy", "gauzy", "cirrocumulus", "veil", "rain", "shower" and "thunder" clouds. When the mightily swelling cumulus clouds rise high into the blue sky, we know that summer is at its height.

Am wolkenlosesten ist Finnlands Himmel im Juni—Juli, am bewölktesten im November—Dezember. Die Zahl der Erscheinungsformen der Wolken ist unbegrenzt. Bestimmte wiederkehrende Formen hat man dennoch klassifizieren und benennen können, so Feder-, Schleier-, Schäfchen-, Haar-, Regen- und Gewitterwolke. Das Aufziehen der gewaltig schwellenden Schönwetterhaufenwolken am blauen Himmel signalisiert: der Mittsommer hat seinen Höhepunkt erreicht.

Siikalahti

In the eastern part of the Finnish Lake District set in the middle of a lush landscape lies Simpelejärvi with its numerous islands and arms. One of these arms, about five kilometres long and no more than a kilometre wide, is Siikalahti Bay, the shores of which are dominated by willow groves, waterside meadows and stands of sedge. Before one reaches the small area of open water one must pass through large expanses of sedge, reeds and bulrushes.

Birds are an essential part of the Siikalahti scenery in spring. The first swans arrive to sit on the ice of the lake as early as the end of March. The ice gradually retreats before the areas of open water and thawing waters from the surrounding land raise the level in the bay. When this happens, great migratory flocks of duck, geese and swans rest on its waters.

Siikalahti is at its most memorable on a mild night in early summer, when it is full of sounds. The unaccustomed ear can not distinguish the accompaniment of a hundreds-strong choir of sedge warblers from the song of rarer species, but the plaintive cry of the bittern will attract the attention of anybody and the mellow song of the nightingale trills from the verdant banks.

Even on rainy autumn days there is still plenty to see and hear at Siikalahti.

Siikalahti is one of Finland's finest bird bays. The cry of the bittern (1) carries far on early-summer nights. Cirl buntings (3) and mysterious, furtive spotted crakes (4) also contribute to the nightly concerts.

Siikalahti in Parikkala ist eines der wertvollsten Vogelgewässer Finnlands (2). Das Blasen der Rohrdommel erschallt hier in frühsommerlichen Nächten (1). Weitere Solisten des nächtlichen Konzerts sind der Feldschwirl (3) und das Düpfelsumpfhuhn (4).

Der Mittelpunkt des östlichen Seengebiets ist der inselreiche See Simpelejärvi, dessen Bucht Siikalahti wie ein Keil fünf Kilometer weit und zumeist weniger als einen Kilometer breit ins Land eindringt. Weidengehölze, Uferwiesen und Riedgrasflächen beherrschen die Ufer der Bucht. Vor der schmalen freien Wasserfläche im Mittelstreifen der Bucht liegen noch Rohrkolben-, Schilf- und Schachtelhalmdickichte.

Ein wesentliches Element der Landschaft von Siikalahti sind die Vögel. Die ersten Schwäne sitzen oft schon Ende März auf dem Eis. Wenn später die Schneeschmelze den Wasserspiegel der Bucht hebt, rasten hier die Zugschwärme der Enten, Gänse und Schwäne.

Am wesenseigensten ist Siikalahti jedoch in milden frühsommerlichen Nächten — voller Laute und Stimmen. Das ungeübte Ohr kann zwischen dem vielhundertköpfigen Schilfrohrsängerchor nicht den Gesang seltenerer Arten heraushören. Das dröhnende Geächze des Rohrdommelmännchens fällt allerdings jedem auf.

Auch wer erst an einem regnerischen Herbsttag, wenn die meisten Vögel schon aufgebrochen sind, nach Siikalahti kommt, bekommt hier noch viel zu sehen. Man braucht kein Pflanzenkenner sein, um zu begreifen, dass die Bucht zu den üppigen Extremfällen der finnischen Natur gehört.

Pihlajavesi

Lake Pihlajavesi, which lies to the south of Savonlinna, comprises several large expanses of open water separated by a labyrinth of islands. Handsome, sheer walls of rock give an exceptionally steep appearance to the channels connecting the different parts of the lake. The moraine ridges in the area are valuable geological, scenic and flora reserves. The wildlife is scarce, as is to be expected in a bleak, large lake area.

Lake Pihlajavesi is a Finnish lakescape at its most typical — a kind of national scenery type in which water, shores, forests and exposed rock form a beautiful mosaic. A national park is planned for the district.

Der südlich von Savonlinna gelegene See Pihlajavesi besteht aus mehreren ausgedehnten, offenen Seenflächen, welche durch labyrinthartige Inselgruppen voneinander getrennt sind. Prächtige steile Felswände verleihen den zwischen den Inseln durchführenden Passagen ein ungewöhnlich wildes Antlitz.

Die Oser des Pihlajavesi sind wertvolle geologische, landschaftliche und botanische Schutzobjekte. Die Fauna ist ausgesprochen dürftig, was für karge grosse Seen nur natürlich ist.

Im Pihlajavesi zeigt sich die finnische Seenlandschaft von ihrer besten Seite — dieser See ist sozusagen eine Nationallandschaft.

Linnansaari

Linnansaari is an internationally known national park representing one of the finest examples of Finnish lake-archipelago scenery. Its islands, groups of islands and expanses of open water make it an unique scenic totality. The national park is in Lake Haukivesi and covers an area of 8 km². It includes one large island, Linnansaari, and 61 smaller islands and islets. The topography, flora and fauna of the area are richly varied. Most of the forests have not yet reached the culmination of their natural development after slash-and-burn agriculture and logging, as can be seen from the abundance of hardwood varieties, but the forest nature is nevertheless rich in variety.

Ospreys and black-throated divers are the most conspicuous of the great number of indigenous avian species to be seen in the area.

The waters of Linnansaari National Park are one of the most important remaining haunts of a rare species of freshwater ringed seal called "saimaannorppa". Unfortunately, these creatures are dwindling threateningly in number owing to water pollution.

Linnansaari is the only national park in a lake area in Finland. The greatest difficulties in preserving lake environments stem from the sheer size of the water areas involved.

Linnansaari ist auch auf internationaler Ebene ein sehr bedeutender Nationalpark. Er repräsentiert die Inselwelt Seen-Finnlands und bildet einen Landschaftskomplex aus Inseln, Inselgruppen und weitläufigen offenen Seenflächen. Linnansaari befindet sich im See Haukivesi und hat eine Landfläche von acht Quadratkilometern. Zum Nationalpark gehören eine grosse Insel sowie 61 kleinere Inseln und Klippen. Topographie, Fauna und Flora des Nationalparks sind vielseitig. Der Hauptteil der Wälder hat wegen einstiger Brandrodung und Einschläge seine Rückentwicklung zum Naturzustand noch nicht abgeschlossen, weshalb örtlich noch Laubhölzer dominieren, aber dennoch ist die Waldnatur mannigfaltig. Fischadler und Prachttaucher sind die stattlichsten Vögel der urtümlichen Seennatur. Die Gewässer von Linnansaari sind das wichtigste Verbreitungsgebiet der Saimaa-Ringelrobbe. Leider verringert sich der schon seit jeher kleine Robbenbestand bedrohlich, da die Verschmutzung des Wassers spürbar zugenommen hat.

Linnansaari ist der einzige Nationalpark der Seenplatte. Die grössten Probleme beim Schützen der Seennatur rühren von der Weitläufigkeit der Seen her: es ist nicht möglich, wasserwirtschaftlich oder landschaftlich selbständige Komplexe unter effektiven Gewässerschutz zu stellen.

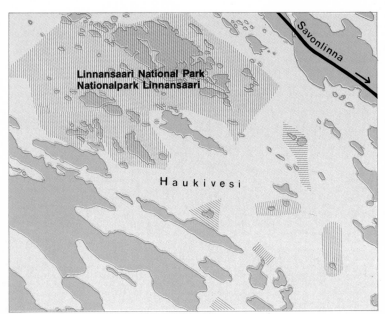

Linnansaari National Park
Nationalpark Linnansaari

Savonlinna

Haukivesi

The osprey is almost a part of the landscape in the Finnish Lake District. In flight, it can be recognized by its long wings, which are white below and dark brown on top. Its nest rests on stout branches and is lined with plants.

Der Fischadler gehört schlechthin zum seen-finnischen Landschaftsbild. Sein Artenbestand nimmt jedoch ab. Man erkennt ihn an seinen langen, an der Unterseite weissen und oben dunkelbraunen Flügeln. Sein Nest besteht aus kräftigen Zweigen und ist mit Pflanzen ''eingerichtet''.

Floods
Hochwasser

The growth and luxuriance of both crops and natural vegetation during the early part of spring is to a great extent dependent on the adequacy of the water absorbed by the ground during this period. Thus abundant spring floods are often an omen of a good growing season.

However, a sudden thaw after a very snowy winter and heavy spring rains can lead to floods causing damage — in some cases quite severe. The clayey, frozen soil is often unable to absorb the meltwaters from the snow.

The comparatively shallow, sluggish rivers are not able to cope with their extra burden. They fill, overflow their banks and flood the surrounding farmlands. In the worst cases, the water can rise as much as nine metres above its summer level and the volume of water in the rivers can be two hundred times normal. "Icejams" make the floods worse.

Floods are also an important ecological factor; many plants thrive only in occasionally-flooded areas.

Das frühsommerliche Wachstum und die Üppigkeit der Anbau- wie auch der Naturpflanzen steht in enger Verbindung mit dem Ausreichen der vom Boden aufgesaugten Schmelzwässer. Daher ist das Frühjahrshochwasser oft eine Garantie für ein gutes Wachstum im Sommer.

Eine plötzliche Hitzewelle, die auf einen schneereichen Winter und auf heftige Frühjahrsregen folgt, kann jedoch Überschwemmungen auslösen. Oft vermag der lehmige und gefrorene Boden die Schmelzwässer nicht schnell genug in sich aufzusaugen.

Flachere Flüsse, die nur geringe Wassermengen führen und langsam fliessen, können die zusätzlichen Wassermengen nicht verdauen, so dass das Wasser über die Ufer tritt. In Extremfällen steigt der Wasserspiegel bis zu neun Meter über das sommerliche Niveau, und die vom Fluss geführte Wassermenge ist zweihundertmal grösser als normal. Eisstauungen können die Überschwemmungen verschlimmern.

The Kolovesi lake area is part of the projected Greater Saimaa National Park. As opposed to Lake Pihlajavesi with its broad expanses of open water, Kolovesi is an archipelago-like lakescape at its best. Narrow, winding strips of water pass between rocky, sometimes steep shores. Sheer cliffs up to 40 m high rise straight up out of the water and the fjord-like sounds are in places 30 m deep.

The terrain is very broken and difficult to travel through. Most of the forests are old and in a natural state. The water of Kolovesi remains pure and the ringed seal population is fairly numerous.

Der See Kolovesi gehört zum Gebiet eines geplanten Nationalparks im Gross-Saimaa. Im Gegensatz zum Pihlajavesi mit seinen weitläufigen, offenen Seenflächen ist der Kolovesi binnenschärenartige Seenlandschaft. Charakteristisch sind schmale, stellenweise von steilen Felsen gesäumte Wasserpassagen. Die bis zu vierzig Meter hohen Felswände ragen senkrecht aus dem See auf. Die fjordähnlichen schmalen Buchten sind bis zu dreissig Meter tief.

Das Terrain ist zerrissen und schwer begehbar. Die Wälder sind zumeist alt und naturwüchsig.

Das Wasser des Kolovesi ist sauber und die Saimaa-Ringelrobbe ist relativ häufig anzutreffen.

Narrow, winding sounds are a charactristic feature of the Kolovesi area (1). The highest island in the area, Ukonvuori (2). Submerged trees add a wilderness touch (3). Sheer cliffs rise out of the water (4).

Schmale, gewundene Wasserrouten charakterisieren den Kolovesi (1). Ukonvuori, die höchste Insel des Gebiets (2). Auf dem Grunde liegende Baumstämme unterstreichen die Wildnisatmosphäre (3). Senkrechte Felswände ragen aus dem Wasser auf (4).

Summer Evenings Sommer-abende

The light and shade contrasts on the landscape are not so severe in Finland as in countries closer to the Equator, where the sun moves across the top of the sky. Even on the clearest day in high summer the sun's rays fall obliquely through the softening atmosphere. Even the darkest shadows are relieved by diffused light.

Using the meltwaters of the claciers, nature has strewn nearly 60,000 lakes on the boundless and perhaps somewhat gloomy and monotonous green carpet of the forests. On a calm, warm summer evening, these mirrors, large and small, reflect the clouds and the lights and colours of the shores in a myriad of delicate nuances.

Die Lichter und Schatten der Landschaft sind in Finnland nicht so grell wie in den näher am Äquator gelegenen Ländern, wo die Sonne ihre Bahn über das Himmelsgewölbe beschreibt. Auch an den hellsten Mittsommertagen fällt das Sonnenlicht schräg durch die Atmosphäre ein und wird gefiltert. Selbst die dunkelsten Schatten weisen eine gewisse Helligkeit auf.

Über den Teppich der unendlichen und im Grunde genommen vielleicht auch etwas bedrückenden und monotonen Wälder hat die Natur in Form von endeiszeitlichen Schmelzwässern fast 60 000 Seen verspritzt. An ruhigen, warmen Sommerabenden wiederholen sich die Wolken und die bewaldeten Ufer in fast sechzigtausend Spiegeln.

Midsummer Night
Mittsommernacht

The origins of the tradition of Midsummer Night are lost in the mists of history. From time immemorial this festival marking the summer solstice has been celebrated with much ado. It is celebrated on the Saturday between 20th and 26th June and is an occasion when the blue-and-white flag of Finland is flown everywhere.

At dusk on Midsummer Eve, the "juhannus" bonfires are lit. The blazing fires and their shimmering reflections on the shining surface of the water is a sight that cannot fail to impress.

Die Wurzeln des Mittsommernachts- oder Johannisfests reichen weit zurück. Seit uralten Zeiten wird dieser Wendepunkt von Licht zur Dunkelheit mit vielerlei Zeremonien gefeiert. In Finnland feiert man das Johannisfest am Samstag der Woche zwischen dem 20. und 26. Juni. Er ist auch der Tag der finnischen Flagge.

Wenn der Abend dämmert, werden überall Johannisfeuer entzündet. Die flackernden Feuer und ihre lodernden Spiegelungen in den Seen sind ein eindrucksvoller Anblick.

Korkeakoski

Rapids are fast flowing parts of a river caused by increases in the slope of its bed. Only where there are prominent breaks of slope do cataracts or waterfalls occur. Such "thresholds" are usually caused by the bedrock configuration, but can also be formed by deposits of loose soil.

Finland's highest waterfall, Korkeakoski at Maaninka in Northern Savo, was declared a nature reserve in 1947. It plunges into the end of a gorge eroded from a fissure in the earth's crust. The head of the fall, which is surrounded by a dense grove of fir and lies over 40 metres above the floor of the gorge, is a narrow defile only a couple of metres across, through which the water must force itself before falling a couple of scores of metres to the jagged tangle of rocks below.

Rapids and cataracts are a very important part of the Finnish landscape, for which reason the remaining ones should be preserved untouched for the enjoyment of future generations.

Stromschnellen sind Flussabschnitte, in denen wegen überdurchschnittlichen Flussbodengefälles eine starke Strömung entsteht. Ausgelöst wird das wilde Schäumen der Stromschnelle durch eine Schwelle im Flussbettboden, über die das Wasser sich ergiesst. Gewöhnlich bildet die Struktur des Felsgrundes, manchmal aber auch loses Gestein im Flussbett die Schwelle. Wenn die Schwelle sehr steil abfällt, spricht man von einem Wasserfall.

Finnlands höchster Wasserfall, der in der Gemeinde Maaninka in Nord-Savo geglegene Korkeakoski, wurde 1947 unter Naturschutz gestellt. Er befindet sich am Rande einer Schlucht, die in einem Erdriss entstanden ist. Der Oberteil des Falls, der vierzig Meter über dem von dichtem Fichtengehölz bewachsenen Tal der Schlucht liegt, bildet einen engen Schlund. Hier muss sich das Wasser durch eine zwei Meter grosse Öffnung zwängen, wonach es auf Dutzende von Metern tiefer gelegenes Geröll prasselt.

Contrasts
Kontraste

Seasonal fluctuations mean a complete change in the appearance of the landscape and put nature's adaptability to a severe test. In autumn, nature makes careful preparations for the coming of winter. Deciduous trees grow a cork-like protective layer over the scars left where their fallen leaves peeled off, migratory birds set off in good time for warmer climes and hibernating animals grow listless as they await the coming of winter. The first thin layer of ice begins forming on the lakes.

When springs breaks the shackles of winter, nature's revival is phenomenally rapid. The massive waves of returning birds of passage, rapidly melting piles of snow and crumbling ice are powerful signs of this.

The strong pulse of spring also brings new life in the form of tourists. The lakescapes of the Savo district are a powerful magnet for visitors because of its untouched character and special attractions such as seine-net fishing and lakeside fish parties in the evening.

Die Jahreszeitenwechsel bedeuten totale Veränderung des Landschaftsbildes, zeigen die grosse Anpassungsfähigkeit der Natur. Im Herbst bereitet die Natur sich sorgfältig auf die Ankunft des Winters vor. Wie als Schutz für die kommende strenge Ruhezeit bilden die ihre Blätter abwerfenden Bäume an den Ansatzstellen ihrer Blattstiele Korkgewebe. Die Zugvögel brechen beizeiten nach wärmeren Regionen auf. Die Seen beginnen sich mit Eis zu überziehen. Die winterliche Landschaft ist eine Landschaft der Stille.

Wenn der Frühling die Fesseln des Winters sprengt, erwacht die Natur in unglaublich kurzer Zeit wieder zum Leben. Unübersehbare Zeichen sind die massive Rückkehr der Zugvögel, das rasche Schmelzen des Schnees und die Auflösung der Eisdecke.

Der intensive Pulsschlag des Sommers bringt mit Feriengästen zusäztliches Leben ins Land. Diese fühlen sich von der Naturnähe der Seenlandschaft von Savo angezogen.

Arctic Frosts
Klirrender Frost

Winter, when the average temperature drops below 0°C, lasts about four months on the South coast and nearly six months at Kajaani, about 600 km to the North. The most intense frosts are experienced around the beginning of February.

On the coldest winter days, the landscape assumes an almost unreal, illusory appearance. It is unmoving, white and silent. Rime frost decorates the forests and buildings with glittering crystals. The cold contracts and tightens telephone wires to strings quivering in the sighing wind. Footsteps crunch in the snow and only the gurgling of a spring-fed brook breaks the enchanted silence of winter.

Der Winter, wenn die Durchschnittstemperatur unter den Gefrierpunkt sinkt, dauert an der finnischen Südküste rund vier, in der Gegend um Kajaani fast sechs Monate. Die schärfsten Frosttage fallen auf den Februarbeginn.

An den strengsten Mittwintertagen sieht die Landschaft fast wie ein Phantasiegemälde aus. Die Landschaft ist reglos, weiss und totenstill. Mit funkelnden Eiskristallen dekoriert der Reif Bäume und Häuser. Die Kälte strafft die Telefonleitungen zu vibrierenden Geigensaiten. An den Ecken knistert und knarrt es. Nur das Murmeln des Quellbachs bricht die Stille. Ein arktisches Erlebnis, der Zauber des Winters.

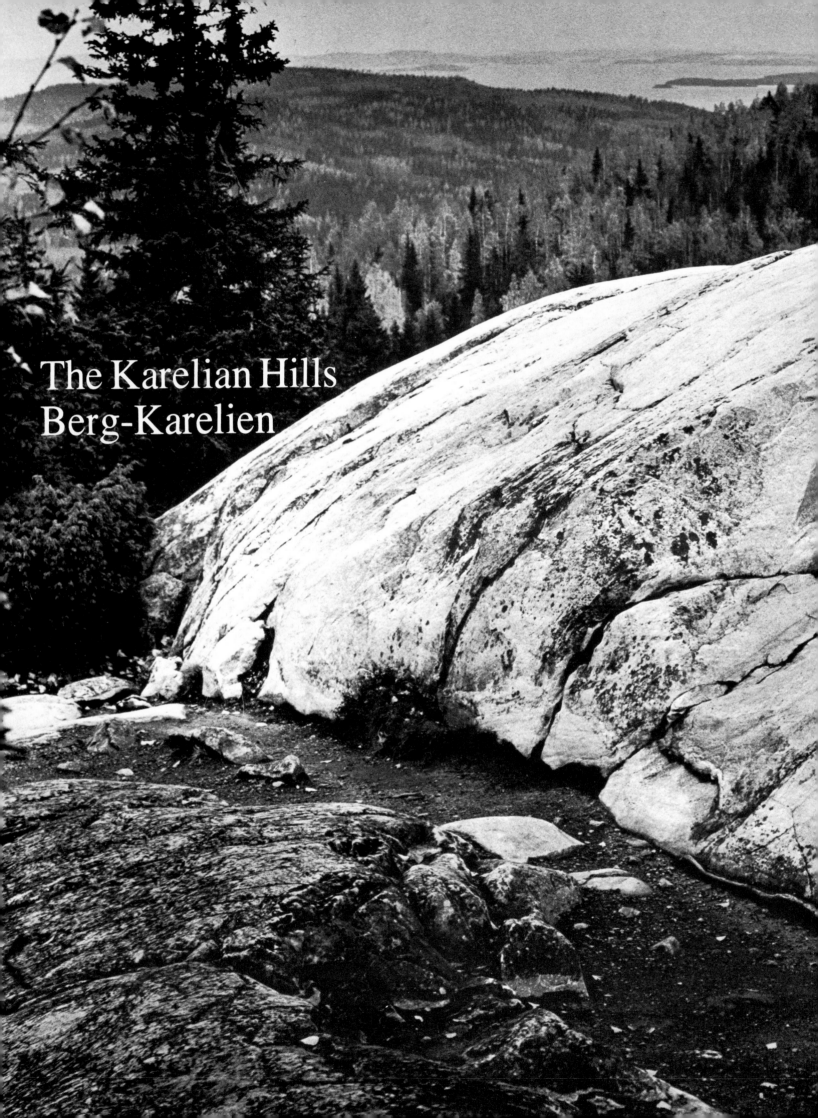

The Karelian Hills
Berg-Karelien

The Blue Hills of Karelia by/von Heikki Turunen

In the course of the past century, the hills, lakes and wilderness areas of Karelia have become concepts about which it is difficult to write without running the risk of plunging into an infinity of cottony metaphors. Even the most genuine-sounding poetic enthusiasm seems destined to dry up into clichés; no matter how fervently I should like to be the first literary person to notice the unique magnificance of the Karelian hills, this honour is denied me.

However, a lot of things have taken place since the Karelianists of the 19th century and the national romantics of the early years of the 20th wandered along the Karelian cattle tracks seeking concrete expressions of the nationalist feelings fired by the Kalevalan literary renaissance. Today, the famous Karelian rapids are harnessed for energy, the curves of the idyllic cattle trails have been straightened out (although many motorists would say the opposite) and covered with tarmacadam, picturesque little villages and hamlets are crammed with shopping centres, blocks of flats and filling stations. A place that once inspired the Finnish writer Juhani Aho to write one of his short stories may well be covered by a holiday village or camping site.

For some reason, I also have the impression that many of those who wandered and discovered Karelia in the past were itinerant, romantic "masters of poetry", more interested in seeking their personal far-off land and exoticism here in this borderland wilderness than genuinely searching for reality. They simply refused to see anything more in this landscape than its most representative silhouettes, the wonderful evening atmospheres of villages grey with poverty, just the main features and nuances that best served their own ends and lyrical enthusiasm.

Today's tourists follow in the footsteps of those old aesthetic dreamers and folklorists such as Lönnrot. They seek exoticism, but also the peace of nature — an increasingly rare commodity in this world —, unspoilt nature and clear, swift streams teeming with fish. And when there are enough of those tranquility-seekers, not many will find it. Virginity has become a trade mark, but it can be found only off the beaten tourist track, where cars and caravans cannot go.

On the other hand, the peace of nature grows deeper in those remote hill villages year by year. New idylls that would serve as the subjects of literary works are created every day, at the same rate as new, polished tombstones rise in the graveyards and a permanent layer of mud erases the tyre tracks of the removal vans.

As the result of a kind of demographic development, the hill region of Karelia is returning almost to its original state. As I sit on the moss-grown steps of a deserted house in Upper Karelia and watch a truck thundering by with a load of Karelian red pine, more raw material for the industries of Southern Finland, I cannot help recalling the painter Pekka Halonen, whose artistic eye was once disturbed by the sight of a tugboat towing a string of log rafts across Lake Pielinen. "It did to the atmosphere what a barrel organ would do to a good concert," he said.

Even Pekka Halonen would feel well by the Lake Pielinen of today. To be sure, log rafts are still outlined as reddish squares on our blue sheets of water, but at least the old fishermen and the unmelodic rat-tat-tatting of their small outboard motors won't bother us for much longer.

There is nothing wrong with the silence of a remote Karelian hill village, except for the fact that it resembles the silence of death.

Perhaps I shall be able to add something new to this landscape painting of mine after all. Maybe I'll be able to avoid clichés in describing my home district. Perhaps I have something the Kalevalan romantics lacked — a great deal of sorrow and anxiety, not only for this landscape, but also for the people who lead their unpoetic lives in it.

I was born on the eastern shore of Lake Pielinen, my home port, where I learned to swim, pray, create poetry and swear. On the opposite side of the lake one can see the Koli Hills, rising above the water like two gigantic waves, changing their shades of colour according to the weather, time of day and season.

Viewed from Vuonislahti Bay, the third hump of Koli, higher than the other two, is partly hidden behind them, and the ridges one sees resemble an enormous hairy arm. The mystically-inclined mind of a child made the hill on the other side of the lake into a reclining giant.

Then one winter, after a poor hay crop the previous summer, an old man came across the ice in a cart to buy hay from us. He insisted that the big mysterious thing there in the distance was a village and that beyond that, endlessly, there were other, similar villages.

Since then my world has been slowly opening up.

Since I have spent the best years of my youth close to water, I find it difficult to try to imagine the Karelian Hills without lakes, ponds and rivers. The basic character of the other lakes of Northern Karelia, for example Lake Höytiäinen, Pyhäselkä and Orivesi, hardly differs from that of Pielinen and Koitere. Without these lakes the landscape would not be what it is. Summer or winter, these sheets of water contain something which, apart from emphasizing height differences, also gives the landscape its soul and softens its stern expression.

Or maybe it is the other way round: the distinctive enchantment of the Karelian lakes is in the stern, guarding hills surrounding them.

In my mind, they blend into a single entity. As a boy I wrote poems on a stump by a hill slope (not merely for the surroundings, but also because I was embarrassed about doing that kind of thing when others could see me). It remained alive inside me like a painting or an image, but not in the usual sense; instead, it kept everything with it, lights colours and their different nuances, fragrances and even warmth and taste. The major elements were hills, lakes and the sky, the trinity of the Karelian Hill Country. The pines, with coarsely barked trunks at the bottom but rustling like torn silk at the top, dark brown near the ground but lightly reddening at their crowns, stood loftily, stretching their warped arms of branches towards the sky and the surface of the water, which changed its expression like the mood of a young poet. Lower down, by the shore, birches and alders, grassy stumps and stones. And behind it all distant proud hills, which when viewed from a high place gradually changed from a shadowy green and brown to ever deeper shades of blue until, tremenduously far away, where the hillocky clouds seemed to merge with the waves of the earth, the land lost its stony weight and changed into fluttering light, free of gravity and blue like my mother's scarf when she called the cows from the birchy pastures.

And not even that is the complete picture. Blue is the colour of distance and of that group of hills, rising from a solid crust, gradually turning to blue in different shapes and heights, creating an image of endlessness, a perspective impression of distance that not even the most skillful of photographers can totally imprison on celluloid. This is because the sensual experience formed from the details, fragrances and movements of the observation point are a fundamental part of this impression. I should almost go so far as to say that this impression of depth, as I have experienced it, cannot be gained unless one is aware of the social situation of the environment. The more distant and blue the horizon seems, the greyer are the walls in the valleys.

My Karelia of the Hills is more than a picture, it is the balance between the various elements, it is life and depth.

Karelien — Land der blauen bewaldeten Berge

In den letzten hundert Jahren sind Kareliens Berge, Seen und Wildnis zu Begriffen geworden, über die zu schreiben schwer ist, ohne in abgedroschene Phrasen zu verfallen. Auch die Früchte aufrichtig erscheinender poetischer Inspirationen drohen zwangsläufig zu Klischees zu vertrocknen. So sehr ich es als Mann der Feder auch wünschte, bin ich nicht der erste, der die wesenseigene Grandiosität Bergkareliens bemerkt hat.

Viel ist jedoch geschehen, seit Ende letzten Jahrhunderts die Karelienisten und zu Beginn dieses Jahrhunderts die Nationalromantiker über die karelischen Kuhpfade pilgerten, um nach konkreten Gegenstücken zum Nationalgefühl, welches durch das Kareliertum geweckt worden war, zu suchen. Heute sind die berühmten karelischen Stromschnellen der Energiewirtschaft unterjocht, die Kurven der idyllischen Viehpfade begradigt (auch wenn manch ein Autofahrer das Gegenteil behauptet) und mit Ölkies verspachtelt, die malerischen Kirchdörfer mit Warenhäusern, Etagenhäusern und Tankstellen vollgepfropft. Dort, wo der Schriftsteller Juhani Aho das Material für seine Skizzen gefunden hat, steht heute vielleicht ein Feriendorf oder ein Campingplatz.

Davon abgesehen erscheinen mir die meisten der damaligen Pilger und Karelienfinder aus irgendeinem Grunde als wandernde romantische "Gedichtsmeister", die im grenznahen Herzland Kareliens eher nach Befriedigung ihrer eigenen Fernweh und nach Exotik denn nach Alltagsrealität suchten. Sie sind einfach nicht bereit gewesen, in dieser Landschaft anderes zu suchen als deren repräsentativsten Umrisse, die wunderliche Atmosphäre der armgrauen Landdörfer, jene Hauptcharakteristika und Nuancen, welche ihren eigenen Absichten und lyrischen Inspirationen am besten entgegenkamen.

Jetzt folgen die Touristen in den Spuren jener alten ästhetischen Schöngeister und Lönnrots. Sie suchen Exotik, aber auch etwas, das in dieser Welt immer seltener wird, nämlich Naturfriede und Stille, unverschandelte Landschaft, blitzendreine Fischwässer. Und wenn die Zahl jener, die nach Stille suchen, gross genug wird, haben nur noch wenige Erfolg bei ihrer Suche. Jungfräulichkeit ist zum Warenzeichen geworden, aber man findet sie nur noch abseits der beliebten Reiserouten, dort, wo Autos und Wohnwagen nicht hinkommen.

In den abgelegenen Bergdörfern hingegen vertieft sich der Naturfriede von Jahr zu Jahr. Neue Idylls als Themen für Skizzen entstehen täglich, im gleichen Takt wie auf den Friedhöfen neue polierte Steine errichtet werden und der ewige Morast die Spuren der Umzugautos füllt.

Im Zuge der Bevölkerungsentwicklung nähert sich Bergkarelien wieder seinem Urzustand. Wenn ich auf der moosüberwachsenen Holztreppe einer oberkarelischen Wildnishütte sitze oder zusehe, wie die Lastwagen dröhnend das rote karelische Holz als Rohmaterial für die südfinnische Industrie abtransportieren, muss ich unwillkürlich an Pekka Halonen denken, dessen Künstlerauge sich einst am Qualmen eines Flössholzschleppers auf dem See Pielinen störte: "Es verdarb vollständig die Stimmung, wie das Spiel einer Drehorgel ein erstklassiges Konzert…"

Vielleicht würde Halonen sich am heutigen Pielinen wohlfühlen. Sicher, die Flössholzbündel zeichnen sich immer noch rot auf dem Blau unserer Seen ab, aber die alten Fischer in ihren tuckernden Kähnen fallen bald niemandem mehr lästig.

Nichts anderes stört an der Stille der bergkarelischen Einöddörfer, als dass sie an Totenstille erinnert.

Vielleicht kann ich meinem bergkarelischen Landschaftsportrait doch noch etwas Neues hinzufügen. Vielleicht kann ich bei der Beschreibung meiner Heimat trotz allem Klischees vermeiden. Vielleicht habe ich etwas, was die Kalevalaromantiker nicht gehabt haben. Nämlich ein gehöriges Mass Angst und Trauer, nicht nur um diese Landschaft, sondern auch um die Menschen, die in ihr ein unpoetisches Leben führen.

Ich bin am Ostufer des Sees Pielinen geboren. Vom Hafen meines Heimatorts aus, wo ich schwimmen, beten, dichten und fluchen gelernt

habe, war der am Gegenufer liegende Berg Koli als doppelte Riesenwoge zu erkennen, die ihre Farben je nach Wetter, Tages- und Jahreszeit änderte.

Von Vuonislahti gesehen, versteckt sich der dritte und höchste Gipfel des Koli teilweise hinter den beiden kleineren, und jene Bergrücken, die im Blickfeld verbleiben, erinnern an einen behaarten riesigen Arm. Kein Wunder, dass meine zur Mystifizierung neigende kindliche Phantasie die Berge hinter dem See in einen liegenden Riesen verzauberte.

Bis eines Wintertages, nach einem schlechten Heusommer, irgendein in Lumpenpelz gekleideter Greis vom Koli, der mit einem Heuschlitten über das Eis gekommen war, um uns Torfstreu abzukaufen, behauptete, dass das Blaue und Geheimnisvolle dort drüben, dass das ein Dorf sei, und dass dahinter eine endlose Zahl ähnlicher Dörfer läge.

Von jenem Augenblick an begann die Welt sich mir zu öffnen.

Da ich die besten Tage meiner Jugend am Wasser verlebt habe, kann ich mir Karelien nur schwerlich ohne Seen, Teiche und Flüsse vorstellen. Von ihrem Charakter her unterscheiden sich die anderen bedeutenden Seen Nordkareliens, der für seine Seesenkung bekannte Höytiäinen und die südlicher gelegenen Seen Pyhäselkä und Orivesi, die zum nördlichen Saimaa abfliessen, kaum vom Pielinen und vom Koitere. Ohne sie wäre diese Landschaft nicht das, was sie ist. Die Ebenheit ihrer offenen Seenflächen birgt sommers und winters etwas, das, ausser die Höhenunterschiede der Landschaft zu betonen, der Landschaft ihre Seele verleiht und deren strenges, manchmal mürrisches Antlitz mildert.

Oder andersherum gesehen: der eigenartige Zauber der karelischen Seenlandschaft liegt in den steilen Bergen begründet, welche sie wie Wächter einkreisen.

In meiner Phantasie verschmelzen beide zu einem, zum selben Ganzen. Als Junge schrieb ich an einem Berghang auf einem Baumstumpf sitzend Gedichte (zugegebenermassen nicht allein der Umgebung wegen, sondern auch weil es mir peinlich gewesen wäre, dies unter den Augen der anderen zu tun). Jene Augenblicke bleiben in meinem Leben wie ein Gemälde oder wie ein Bild haften, aber nicht in herkömmlichem Sinne, sondern in einer Form, welche alles enthält: Licht, Farben und deren Nuancen, Gerüche, selbst Wärme und Geschmäcke, und als Hauptelemente Berge, Seen und Himmel, diese bergkarelische Dreieinigkeit. Die an ihren Wurzelenden grobrindigen, weiter oben wie zerfetzte Seide rauschenden, unten dunkelbraunen, in ihren Kronen hellroten Föhren reckten ihre gekrümmten Astarme zum Himmel und zum See, welcher sein Antlitz wechselte wie der junge Gedichteschreiber seine Launen. Weiter unten am Ufer Birken und Erlen, baumstumpf- und steinübersäte Heide, und im Hintergrund immer die fernen stolzen Berge, die, aus der Höhe gesehen, ihr schattiges Grün und Braun stufenweise immer blauer werden liessen, bis das Land in atemberaubender Ferne, dort wo die hügligen Wolken mit dem gewellten Land zu verschmelzen schienen, seinen steinernen Ballast abwarf und zu flackerndem Licht wurde, schwerelos und blau wie das Kopftuch meiner Mutter, wenn diese die Kühe von der Birkenweide ins Gatter zurückrief.

Und damit noch nicht genug: Blau ist die Farbe der Ferne, und diese aus der starren Erde aufragenden, stufenweise blauer werdenden Berge liessen die Illusion der Unendlichkeit entstehen, einen perspektivischen Eindruck der Entfernung, den wohl auch der fähigste Fotograf nicht auf Zelluloid zu bannen imstande wäre. Ein wesentlicher Bestandteil dieses Eindrucks ist nämlich das aus den Details der näheren Umgebung des Betrachters, den Gerüchen und Bewegungen bestehende Sinneserlebnis. Ich möchte sogar fast behaupten, dass dieses Gefühl der Tiefe — so wie ich es erlebt habe — nur entstehen kann, wenn man sich der sozialen Lage der Umgebung bewusst ist; desto blauer und ferner scheint der Horizont, je grauer die Häuserwände im Tal sind und je kürzer der Weg zwischen Häusern und Schuppen ist.

Mein Bergkarelien ist mehr als nur ein Bild, es ist das Gleichgewicht verschiedener Elemente, es ist Leben und Tiefe.

The Eastern Forests

Die östlichen Wälder

Forests, water bodies and bogs — those are the basic elements of the Northern Karelian landscape, combining with varying surface formations to create a distinctive natural picture. Everywhere in Northern Karelia forests cover at least 2/3 of the land area. They are least common in the Nurmes—Valtimo district and around Ilomantsi, where bogs abound.

Although spruce is also seen, pine is the dominant variety in this district. As a consequence of slash-and-burn methods of agriculture which continued until fairly recently, Northern Karelia has relatively many birch-dominated forests, which are most numerous to the south of Lake Pielinen.

Present-day silvicultural methods are designed to obliterate the traces left by slash-and-burn clearance. Cutaway areas, seedling stands and drained bogs are now beginning to dominate the landscape. In the southern part of the district the forests are lush, but outright deciduous groves are nevertheless rare.

Wälder, Gewässer und Moore — das sind die Grundelemente der nordkarelischen Landschaft, die zusammen mit den wechselhaften Oberflächenformen eine eigentümliche Naturlandschaft bilden. Überall in Nordkarelien bedecken die Wälder mindestens zwei Drittel der Erdoberfläche.

Obwohl die Fichte ein wichtiger Faktor in der bewaldeten Berglandschaft ist, nimmt die Kiefer die Vormachtstellung in Nordkarelien ein. Da die Brandrodung in dieser Gegend erst spät eingestellt wurde, wachsen hier relativ viele von Birken dominierte Wälder.

Die moderne Forstwirtschaft trägt jedoch Sorge dafür, dass die Spuren der Brandrodung allmählich verschwinden. Kahlschläge, Anpflanzungen und Moorabzugsgräben nehmen eine zunehmend beherrschende Stellung in der Landschaft ein. Mit Ausnahme des Salpausselkä sind die Wälder in den Südteilen der Provinz üppig: frische Waldböden bestreiten mehr als die Hälfte der Waldfläche. Ausgesprochene Laubhaine gibt es hingegen nur wenige.

Hill Farming
Berghöfe

Hill farming, common in Eastern
Finland, is also practised in the
Suomenselkä and Tammela districts.
The fields are often fringed by piles
of stones made when the moraine land
was being cleared. More stones are
thrown up by the winter frosts.

*Die für Ostfinnland charakteristische
Hochbesiedlung findet man auch im
Suomenselkä und im Hochland von
Tammela. Die Raine der Bergäcker
sind von Steinen gesäumt, welche
beim Roden des Moränenlands
aufgehäuft wurden. Das Gefrieren des
Bodens hebt weitere Steine an die
Oberfläche.*

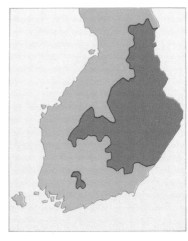

Hill farming is the most common type of agriculture in Eastern Finland. In the Karelian Hills it was formerly the only type of agriculture if one excludes a slight amount of farming in the lakeside strips. A typical feature of hill farming is that both buildings and cultivated land are on the rounded crowns or slopes of the hills.

This choice of location partially stems from the topography. The landscape in the Karelian region is characterised by parallel rocky ridges running in NE—SW direction with depressions in between.

The narrow valleys are boggy and the slopes often steep, so the largest level areas are on the crowns of the hills. The hills were earlier burned over to create arable land, and when this method gradually gave way to permanent fields the farmhouses were also built on the high ground. The greatest advantage of hill farming is a microclimatic one; on cold nights, the heavier cool air flows down the slopes and accumulates in the hollows. The summits are like warm islands in a sea of cold air, sometimes several degrees warmer.

Berghöfe sind die übliche Siedlungsform in Ostfinnland. Mit Ausnahme von geringfügiger Uferbesiedlung waren sie in Bergkarelien vormals die einzige Siedlungsform. Beim typischen Berghof befinden sich sowohl Gebäude wie auch Äcker im Gipfelbereich oder an den Hängen der Berge.

Die Geländestruktur hat zur Bevorzugung der Berglage beigetragen. Im karelischen Schiefergebiet charakterisieren parallel von Nordwest nach Südost verlaufende Felsrücken und die dazwischen gelegenen Senkungen die Landschaft. Die engen Talsohlen sind versumpft und die Hänge steigen oft steil an, so dass sich die ausgedehntesten ebenen Gebiete im Gipfelbereich der Berge befinden.

Der grösste Vorteil der Berglage liegt im Mikroklima: in kühlen Nächten strömt die kalte Luft die Berghänge hinab und sammelt sich in den Niederungen an. Dann ragen die Berge als warme Inseln aus dem Meer der kalten Luft auf. Die täglichen Tiefsttemperaturen liegen auf den Berggipfeln um mehrere Grade über dem Niveau der frostanfälligen Täler.

Slash and Burn
Brandrodung

The Finns adopted the slash-and-burn method of land clearance from the Russians in the Middle Ages and it continued to be practised in parts of Eastern Finland until well into the present century.

During the centuries this method was practised, forests close to settled areas were burned over many times, while further away only a few crops were won from clearings. In these areas, the vegetation developed in the same way as after natural forest fires: spruce had to yield to broad expanses of pine and, on more recently burned patches, stands of birch. By contrast, the deciduous areas near settlements were re-burned at regular intervals. Because of this, softwood varieties were not able to hold their own and the land was taken over by birch, alder and poplar, the most intensively cultivated areas by alder.

The marks left by slash-and-burn forest clearance can still be seen in Eastern Finland, in the form of bright stands of birch and alder and poplar growths near towns and villages.

Die Finnen übernahmen die Brandrodungstechnik im Mittelalter von den Russen. In Ostfinnland wurde sie bis weit in unser Jahrhundert hinein praktiziert. In die weiterab gelegenen Wälder wurden Schwenden gebrannt, die man jeweils nur für einige wenige Ernten benutzte. In ihnen entwickelte der Wald sich wie unter Einwirkung natürlicher Waldbrände: die Fichten mussten vor ausgedehnten Kiefernwäldern und auf frischeren Böden vor Birkenwäldern weichen. In der Nähe der Dörfer hingegen wurde die Brandrodung in regelmässigen Abständen wiederholt. Die dazwischenliegenden Wachstumsperioden waren nicht so lang, dass die Nadelbäume sich hätten behaupten können, weswegen diese Gebiete von Birke, Erle und Esche erobert wurden.

Die Spuren der Brandrodung sind noch sichtbar. Auf Schwenden gewachsene Birkenwälder, die Dörfer säumende Erlenwälder und Waldweiden sind bis heute wesentliche Elemente der nordkarelischen Kulturlandschaft.

The Ilomantsi Bogs

Die Moore von Ilomantsi

An aerial view of Kesonsuo Bog.

Luftansicht des Kesonsuo-Moores.

Northern Karelia is not a wetland region to the same extent as Ostrobothnia or Kainuu — not to mention Peräpohjola. On the contrary, there are quite few bogs in the lake district of Northern Karelia and this landscape feature is of significance only in the northernmost part of the region and around Ilomantsi, where peatlands cover no less than half the total land area.

As elsewhere in Finland, drainage has destroyed the bogs' character. Over 50 % of the more than half million acres of bog have already been drained and only a tiny area of peatland remains in its natural state in the southern part. In the east, however, several of the best known and most interesting bogs in Finland have been preserved, all around Ilomantsi.

Nordkarelien ist keine Moorlandschaft wie beispielsweise Kainuu oder Österbotten. Im Gegenteil: Nordkarelien ist eine sehr moorarme Gegend. Erst im Nordteil der Provinz und in Ilomantsi, wo Moore rund die Hälfte der Gemeindefläche bestreiten, nehmen die Moore eine landschaftlich prägnante Stellung ein.

Wie auch in den anderen Teilen des Landes ist die Moornatur Nordkareliens durch Dränierung zerstört worden. Mehr als die Hälfte der gut einer halben Million Hektar Moorfläche der Provinz sind schon dräniert. In den südlichen Gemeinden gibt es nur noch eine Handvoll naturwüchsiger Moore, im Osten hingegen sind eine Reihe der bekanntesten und wissenschaftlich interessantesten Moore erhalten geblieben: Kesonsuo, Patvinsuo, Koivusuo — allesamt im Gebiet von Ilomantsi.

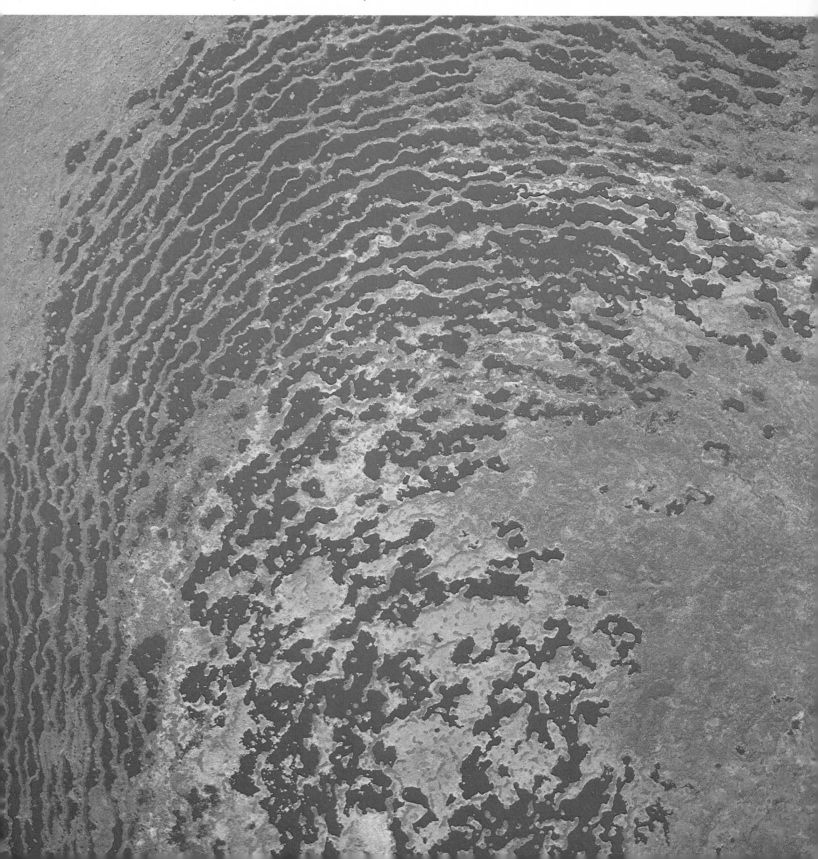

Kesonsuo

Formed in a meander of the River Koitajoki, Kesonsuo Bog is an almost circular, puddly peatland area with abundant hummock banks (''kermis''). The peat is calculated to have been developing for 9,500 years, allowing it to form an exceptionally mature and scenically unique bog.

The bog's situation right beside the river means that its outer sloping edge has developed particularly well. Inside a narrow strip bordered by the river and surrounding mineral soil, the different peat zones have formed a forest, in which the surface of the bog is rising fastest of all. In the flat central area of the bog, two distinct zones can be discerned (see the aerial photograph on p. 185). Concentric configurations of long mossy mounds and watery hollows predominate in the outer zone, while the central area contains amorphous pools and depressions in the peat.

Kesonsuo is the largest parcel of privately-owned land covered by a conservation scheme (since 1976) and is included in many international conservation programmes.

Das im Inneren einer Windung des Flusses Koitajoki liegende Moor Kesonsuo ist ein fast rundes, von Tümpeln durchsetztes Stranghochmoor. Seine Versumpfung hat schon vor 9500 Jahren begonnen, so dass es sich zu einem strukturell ungewöhnlichen und landschaftlich einzigartigen Moor entwikkeln konnte.

Die Lage des Moors am Koitajoki hat bewirkt, dass seine Aussenbereiche, der Rand und das Randgehänge, sehr gut entwickelt sind. Auf dem umgebenden Mineralboden sowie im Inneren des an den Fluss grenzenden Moorrandes befindet sich ein Randbestand aus verschiedenen Reisermooren, in dessen Bereich die Oberfläche des Moors am stärksten ansteigt. In der Mitte des Moores, auf der Hochfläche, können deutlich zwei Gürtel — siehe auch Luftaufnahme S. 185 — voneinander unterschieden werden: aussen Stränge und Rundschlenken, im Inneren ein diffuses Gebiet mit Tümpeln und Morastsenken.

Das 1976 unter Naturschutz gestellte Kesonsuo-Moor ist in viele internationale Naturschutzprogramme einbezogen worden.

The bird population in Kesonsuo Bog's pools is considerably denser than in ordinary bogs (1). Stunted pines grow on the peaty fringe of the bog (2). The wood sandpiper (3) and the bean goose (4) are typical species in the Kesonsuo bird paradise.

Die Vogeldichte des Kesonsuo-Moores liegt bedeutend über der gewöhnlicher Moore (1). Auf den Randgehängen des Kesonsuo-Moores wachsen Krüppelkiefern (2). Bruchwasserläufer (3) und Saatgans (4) sind typische Arten des Vogelparadieses Kesonsuo.

The Land of Blue-Tinged Hills
Das Land der blau schimmernden Berge

From the viewpoint of its phyto-geography, Northern Karelia is a watershed area. The southern part of the region is still a typical southern boreal evergreen forest zone, like the rest of the Finnish Lake District, while the northern part is considered to belong to the intermediate boreal Ostrobothnia — Kainuu zone. The dividing line runs through the region north of Lake Pielinen, bends southwards to Koitere and from there moves east again. The transformation is a gradual one. The appearance of the forests does not change rapidly as one moves northwards and the only changes that one notices in the undergrowth are an increase in the number of crowberries and the encroachment of whortleberries onto even the freshest of heaths.

The vegetation of Northern Karelia is generally poor and not very varied. The northern limit of the lime tree runs through the region. However, some oases can be discerned in its bleakness. Some fragments of the so-called Sortavala deciduous belt remain in, e.g., the Kitee—Tohmajärvi area.

Northern Karelia is still so sparsely inhabited and so many patches of wilderness remain there that two of Finland's large predators, the bear and the lynx, are permanent inhabitants, while the wolf is at least a regular visitor.

The most endangered species alongside the wolf are the wild

Nature Reserves are the last refuges of primeval forests and the creatures that live in them (1).
Living its inconspicuous life, the wood lemming (2) is a typical inhabitant of old forests.
The spruce has a prominent role in the hill landscapes of Northern Karelia, although the principal tree in the region is pine (3).

Naturschutzgebiete sind die letzten Reservate der alten Wälder und der von ihnen abhängigen Lebewesen (1). Ein typischer Bewohner alter Wälder ist der unauffällig lebende Waldlemming. Er ist aus der sibirischen Taiga nach Finnland gekommen (2). Obwohl die Kiefer dominiert, nimmt die Fichte eine markante Stellung in der nordkarelischen Landschaft ein (3).

forest reindeer (as opposed to the domesticated reindeer of the Lapps) and the Saimaa ringed seal, some dozens of which remain in the Orivesi—Pyhäselkä lake district. Wild forest reindeer were first observed in the area between Ruunanjärvi and the Soviet frontier in the early 1960s, and since then a smallish permanent colony has established itself.

In addition to the wild forest reindeer, another of Northern Karelia's animals that had earlier become extinct in the region, the beaver, has returned. The beaver population there is now one of the most firmly established in the country, and is even beginning to cause damage by flooding forests.

The easterly situation of Northern Karelia is also reflected in the fauna. Siberian varieties are numerous: in addition to the wild reindeer they include many small mammals, e.g. the extremely rare pygmy shrew, one of the world's smallest mammals.

The hills in the south-western part of Northern Karelia rise to no more than 100 metres in height, but around Lake Pielinen they soar to over 300 m. Koli is the best known of these rugged rocky hills. Height differences are quite pronounced, but north of the large lakes the landscape smoothens out into a fertile alluvial plain, rising again as it approaches the Soviet frontier.

———————

Pflanzengeographisch ist Nordkarelien Wasserscheidengebiet. Sein Südteil ist noch typisches Seen-Finnland, südboreale Nadelwaldzone. Der Nordteil wird schon zur mittelborealen Österbotten-Kainuu-Zone gerechnet. Die Grenze zwischen den beiden Zonen verläuft durch den Nordteil des Sees Pielinen, dringt auf dem Koitere-See nach Süden vor und verläuft von dort wieder nach Osten. In der Natur schlagen sich die Unterschiede zwischen den Zonen nur geringfügig nieder. Das Äussere der Wälder ändert sich nach Norden hin anfänglich noch nicht, und in der Bodenvegetation erkennt man den Unterschied nur an der zunehmenden Verbreitung der Krähenbeere sowie am Vordringen der Preisselbeere auch auf frische Waldböden.

Die Vegetation Nordkareliens ist zumeist dürftig und artenarm. Einige Oasen findet man allerdings auch in dieser kargen Umgebung. So sind in der Gegend Kitee—Tohmajärvi Überreste des sogenannten Laubhainzentrums von Sortavala erhalten.

Immerhin so dünn ist die Besiedlung und so viel mehr Wildnisreste sind in Nordkarelien bewahrt geblieben, dass von den grossen Raubtieren noch Bär und Luchs zu den ständigen Waldbewohnern gehören und auch der Wolf zumindest ein regelmässiger Gast ist. Neben dem Wolf die bedrohtesten Arten sind das Waldrentier und die Saimaa-Ringelrobbe. Waldrentiere wurden erstmals Anfang der sechziger Jahre im Gebiet zwischen dem See Ruunanjärvi und der finnischen Ostgrenze gesehen, wo seitdem ein kleiner Bestand fest ansässig geworden ist. Ausser dem Waldren ist auch ein zweites Tier nach Nordkarelien zurückgekehrt, das man einst ausgerottet hatte, nämlich der Biber. Der Biberbestand Nordkareliens ist der grösste Finnlands, und er beginnt allmählich spürbare Schäden anzurichten.

Der Südwesten Nordkareliens ist noch typische Seenplatte. Die Umgebungen der Seen Orivesi, Pyhäselkä und Höytiäinen sind sanft ansteigendes Flachland, das nur ausnahmsweise mehr als hundert Meter über dem Meeresspiegel liegt. Am Rande des Salpausselkä und der sich ihm anschliessenden Jaamankangas-Kiesrücken erstrecken sich ausgedehnte sandige Waldböden, und vor allem nördlich der grossen Seen breiten sich fruchtbare Tonebenen aus.

Die Ufer des grossen oberkarelischen Pielinen-Sees hingegen sind von bis zu 300 Metern hohen felsigen Bergen gesäumt, unter ihnen der Koli. Die Höhenunterschiede in diesem von Südost nach Nordwest durch die Provinz verlaufenden Berggürtel sind gross. Im östlichen Hinterland des Pielinen wird das Profil wieder ausgeglichener, obwohl die mittlere Höhe nach Osten weiter ansteigt.

Kolvanan Uuro

Kolvanan Uuro is the name of a rift valley running over ten kilometres in a SSW—NNE direction along the border of the Eno and Kontiolahti districts and resembling a canyon in places. A similar gash runs through the landscape about 5 km to the west. Kolvanan Uuro is deepest towards its southern end, where the western walls are steep, in places soaring quite perpendicularly to nearly 100 m above the valley floor.

According to botanists, Kolvanan Uuro was one intermediate stage in the migration of flora from the Lake Ladoga region to the Kuusamo area during the late Pleistocene. There are also other similar places in the Karelian schist area. The flora in Kolvanan Uuro contain much evidence supporting the botanists' theory.

With the exception of the steepest places, the valley's slopes are covered with old, dense stands of spruce, the dark shade of which is relieved by silvery birches in places. The lower slopes and valley floor are in places nearly bare and covered by loose rocks, while elsewhere they are covered by lush vegetation.

Kolvanan Uuro is one of the most important nature conservation areas in the region and ought to be declared a completely protected zone with the greatest possible urgency.

Kolvanan Uuro an der Gemeindegrenze von Kontiolahti und Eno ist ein mehr als zehn Kilometer langer, fast cañonartiger Senkungsgraben. Vier bis fünf Kilometer weiter westlich verläuft ein ähnlicher Schnitt durch die Landschaft. Am steilsten ist das Tal in seinem Südteil — vor allem die westlichen Wände ragen teilweise bis zu hundert Metern senkrecht auf.

Den Botanikern zufolge war Kolvanan Uuro eine Zwischenetappe auf der Wanderung der Fjällvegetation aus der Gegend des Ladogasees nach Kuusamo. Im karelischen Schiefergebiet gibt es noch weitere derartige Orte, so der Berg Hiidenvaara in Tohmajärvi, der Berg Koli sowie der Berg Niinivaara in Kaavi. Im Kolvanan Uuro findet man viele Beweise für die Theorie der Botaniker. Auf dem gleichen Felsabsatz gedeihen nordische und südliche Pflanzenarten nebeneinander.

Ein dichter alter Fichtenbestand bedeckt mit Ausnahme der steilsten Stellen die Talhänge, und hier und da hellen Birken das dunkle Grün der Fichten auf. Die unteren Talhänge sowie der Talgrund sind stellenweise pflanzenloses Geröll, anderswo wächst auf ihnen wieder eine üppige Vegetation.

Das Tal Kolvanan Uuro ist eines der wichtigsten Naturschutzobjekte Nordkareliens.

The Koli Hills and Lake Pielinen
Der Berg Koli und der Pielinen-See

The bedrock of Northern Karelia is divided into two separate zones, which differ from each other both in age and structure, the granite-gneiss area of Eastern Finland and a younger schist region to its west. A continuous belt of quartzite, which achieves its greatest size in the Koli district, runs along the eastern edge of the schist region. The striated nature of the landscape bears witness to ancient folding. Ridges, chains of hills and the valleys between them run in parallel lines towards the north-west.

Koli is the most famous feature of Northern Karelia. A wooded ridge a score or so kilometres in length runs south of Lake Pielinen as a continuation of the Koli-Vesivaara hill chain. Ukko-Koli ("The Old Man of Koli") is the highest of the three summits and also the highest point in the whole of Northern Karelia (347 m above sea level and 253 m above the surface of Lake Pielinen).

With an area of 867 km^2, Lake Pielinen is Northern Karelia's largest sheet of water, although it is divided into several separate open areas by the dozens of islands it contains. Except near Lieksa, Nurmes and Juuka, the lake remains in its natural condition, with excellent fishing.

In Nordkarelien kann man zwei von Struktur und Alter her verschiedene Felsgrundgebiete unterscheiden, im Osten das ostfinnische Granitgneissgebiet und im Westen ein jüngeres Schiefergebiet. Durch den Osten des Schiefergebiets verläuft von Tohmajärvi nach Nordnordwest ein zusammenhängender Quarzitgürtel, der seine grösste Ausdehnung im Gebiet des Bergs Koli erreicht.

Die alte Faltung der Erdoberfläche erkennt man an der Streifigkeit der Landschaft, an den von Südost nach Nordwest verlaufenden Höhenzügen, an den Bergen und den zwischen ihnen gelegenen Tälern.

Der Berg Koli ist Nordkareliens bekannteste Sehenswürdigkeit. Die Bergkette Koli-Vesivaara ragt als zwanzig Kilometer langer Höhenzug auf. Der Ukko-Koli, der höchste der drei Koli-Gipfel und die höchste Erhebung Nordkareliens (347 Meter über dem Meeresspiegel), liegt 253 Meter über dem Pielinen-See.

Der Pielinen ist mit 867 Quadratkilometern Nordkareliens grösster See. Dutzende von Inseln teilen ihn in mehrere offene Seenflächen auf. Ausser vor Lieksa, Nurmes und Juuka befindet sich der Pielinen noch im Naturzustand, ist karg und von Humusstoffen leicht bräunlich gefärbt.

1 2

3

Kainuu-Koillismaa

This is Koillismaa

by/von Reino Rinne

Koillismaa means "the North-Eastern Land", and it was shaped by the embrace of an icy god during an era that has now receded ten millenia into the history of life. The ice sheet was exceptionally active here. As it advanced slowly from west to east it shaped the landscape, dredged valleys, gouged out depressions and heaped up moraine ridges, even hills, during the intermediate stages. The roots of mountains dating back to an era millions of years before did not completely crumble under this mighty sledge-hammer. A hundred hills and ten arctic fells still stand in Koillismaa.

Under the exhausting weight of the ice sheet, or perhaps because of their igneous origin, the surface rocks cracked in places. Depressions and fault blocks were formed. These can be seen as gorges, some with walls close to a hundred metres high: Julma-Ölkky, Korouoma, Ristikallio, the valley of the River Kitkajoki, Lake Porontimajärvi and so on.

How long was Koillismaa desolate and empty after this enormous work of sculpturing?

Perhaps a thousand years.

Had any seed of life been preserved in the mutilated ground?

The seed of life had obviously been diminished almost to non-existence, but when the way had again been cleared with the melting of the ice and the water had settled into lake and pond basins, nature began to restore life to this area close to the Arctic Circle. The advance of life on this return journey was a continuous upward climb. The central region of Koillismaa is in the Maaselkä Uplands, 250 metres above sea level.

Nature began a new work of creation. She sent the sea buckthorn bush as a pioneer moving in from the White Sea shore. This bush and, later the birch and other deciduous trees, eventually reached the uplands of Kuusamo — although the names Kuusamo and Koillismaa were not uttered until much later.

The sea buckthorn eventually wandered on to the Gulf of Bothnia coast, but birch remained to occupy the land everywhere along its migration route. In its wake spread Finland's only indigenous pine species, which soon dominated Koillismaa. Spruce was one of the last arrivals. It spread into the region about 7,000 years ago, adding further expression to Koillismaa's diversifying forests.

With the development of the forests, the fauna driven into exile by the ice sheet also returned. Thus the forest pattern again became whole. The water dwellers had already returned; some of them had even remained throughout the long Ice Age.

The earliest human inhabitants of Koillismaa — I began calling the region by this name at the beginning of the 1950s — arrived about 1,000 years after spruce had established itself, some 6,000 years before our day. This tribe was probably of Indo-Aryan origin. Where did it go? Did it move on somewhere else, or did it fade away completely from the pattern of life? It is quite possible that some of the hidden places of Koillismaa preserve notes hewn in the rocks by these Stone-Age people.

Then came the Lapps. They came to move on rather than to stay, for about 400 years ago the industrious Finns moved in to occupy Koillismaa. These latest arrivals, formed from the excess populations of numerous Finnish tribes, were the first human inhabitants to really move in for keeps and create permanent "jobs" here.

Did Koillismaa welcome them with open arms and cheers, or did it watch them with frowning suspicion? The latter course was taken by those Lapps who had not managed to flee. They were driven away or subjugated. Perhaps nature was not yet afraid of the human ants.

The axe and other iron weapons were introduced by the forefathers of today's Koillismaa people 14 generations ago. They soon began to show their environment the power and intelligence of man. They slashed and burned out clearings in the forests, built houses, cleared fields, lowered the levels of lakes and diverted streams into bogs to create meadows.

But it was only the generation that reigned most recently — and is

still in power to some extent — that brought a mighty machine technology to Koillismaa and began planning the utilization of nature in such a way that the changes threatened to be total. The rapids were to be harnessed to the last, the rivers regulated, the bogs and marshes drained and the primeval forests transformed through a generation change.

What is the Koillismaa landscape like today?

It is shackled, split into blocks by metalled roads. Instead of paths one finds forest roads, country roads, national highways. The architecture in the urban settlements is so typically Finnish that hardly any feature in them says:

"This is Koillismaa."

This is Koillismaa, but its forested hills and pine-covered ridges, spruce wildernesses and natural bogs with their myriad of expressions have had to submit to harsh treatment during the past couple of decades. The primeval forests are gone, the bogs shrunk, the watercourses of the area — Lake Suolijärvi in Posio, the River Kostojoki in Taivalkoski, the River Suininki, the headwaters of the River Iijoki — have lost their natural rhythm, the salmon are barred from the River Iijoki. Otherwise, too the salmenoid fishes of the Koillismaa rivers only live in stories. The same can be said of nearly all the harvest of the forest, its game, the return of which one awaits and wonders at the delay.

Nevertheless, some untouched nature still remains in Koillismaa. The cascades and rapids of the Rivers Oulanka and Kitkajoki, Lakes Livojärvi, Kuusamojärvi, Muojärvi and Joukamojärvi and hundreds of other smaller water bodies remain in their natural condition. There are still miniature wildernesses around Riisitunturi Fell in Posio and Iivaara Fell in South-eastern Kuusamo, Kylmäluoma, Syöttee... some areas of blanket bog remain untouched, but an aapa bog with its rushes and sedges that has been spared the ravages of machinery can hardly be found any longer.

The permanent inhabitants of Koillismaa made the beaver extinct there three centuries ago. The elk is protected by law, but the bear, persecuted by reindeer herdsmen and other hunters, lives on a permanent battlefield and hardly finds adequate sanctuary outside the Oulanka National Park, the only nature reserve in the Koillismaa area. The wolf is the least protected of all; hated, persecuted. Both it and the bear will ultimately suffer the same fate that once befell the beaver. And yet both wolves and bears roamed these lands long before man.

Koillismaa no longer has a large, complete, living forest, the kind of forest in which all the elements belonging to it — trees, fauna, flora — are still alive. The landscape of Koillismaa is like a used car; there are even parts missing. It is true that there are not so many missing parts that it wouldn't run, but one can feel an absence of smoothness, of certainty, in its operation.

Hopefully we shall have the patience to let nature restore her creation to full perfection.

Dies ist Koillismaa

Die Formen von Koillismaa, der östlichen Schwelle zu Lappland, entstanden in der Umarmung des Gottes der Kälte zu einer Zeit, seit der unsere Lebensbotschaft schon wieder zehntausend Jahre weitergeeilt ist. Das Inlandeis legte hier ungewöhnliche Aktivitäten an den Tag. Indem es Schritt für Schritt von Westen nach Osten vordrang, formte es die Landschaft, baggerte Täler aus, furchte Senkungen und wühlte dazwischen lange Moränen-Oser, selbst Hügel auf. Die aus Jahrmillionen zurückliegender Vorzeit stammenden Bergwurzeln gingen unter dem gewaltigen Eishammer nicht vollständig in die Brüche — Koillismaa hat hundert Berge und zehn Fjälls.

Unter dem erdrückenden Gewicht der Eisdecke oder vielleicht auch wegen des vulkanischen Ursprungs des Bodes barst stellenweise die Felsoberfläche. Es entstanden Brüche, Schluchttäler. Die mächtigsten von ihnen haben fast hundert Meter aufragende Steilwände: Julma Ölkky, Korouoma, Ristikallio, das Flusstal des Kitkajoki, der See Porontimajärvi.

Wie lange blieb Koillismaa nach dieser gewaltigen Formung öde und leer?

Vielleicht tausend Jahre.

Hatte der Keim des Lebens in seinem zermalmten Bett überlebt?

Offenbar war der Keim des Lebens bis auf einen kleinen Rest vernichtet worden, aber als das schmelzende Eis den Boden wieder freilegte und die Schmelzwässer sich in den Seen- und Teichbecken etabliert hatten, begann das Leben in dieses an den Polarkreis gelehnte Gebiet zurückzukehren. Das Vordringen des Lebens auf seiner Rückkehr war ein ständiges Klettern. Das Zentrum von Koillismaa liegt auf der Hochebene Maanselkä, 250 Meter über dem Meeresspiegel.

Die Natur begann ein neues Schöpfungswerk. Schickte den Sanddorn von irgendwo aus der Gegend von Archangelsk als Pionier vor. Dieser und die ihm auf den Fersen folgende Birke wie auch die anderen Laubbäume erreichten schon bald die Hochebene von Kuusamo — die Namen Kuusamo und Koillismaa kamen natürlich erst viel später zum ersten Mal über die Lippen eines Menschen.

Der Sanddorn gelangte auf seinem Durchmarsch irgendwann zur Küste des Bottnischen Meerbusens. Die Birke hingegen setzte sich überall an ihrer Wanderroute fest, um die Landschaft zu erobern. In ihrem Schutze drang die Föhre vor, die einzige ursprüngliche Kiefernart des Landes. Sie wurde zum Herrscher der Wälder von Koillismaa. Einer der letzten Rückwanderer war die Fichte. Sie breitete sich vor etwa 7000 Jahren hier aus, um das Antlitz der Waldnatur anzureichern.

Indem der Wald sich entwickelte, kehrte auch die vom Inlandeis ins Exil vertriebene Tierwelt zurück. Die Wasserbewohner hatten sich schon früher wieder niedergelassen, teilweise auch während des langen Eiswinters im Lande ausgeharrt. Koillismaa — diesen Namen gab ich der Landschaft im Morgengrauen der fünfziger Jahre — empfing seine ersten menschlichen Bewohner vielleicht tausend Jahre nachdem die Fichte sich niedergelassen hatte, also vom heutigen Tage vor 6000 Jahren. Jener Menschenstamm dürfte indogermanischer Abstammung gewesen sein. Wohin ging er von hier? Zog er weiter oder verschwand er vollständig von der menschlichen Landkarte? Gut möglich, dass Koillismaa irgendwo die in Fels gehauenen Aufzeichnungen jener Steinzeitler verborgen hält.

Dann kamen die Samen. Eher auf der Durchreise denn zu bleiben. Nämlich vor rund 400 Jahren eroberten die emsigen Finnen Koillismaa. Jenes Gemisch aus Resten vieler finnischer Stämme war die erste menschliche Bevölkerung, welche dieses Gebiet wirklich für sich selbst eroberte und hier ”neue beständige Arbeitsplätze” zu schaffen begann.

Begrüsste die Natur von Koillismaa diese Ankömmlinge freudig und jubilierend oder sah sie diese vielleicht schräg an? Schräg angesehen wurden sie zumindest vom Volk der Samen, das es nicht geschaft hatte, beizeiten die Flucht zu ergreifen. Die Samen — heute vielen besser als Lappen bekannt — wurden vertrieben oder unterworfen. Vielleicht hat die Natur zu jenen Zeiten die menschlichen Ameisen noch nicht allzu sehr gefürchtet.

Die Axt und andere eiserne Werkzeuge wurden von jenen vor vierzehn Generationen nach Koillismaa eingereisten Stammopas mitgebracht. Schon bald lehrten sie die Natur, Kraft und Intelligenz des Menschen zu fürchten: sie brannten Schwenden, bauten Häuser, rodeten Felder, senkten die Seenspiegel und lenkten die Wässer der Bäche in die Moore ab, um neues Anbauland zu schaffen.

Aber erst eine Generation der allerjüngsten Zeit, eine, die teilweise immer noch am Ruder ist, rief die gewaltige Maschinentechnik nach Koillismaa und begann, die Nutzung der Natur derart gründlich zu planen, dass die Veränderungen in ihrer Totalität bedrohlich wurden: es war beabsichtigt, auch die letzten Stromschnellen zu unterjochen, die Seen zu regulieren, die Moornatur trockenzulegen, die Urwälder durch Baumgenerationswechsel zu erneuern.

Wie ist die Landschaft von Koillismaa heute?

Asphaltierte Strassen binden sie, zerschneiden sie in Streifen. Anstelle von Pfaden Autostrassen quer durch die Wälder, Landstrassen, Fernverkehrsstrassen. Die Architektur der Gemeindezentren ist so allgemeinfinnisch, dass sie praktisch nichts enthält, das erzählte:

Dies ist Koillismaa.

Dies *ist* Koillismaa, aber seine bewaldeten Berge und kiefernbestandenen Bergrücken, Fichtenödwälder und — wenn im Naturzustand befindlich — vielgesichtigen Moore haben sich in den beiden letzten Jahrzehnten einer strengen Behandlung unterwerfen müssen. Die Urwälder sind verschwunden, die Moore verkümmert, die Randgewässer dieses Gebiets — die Suolijärvet-Seen in Posio, der Kosto in Taivalkoski, der Suininki in Kuusamo, der Fluss Iijoki und die Seen an seinem Oberlauf — sind aus ihrem natürlichen Takt geraten, der Iijoki ist den Lachsen versperrt. Auch sonst leben die Lachsfische der Gewässer von Koillismaa nur noch in Erzählungen fort. Wie auch fast das gesamte ”Getreide der Wälder”, das Wild, nach dessen Rückkehr Ausschau gehalten wird und über dessen Ausbleiben man sich wundert ohne zu merken, dass die Heimatgründe des Wilds übel mitgenommen sind.

Selbstredend, Überbleibsel urwüchsiger Natur sind in Koillismaa noch erhalten. Die Oulanka-Wasserfälle, die Kitkajoki-Stromschnellen, die Seen Kitkajärvi, Livo, Kuusamojärvi, Muojärvi und Joukamojärvi und Hunderte von kleineren Gewässern; der Riisitunturi-Fjäll in Posio, die Wildnis von Iivaara im Südosten von Kuusamo, der Kylmäluoma-See in Talvakoski, die Gegend von Syöte in Pudasjärvi... Hier und da findet man noch ein unzerstörtes Hangmoor, aber Rimpimoore oder prächtige Aapamoore, welche samt ihre Umgebung den gierigen Klauen der Maschinen entgangen wären, trifft man kaum noch an.

Der Biber wurde vor 300 Jahren von den ständigen Bewohnern Koillismaas ausgerottet. Unter den grösseren Säugern ist der vom Gesetz geschützte Elch in seiner Existenz nicht sonderlich bedroht, aber der von Rentierzüchtern und Jägern aller Art verfolgte Bär, der ausserhalb des einzigen Naturschutzgebiets von Koillismaa, dem Nationalpark Oulanka, kaum noch gebührenden Schutz in den Wäldern findet, lebt wie auf einem ewigen Kriegsschauplatz. Der Wolf ist der schutzloseste von allen, gehasst, gejagt. Ihn wie auch den Bären erwartet in Koillismaa das Schicksal des Bibers. Und dies, obwohl Wolf und Bär schon lange vor dem Menschen hier lebten.

In Koillismaa findet man keine unversehrten grossen und lebendigen Wälder mehr, in denen sämtliche im Idealfalle vorhandenen Elemente — Bäume, Tiere, alle möglichen Pflanzen — erhalten wären. Die Landschaft von Koillismaa ist wie ein Gebrauchtwagen: es fehlen sogar ganze Teile. Allerdings in dieser Landschaft nicht in derartigem Ausmass, dass es nicht doch irgendwie ginge. Aber im Ablauf ihrer Naturprozesse kann man Ungleichmässigkeiten, Unsicherheit verspüren.

Hoffentlich sind wir Finnen so vernünftig, die Natur ihre eigene Schöpfung voll wiederherstellen zu lassen.

Lake Chains
Seenketten

2 Two labyrinthine lake chains give the Kainuu region its distinct character. The long Hyrynsalmi chain begins on the Maanselkä isthmus near Kuusamo and continues Southwest along the River Kehimäjoki, which in turn flows into Lake Oulujärvi. The numerous lakes of the Sotkamo chain begin at Kuhmo and form a serpentine necklace of water-bodies also discharging into Lake Oulujärvi.

The landscapes around the headwaters of the Hyrynsalmi and Sotkamo chains are barren and boggy. The heaths are carpeted with heather or lichen and by the edges of bogs stunted pines watch, destined to dry up and die while they still stand. Even as far downstream as the central lakes of both systems, Kiantajärvi and Lentuajärvi, the forlorn cry of the wilderness can still be heard.

However, as one moves south of Kianta and Lentua, the wilderness landscape is gradually replaced by impressive looking hills and forests more obviously tended by man.

Zwei labyrinthartige Seenketten prägen die Landschaft von Kainuu. Die langgestreckte Hyrynsalmi-Kette beginnt an den Hängen der Hochebene Maanselkä in Kuusamo und führt über den Fluss Kiehimäjoki zum Oulujärvi-See. Die gewundene und seenreiche Sotkamo-Kette beginnt in Kuhmo und verläuft über den Fluss Kajaaninjoki zum Oulujärvi.

Die Landschaften an den Oberläufen beider Seenketten sind karg und sumpfig. Die Waldböden sind mit Heide oder Flechten überwachsen. Krüppelkiefern stehen an den Reisermooren und sehen ihrem Austrocknen entgegen, andere spiegeln sich in stillen Wildnisseen.

Noch in der Umgebung der Zentralseen beider Ketten, des Kiantajärvi und des Lentua, ist die Natur urwüchsig. Gegen Süden weicht allmählich die Wildnisatmosphäre. Hochgewachsene Kiefernwälder säumen die Gewässer. Bewaldete Berge sind weithin sichtbare Landzeichen. Hier sind die Spuren menschlichen Wirkens nicht mehr zu übersehen.

The dark colouring caused by humus is a characteristic feature of the unpolluted lakes in the Kainuu region, such as the largest one, Lake Lentuajärvi. This beautiful lake retains its wilderness character, because these bleak sand beaches have not yet been discovered by holiday residence builders from urban centres. There are plans to include the lake in a projected network of national park areas in Finland.

Die durch Humusstoffe verursachte dunkle Färbung des Wassers ist charakteristisch für Kainuus saubere Seen, so für den Lentua, den grössten See von Kainuu.
Am schönen Lentua herrscht noch Wildnisatmosphäre, da die Ferienbesiedlung noch nicht bis zu diesen kargen Sandstränden vorgedrungen ist. Der Lentua ist mit in die Entwicklungspläne für ein finnisches Nationalparknetz einbezogen worden.

3

Vuokatti

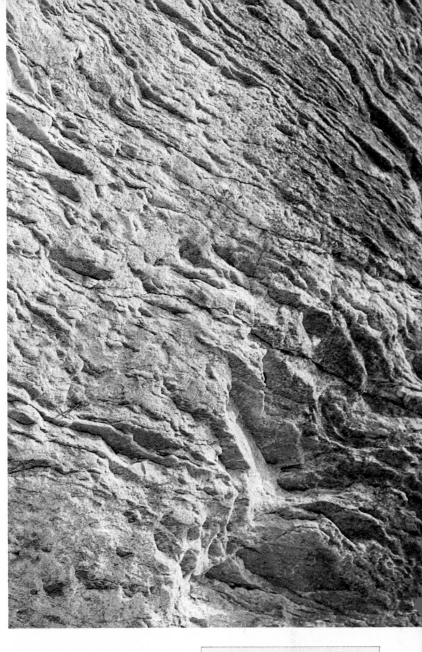

The highest peak of the Vuokatti quartzite ridge is nearly 300 m above sea level and some 200 m above the surfaces of the lakes in the nearby Sotkamo chain. Like Koli, Vuokatti is a relict of the Svecokarelide Range, which was produced when the earth's crust folded some 1,800 million years ago. Most of this range has long since been eroded and only a few upland areas remain. The bedrock relief here, as elsewhere in Finland, would appear to be the same as it was before the Ice Age.

Der höchste Gipfel des Quarzithöhenzuges Vuokatti liegt mehr als 300 Meter über dem Meeresspiegel und fast 200 Meter über der nahegelegenen Sotkamo-Seenkette. Wie auch der Koli ist der Vuokatti ein Relikt des vor über 1800 Millionen Jahren gefalteten Svekokareliden-Gebirges, das schon seit langer Zeit eingeebnet ist. Das Profil des Felsgrunds dürfte hier wie auch in den anderen Landesteilen schon vor der Eiszeit in seinen Grundzügen dem heutigen entsprochen haben.

"Relict mountain" is the term used to describe any upland feature that has been peneplaned, i.e. is almost flat on top. In Finland, they include the watershed areas, not all of which are made of more erosion-resistant material than the areas in which they are situated. It is simply that the forces of erosion have not yet managed to wear them down more. Most relict mountains, however, are made of tougher material than that surrounding them and thus remain as prominent features in areas of denudation. The quartzite areas of the Svecokarelides or Svecofennides of Southern Finland (light brown on the map) and the Karelides of Eastern Finland (dark brown on the map) contain many such relict mountains. However, it must be noted that these mountain chains about 1,800 million years old had already been peneplaned about 1,300 million years ago, and it was only a few million years ago that erosion set in again. Thus the present peaks, Vuokatti, Koli and Pyhätunturi are not necessarily the stumps of the ancient mountains' highest summits, but rather are evidence of the durability of quartzite and the other materials they contain.

Als Restberge bezeichnet man flach abgetragene Erhebungen, die inmitten einer Fastebene — Peneplain — erhalten geblieben sind. Derartige Restberggebiete sind in Finnland beispielsweise die Wasserscheiden, welche nicht immer aus härteren Gesteinen als ihre Umgebung bestehen, sondern deren Abtragung einfach noch nicht weiter vorangeschritten ist. In den meisten Fällen jedoch sind Restberge härteres Gestein, welches im Gegensatz zur Umgebung der Abtragung widerstehen konnte. Beispiele hierfür sind die Quarzitgebiete der Svekokareliden, also der südfinnischen Svekofenniden (Karte: hellbraun) und der ostfinnischen Kareliden (dunkelbraun). Diese rund 1800 Millionen Jahre alten Bergzüge wurden in Südfinnland schon vor 1300 Millionen Jahren zu Peneplains abgetragen. Die heute höchsten Erhebungen, Vuokatti, Koli und Pyhätunturi, brauchen nicht unbedingt die Stummel der höchsten Erhebungen jener vorzeitlichen Bergketten zu sein, sondern möglicherweise sind sie nur Beispiele für die Widerstandsfähigkeit der Quarzite und anderer in diesem Gebiet anzutreffender Gesteinsarten.

RELICT MOUNTAINS RESTBERGE

OUNASTUNTURI
PALLASTUNTURI
LEVITUNTURI
KUMPUTUNTURI
YLLÄSTUNTURI
LUOSTOTUNTURI
PYHÄTUNTURI
OUNASVAARA
RIISITUNTURI
RUKATUNTURI
VALTAVAARA
KONTTAIS-
TUNTURI
SIIKAVAARA
PALJAKKA
VUOKATTI
TAHKOVUORI
PISA
KOLI
SIMPSIO
LAUHAVUORI
TIIRISMAA

Wild Forest Reindeer

Auf den Spuren des Waldrentiers

After the wild forest reindeer had been made extinct in Finland, it was declared a protected species "in absentia" in 1913. During the war years, wild forest reindeer were found in Eastern Karelia, whence they returned to their old homeland after hostilities had ended. The boggy woodlands along the border between Ilomantsi and Suomussalmi provided refuge for the earliest casual stragglers. Then, however, it was noticed that the Elimyssalo area of Kuhmo suited the animals for summer grazing and breeding purposes. In 1972, all silviculture was prohibited in a 3,000-ha area for 20 years in order to protect the wild forest reindeer.

Elimyssalo bears many expressions. There are primeval forests and every type of bog found in Finland. The wild forest reindeer, not to be confused with the semi-domesticated reindeer of Lapland, thrive there from the calving season in May—June until late autumn. In winter they move on to open heaths, where beneath the snow they find lichen to eat.

Nachdem es in Finnland ausgerottet worden war, hat man das Waldrentier 1913 in "Abwesenheit" unter Naturschutz gestellt. Während des Zweiten Weltkriegs traf man es in Ostkarelien an, von wo es nach Kriegsende von selbst in seine alte Heimat zurückkehrte. Die Ödwälder an der Ostgrenze zwischen Ilomantsi und Suomussalmi nahmen die ersten vereinzelten Waldrentiere auf. Dann bemerkte man, dass die Waldrentiere den Ödwald Elimyssalo in Kuhmo als Sommer- und Kalbungsrevier akzeptierten. Im Jahre 1972 wurden zum Schutze des Bestandes 3000 Hektar des Elimyssalo für zwanzig Jahre von jeglicher forstwirtschaftlichen Nutzung ausgenommen.

Die Landschaft von Elimyssalo ist vielgestaltig. Die Wälder sind urwüchsig. Da man in Elimyssalo alle Haupttypen der finnischen Moore antrifft, fühlt das Waldrentier sich hier den ganzen Sommer über sehr wohl. Im Winter sucht es seine Nahrung auf flechtenbewachsenen Waldböden.

1

Old Tar Lands

Die alten Teerländer

In the 16th century, the Viceroy offered ten peasants from Savo a 3-year tax holiday to move to the wilderness around Lake Oulujärvi, where they were to clear the land by slash and burn methods.

This form of agriculture was practised in the Kainuu region for about three centuries. After that the forests were burned again, this time for tar, and later still logging began to feed the sawmills and paper plants. Through the ages, the forests of Kainuu have paid a heavy toll to man.

Im 16. Jahrhundert lobte der Statthalter der Schwedischen Krone drei steuerfreie Jahre für zehn Bauern aus, die von Savo in die Wildnis am Oulujärvi-See zögen. Damit begann die Brandrodung in Kainuu.

Als 300 Jahre später die Brandrodung in Kainuu eingestellt wurde, begann man erneut, die Wälder abzubrennen, diesmal für die Teergewinnung, bis schliesslich die Ernte ganzer Baumstämme begann, zuerst als Sägeholz, später als Papierrohstoff.

Nearly half the Kainuu region consists of peatlands. Every other farm there was established this century (1). The earliest tax collected from the peasants in the Eastern Kainuu was one and a half pecks of dried pike per year. Thus there is a long tradition of fishing for domestic needs (2). The "tar boom" reached its peak in the Kainuu region around the turn of the century. The tradition is preserved at the Tönölä Camping Site, where a couple of pits are fired each summer as an unusual tourist attraction (3).

Fast die Hälfte von Kainuu ist Moor. Jeder zweite Bauernhof von Kainuu stammt aus diesem Jahrhundert (1). Die ersten Bauern von Ost-Kainuu mussten an den Steuereintreiber jährlich zwei Metzen getrockneten Hecht entrichten. Die Fischerei für den Eigenbedarf blickt also schon auf alte Traditionen zurück (2). Das Teerbrennen erreichte um die Jahrhundertwende seinen Höhepunkt. Die Traditionen werden auf dem Campingplatz Tönölä gepflegt, wo man zweimal im Sommer beim Köhlern einer Teergrube zusehen kann.

Rowing Boats
Ruderboote

It is almost impossible to imagine a Finnish summer landscape without a lake and a boat leaving its wake on the shimmering surface of the water.

The Finnish rowing boat is the result of centuries of practical tests, of real product development. It must be safe, durable and ride the water lightly. Its design has been determined by the prevailing water conditions and the uses to which it is put.

Thus the boats in the lakes are delicately lined, almost keel-less and have low sides. The rougher the water they are used in, the higher the boats' sides are made. The boats in the far North have high bows and sterns, enabling them to weave through the river rapids, the sharp-prowed Savo boats easily cleave the waters of Kallavesi and the straight-bowed boats of Häme are the most suitable design for Lake Päijänne. There are different requirements for coastal waters. Boats must be sturdy and high-sided, and a keel is also essential.

Es ist fast unmöglich, sich die finnische Sommerlandschaft ohne die Seen und die auf ihrer schimmernden Oberfläche Spuren ziehenden Ruderboote vorzustellen.

Die finnischen Ruderboote sind Resultate jahrhundertelangen Experimentierens. Das Boot sollte sicher, haltbar und leicht zu rudern sein. Die örtlichen Wasserverhältnisse sowie der Verwendungszweck bestimmten seine Form.

So sind die Binnenseeboote schlank und flachrandig, fast kiellos. Je stärker der Wellengang, desto hochrandiger die Boote. Die mit hohem Steven und Heck gebauten Flussboote von Peräpohjola schlängeln sich sicher zwischen den Steinen der schäumenden Stromschnellen hindurch, die vorn spitz zulaufenden Boote von Savo durchpflügen mühelos den Saimaa, und die Häme-Boote meistern mit ihrem Steilsteven am besten die Bedingungen des Päijänne. Die Boote der Küstengewässer wiederum müssen hochrandig und stabil sein und zum Verhindern des Kenterns bei hohem Seegang einen Kiel haben.

Hiidenportti Gorge
Die Schlucht Hiidenportti

The easternmost part of the Suomenselkä Ridge acts as a watershed separating the Oulujärvi and Pielinen lake basins. It is also the border between the regions of Northern Karelia and Kainuu. The landscape is bleak and wild, with many bogs.

Here and there in the watershed area, depressions running in a NW-SE direction are to be found. The most famous of these gorges is Hiidenportti near Sotkamo.

Der Ostteil des Suomenselkä scheidet die Wässer des Oulujärvi- und des Pielinen-Sees. Gleichzeitig trennt er Kainuu von Nordkarelien. Die Landschaft der Wasserscheide ist karg. Gute Waldböden sind selten. Moore hingegen gibt es viele, ebenso Bruchwald. Hier und da trifft man auf Brüche, die von Südost nach Nordwest verlaufen. Hiidenportti ist die bekannteste unter den langen Schluchten dieser Gegend.

One of the paths leading to Hiidenportti ("The Demon's Gate") starts at Nimisenselkä and the other at Sivakkavaara, near Valtimo. After the colour display of autumn has been snuffed out by the winter snows, only elk herds move in the boggy woodlands there (1). There is good fishing and hiking in the Peurajärvi area. The "Demon's Gate" is one of the steepest gorges in Finland. It continues all the way to Nurmes (3).

Von Nimisenkangas führt ein Pfad zur Schlucht Hiidenportti ("Dämonenpforte") in Sotkamo, ein anderer von Sivakkavaara in Valtimo. Nach Erlöschen der herbstlichen Farbenpracht und den ersten Schneefällen trifft man im Ödwald des Hiidenportti höchstens noch Elchherden an (1). Das Sportangelgebiet Hiidenportti in Peurajärvi liegt beidseitig der Provinzgrenze (2). Der Grabenbruch Hiidenportti, eine der wildesten Einöden des Landes, führt als schmale Schlucht weiter bis Nurmes (3).

1

Kitkajärvi

The hill country of Kainuu and Kuusamo is almost entirely upland, which in Finland means land with an elevation of more than 200 metres above sea level. Kitkajärvi lies 240 metres above sea level, making it the highest lake of any size in Finland. It is drained by the River Kitkajoki, which flows into Lake Paanajärvi on the Soviet side of the border and from there into the White Sea. Water bodies are plentiful in the Kuusamo — Posio area, where eight per cent of the land is covered by lakes.

Lake Kitkajärvi and its satellite bodies have a total area of 295 square kilometres. It is surrounded by relatively high hills, some of which soar to more than 300 metres above sea level.

Das Bergland von Kainuu und Kuusamo ist fast durchweg Hochland. Der Kitkajärvi liegt 240 Meter über dem Meeresspiegel und ist der höchstgelegene unter Finnlands grossen Seen. Er fliesst über den Kitkajärvi-Fluss in die Sowjetunion ab. Die auf finnischem Territorium liegenden Seen dieses Gebiets gehören zu den Oberlaufgewässern des Koutajoki-Flusses, welcher zum Weissen Meer abfliesst. Die Region Kuusamo—Posio ist relativ seenreich — acht Prozent der Fläche sind Seen.

Die Fläche des Kitkajärvi und seiner benachbarten Seen beträgt 295 Quadratkilometer. Der See ist von relativ hohen Bergen eingerahmt. Etliche Berge der näheren Umgebung erheben sich mehr als 300 Meter über dem Meeresspiegel.

Oulankajoki

The River Oulankajoki rises in the peaty uplands of South Salla in the South-eastern corner of Lapland. It soon plunges into a narrow gorge-like valley, which widens out further downstream. This valley contains several stretches of rapids, the best-known of which is the Kiutaköngäs Cascade in the Oulanka National Park.

Numerous flowering waterside meadows stand out as bright flecks against the background of the wilderness forests. These meadows were originally cleared from forest and scrublands. Many beautifully flowering plants originally quite rare have established themselves here in these meadows.

A well-marked hiking trail leads along the banks of the River Oulanka. There is a biological research station on its north bank.

Der Fluss Oulankajoki entspringt in Lappland im flachen Moorland von Süd-Salla. Schon bald jedoch stürzt sich der Fluss in ein schluchtartiges enges Tal, das später breiter wird. Im Schluchtabschnitt bildet der Fluss viele prächtige Stromschnellen — die bekannteste von ihnen ist der Kiutaköngäs im Nationalpark Oulanka.

Zahlreiche Uferwiesen mit schönen Blumen leuchten als farbige Flecken in der Landschaft des Wildnisflusses. Sie sind einst zu Wiesenland gerodete Uferwälder. Viele vormals seltene schöne Blumenarten haben auf den Wiesen Fuss fassen können.

Die Bärenroute (Karhunkierros), ein gut markierter Wildnispfad, führt am Ufer des Oulankajoki entlang.

No hay has been harvested in these meadows since the 1950s (1 and 4). In places the River Oulankajoki flows between sand embankments it has built itself (2). The brown dolomite cliffs of the Kiutaköngäs Cascade harbour many botanical rarities (3).

Heu wird auf den Wiesen schon seit einiger Zeit nicht mehr geerntet (1 und 4). Stellenweise fliesst der Fluss durch angeschwemmte Sandbänke (2). Auf dem Dolomitfels der Kiutaköngäs-Stromschnellen gedeihen viele seltene Pflanzen (3).

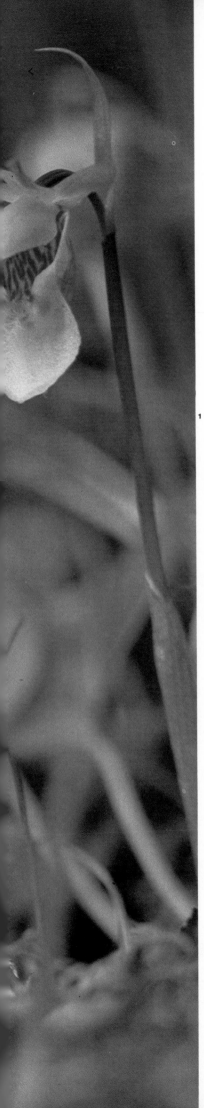

Orchids in the North
Orchideen im Norden

The orchid varieties calypso (1) and lady's slipper (2) grow on lime-rich soils. Few people in Finland have seen these large, rare plants, which are protected by law.

Die in Finnland äusserst seltenen grossblütigen Orchideenarten Calypso-Orchidee (1) und Frauenschuh (2) wachsen auf kalkhaltigem Untergrund.

Both the fauna and the flora in the valley of the River Oulankajoki are varied and abundant. This is because of the valley's favourable microclimatic conditions, its limestone-rich soil and the fact that it opens to the east — as though to welcome back the plants returning after the retreat of the ice sheet. The river itself has also played an important role in the spread of plants and animals since the end of the Pleistocene.

The special feature of the valley is its blend of eastern, southern and northern species. Its limestone cliffs resemble botanical gardens. Many of its varieties are found nowhere else in Finland. Calypso and lady's slipper orchids are two of the most spectacularly flowering varieties.

———

Die Tier- und Pflanzenwelt des Oulankajoki-Flusstals ist mannigfaltig und reichhaltig. Das günstige Mikroklima, der kalkhaltige Felsgrund und die Öffnung des Tals nach Osten sind Grundlagen dieser Fülle. Zusätzlich hat auch der Fluss selbst eine grosse Bedeutung für die Ausbreitung der Tiere und Pflanzen gehabt.

Die östlichen und südlichen wie auch die nordischen Arten verleihen der Fauna und Flora des Oulankajoki ihren wesenseigenen Charakter. Die kalkhaltigen Felsen sind schlechthin botanische Kollektionen. Am Oulankajoki wachsen viele Pflanzenarten, die man sonst in Finnland nicht antrifft. Besondere Erwähnung verdienen Calypso-Orchidee und Frauenschuh.

1 2

Kuusamo

Kuusamo is very rocky. The area is sometimes called "the Switzerland of Finland", a somewhat euphemistic title in view of the fact that the arctic hills here are less than 500 m above sea level and only 200—250 m above the surrounding terrain.

Another special feature of the Kuusamo landscape is the abundance of handsome rocky river gorges: the valleys of the River Oulanka and its tributaries, the ravines of Juuma and the steep-walled canyon lakes Julma-Ölkky and Ruoppijärvi.

Die Mannigfaltigkeit der Natur von Kuusamo hat ihre Ursache im Felsgrund. Die für Kuusamo manchmal gebrauchte Bezeichnung "Finnische Schweiz" ist leicht übertrieben: Die Fjälls und die bewaldeten Berge erheben sich weniger als 500 Meter über dem Meeresspiegel und 200—250 Meter über ihrer Umgebung.

Zu den Eigenarten der Natur von Kuusamo gehören viele Schluchten: die Flusstäler des Oulankajoki und einiger seiner Nebenflüsse sowie die Schluchtseen Julma Ölkky und Ruoppijärvi.

Konttainen and the other arctic fells of Northern Kuusamo are less impressive for their height than for their stark shapes (1). The River Kitkajoki flows through a comparatively narrow gorge 50—80 metres deep and foams over many rapids, the best known of which is the Jyrävänköngäs, 9 metres high, (3) and the Aallokkokoski Rapids, about one kilometre long, (2). One of the beauty spots of Southern Kuusamo is Julma-Ölkky (4), a shimmering lake in a deep rocky valley.

Der Konttainen wie auch die anderen Fjälls von Nord-Kuusamo beeindrucken nicht so sehr mit ihrer Höhe als vielmehr mit ihren steilen Formen (1). Der Kitkajoki fliesst durch ein relativ enges, rund 50—80 Meter tiefes Bruchtal und bildet vielerorts reissende Stromschnellen und Wasserfälle. Die bekanntesten von ihnen sind der neun Meter hohe Jyräväköngäs (3) und der rund ein Kilometer lange Aallokonkoski (2). Eine der einzigartigen Natursehenswürdigkeiten des verhältnismässig flachen Süd-Kuusamo ist der in einer engen Schlucht schimmernde See Julma Ölkky (4).

3

4

The Northern Spruce Forests
Fichtenwald

A belt of spruce forests with a thick carpet of moss begins at Kuusamo and stretches right across Lapland. These sparse forests grow on moraine soils covered by dense layers of finger and leaf mosses. The moraine has a thick peat overlay which inhibits soil heating and aeration and retains water. Tree growth is very slow under these circumstances. The trees are well spaced, often dead at the crown and rotting at the base.

Because of their low timber yield, the mossy spruce forests have become a victim of modern silviculture. Efforts have been made to replace them with pine, although with less success than expected. Nowadays, some districts have only a few remaining fragments of the mossy spruce forests once quite common.

Bei Kuusamo beginnt das Reich des dickmoosigen Fichtenwalds, das sich quer durch Lappland zieht. Dieser lichte Fichtenbestand, der auf Moränenland wächst, ist am Boden mit einem dicken Astmoosteppich bedeckt. Unter diesem befindet sich eine dicke torfähnliche Rohhumusschicht, welche die Erwärmung des Bodens und seinen Luftwechsel verlangsamt und Wasser zurückhält. Daher gehen Wachstum und Regenerierung der Bäume nur sehr langsam vor sich. Die Bäume sind oft an ihren Kronen abgestorben und an den Wurzelenden fäulnisbefallen.

Man hat versucht, diese Fichtenwälder wegen ihres schwachen Holzertrags in Kiefernwälder umzuwandeln, oft mit schlechten Ergebnissen. Örtlich wachsen nur noch Reste des einst so verbreiteten dickmoosigen Fichtenwalds.

The moss-carpeted spruce forests of the North resemble the bilberry-carpeted forests of the South, but are much less dense and slower growing (1). The great grey owl (2) is one of the taiga species in the spruce forests.

Der Dickmoos-Fichtenwald entspricht dem südfinnischen Blaubeertyp, hat aber einen lichteren Baumbestand und ist von schwächerem Wuchs (1). Der Bartkauz gehört zu den östlichen Taigaarten der Fichtenwaldfauna (2).

Snow-laden Trees

Schneelast

When an air current rises to pass over a mountain, it becomes more tenuous and colder. It can no longer carry all the moisture it has absorbed earlier. The surplus moisture condenses, first to fog and then to rain, snow or hoar frost.

The amount of snow that adheres to trees is surprisingly large. Even the smallest tree can carry hundreds of kilogrammes. One spruce 12 metres high was estimated to have a snow load of three tonnes. If the snow adhering to trees were spread on the ground, it would add between 30 and 45 centimetres to the depth of the snow already there.

The sunshine of early spring makes the snow loosen and begin to fall. This can also lead to severe damage. Earlier in the winter, the snow has formed a continuous "tower" extending from the ground to the tree top. If the lower part of this tower collapses, the weight of the snow adhering to the top of the tree can snap the trunk across.

Wenn der Luftstrom zum Überqueren von Bergen aufsteigt, verdünnt er sich und kühlt dabei ab. Die kühlere Luft kann nicht mehr so viel Feuchtigkeit binden. Die überflüssige Feuchtigkeit verdichtet sich erst zu Nebel und danach im Sommer zu Regen und im Winter zu Rauhreif oder Schnee, der an den Bäumen Schneeanhänge bildet.

Die Schneeanhänge der Bäume sind überraschend gross. Schon an kleinen Bäumen wiegen sie viele Zentner. Man hat eine zwölf Meter hohe Fichte gefunden, deren Schneeanhang auf 3000 Kilogramm geschätzt wurde. Die Bäume des Schneeanhanggebiets binden so viel Schnee, dass er, gleichmässig auf dem Boden verteilt, die bereits vorhandene Schneedecke um 30—45 Zentimeter erhöhen würde.

Im Spätwinter, wenn die Sonnenwärme den Schnee, der im Winter von der Erde bis zur Krone einen einheitlichen Schneeturm gebildet hat abbröckeln lässt, kommt es vor, dass in der Krone noch ein grosser Klumpen nassen Schnees verbleibt, unter dessen Last der Stamm bricht.

Blanket Bogs
Hangmoore

Kuusamo and the Kainuu are areas of very high precipitation. The moistness of the climate is revealed with particular clarity in the hills and fells, where sphagnum and other bog mosses manage to grow even on comparatively steep slopes. This results in long, water-logged depressions winding along the slope or blanket peat covering a larger area of a hillside.

Most blanket bogs dry out during the summer, only those with springs under them or another bog uphill from them remaining wet. Because of difference in nutrient supply and moisture, their vegetation varies. The flora of blanket bogs is usually lusher and more varied than that of level bogs.

Klimatisch sind Kuusamo und Kainuu Finnlands feuchtesten Gebiete. Besonders deutlich zeigt sich die Luftfeuchtigkeit an den Bergen und Fjälls, wo das Torfmoos auch an relativ abschüssigen Hängen wachsen kann. Hierbei entstehen sogenannte Hangmoore: Moorsenken, die sich an den Hängen emporwinden, oder grössere

Hangflächen bedeckende Moore.

Viele Hangmoore trocknen im Sommer aus, und nur von Quellen gespeiste oder unterhalb ebener Moore gelegene Hangmoore bleiben auch im Sommer feucht. Zumeist sind sie dank der dünnen Torfschicht und des fliessenden nährstoffhaltigen Wassers üppiger und artenreicher als ebene Moore.

The peat layer in blanket bogs is usually thin, only a few tens of centimetres deep. The green layer in the diagram is sedge peat and the light brown layer sphagnum.

Die Torfschicht der Hangmoore (in der Darstellung Seggentorf grün und Weisstorf hellbraun) ist gewöhnlich relativ dünn, nur wenige Dezimeter stark.

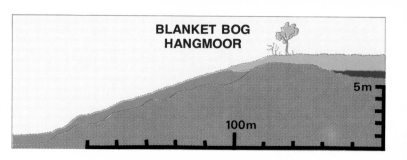

Scenes from Posio
In der Landschaft von Posio

In places the ground water reaches the surface, forming clear pools (1). Beautiful Posio, with its many lakes and ponds, has undeservedly remained in the shadow of its neighbour Kuusamo where tourism is concerned. The beauty spots in the district include Riisitunturi Fell, the Kitkajärvi Lakes, Alttiköngäs Falls, Korouoma Canyon and Livojärvi Lake (2 and 3).

Stellenweise tritt das Grundwasser in Form von kristallklaren Quellen an die Oberfläche (1). Posio ist als Ferienort unverdient im Schatten seiner Nachbargemeinde Kuusamo geblieben, obwohl an Sehenswürdigkeiten kein Mangel besteht: u.a. der Riisitunturi-Fjäll, die Kitkajärvi-Seen, der Alttiköngäs-Wasserfall, das Cañontal Korouoma sowie der See Livojärvi (2 und 3).

Posio contains more lakes than any other parish in Lapland. The whole district is an elevated watershed area, from which the waters flow both to the Gulf of Bothnia via the Rivers Kemijoki and Iijoki and into the White Sea via the River Kitkajoki and Lake Paanajärvi in the Soviet Union. The best known lake is in fact a double lake, Upper and Lower Kitka. Upper Lake Kitka is separated from the waters of the Iijoki system by only a low rock threshold no more than a couple of kilometres wide, so the watershed line is very thin. Lake Livojärvi is crossed by a moraine ridge, which has formed beautiful sand beaches everywhere it intersects the shoreline.

Posio ist Lapplands relativ seenreichste Gemeinde. Die Gegend von Posio ist hochliegendes Wasserscheidengebiet, aus dem das Wasser zu den Fluss-Systemen des Kemijoki und des Iijoki sowie über den Kitkajoki in die Sowjetunion zum Paanajärvi-See und von dort weiter zum Weissen Meer abfliesst. Der bekannteste See ist der Doppelsee Yli- und Ala-Kitka, der sich bis auf das Gemeindegebiet von Kuusamo erstreckt. Der zum Fluss-System des Iijoki gehörende Livojärvi-See ist nur durch eine zwei Kilometer breite und relativ flache Felsschwelle vom Yli-Kitka getrennt. Quer durch den Livojärvi verläuft eine Os-Formation.

3

2

Forest Lapland
Wald-Lappland

Round Trip in the North

by/von Annikki Kariniemi

I was born here, close to the River Ounasjoki, a river which springs from the bright uplands of the fells and ends in the breast of the River Kemijoki at Rovaniemi. It is said that the River Ounas-Kemijoki, with all its tributaries, is nigh on three thousand kilometres in length. It is the watercourse which dominates Peräpohjola and the forested region of Lapland. It also makes fertile these parts of the country considered by so many to be barren and bleak. In my opinion this, the area where I was born, is neither barren nor bleak in fact it is anything but.

When summer holds sway here, the sun follows her path on bright summer nights for days on end without ever dropping, even for a moment, into the bosom of the arctic hills and fells, nor behind the great bogs and countless marshes. It shines for a solid month into this cabin from over there beyond Törmäsjärvi Lake. It begins to stay awake, and to keep us awake, on the fourth of June, and it isn't until late on Hermann's day (12th July) that is has disappeared into the stony ground of the conglomeration of rocky slopes at Koutus, there over Pello way. Then commence the glorious symphonies of colour in the evenings at sunset. They continue until the arrival of winter evenings, before the long, dark polar evenings, though they, too, blaze with the incandescence of the sunset in a glorious panorama gilding the lakeside scenery of Törmäsjärvi with a beauty out of this world.

The old bear hunters of Kittilä used to say that the forest was moving when they heard the bears begin to move with predatory intent. It signified that the whole of summertime creation was rising, as if to wing, to warn that the great predator was now afoot and to say "Beware, all small creatures, for here he comes crashing to seize the first sweet flesh to cross his path."

The forest moves in springtime and in autumn, asserts an inhabitant of the Peräpohjola backwoods. The great movers are afoot, nature awakens into life, and it is the noble rutting time: the time when all who can carry out their designated task of fertilization do: they stud, they bear young, they nurture their litters for future generations here and now to ensure the survival of their species until the end of time.

And then, when Nature grows still to wait for the coming of winter on the great expanses of bog, it is the time of year when the nature lover should, at the latest, set out to wander the reindeer paths. Then the great forests stand silent like large halls ready for a coming festival. A festival is coming — that of winter itself.

But life is not entirely extinguished in the heart of the wilderness. A wood grouse, startled by the walker's footsteps, may take to the air with such a powerful beating of wings that the ground itself almost shakes and vibrates. Or a Siberian jay may unfurl into flight before your eyes, a blue-eyed seducer which seems to say, "Just follow me" and flies from tree to tree, from bough to bough.

Or you may even find yourself amidst a herd of reindeer: it's reindeer separation time and the Forest Lapp has brought his herd to the corral to inspect them for the first time this autumn. Bonfires blaze around the reindeer corrals, a strong aroma of coffee mingles with the smoky smells of burning pine stumps in the frosty air. From time to time you can hear the muted ring of reindeer bells when the stud bull reindeer, standing tethered further away from the corral, munches a lump of lichen dug out from the ground frost.

No-one who has set out from Sodankylä to drive from Rovaniemi during autumn/winter, and has gone up through the Posio country to Salla, and from there to take in Kemijärvi, Pelkosenniemi, Savukoski, Sodankylä, Kittilä and Muonio, and gone down the Muonio-Torniojoki open road, can fail to praise that frontier spirit with which these Peräpohjola and Forest Lapland parishes were opened up for cultivation in the midst of broad bog scenery and gloomy wilderness.

Autumn/winter, when a slight sprinkling of snow begins to cover the countryside, making this huge round trip gives a unique view of what Peräpohjola and Forest Lapland really are.

By starting your journey on a Thursday you can see all the patterns of the late harvest. It is the season for September-spawning fish: in October the seine nets are pulled through the pollan lakes, and the catch can really seem like the Biblical catch of Peter the Fisherman. Further from the painted villages, the smoke saunas puff at weekends: the eye might even chance to spy smoke where grain is being dried, for a certain amount of rye is farmed in these parts, and smoke is good for it.

On clear autumn/winter days festive sights, each more festive than the other, open up before the eye in these little roadside villages. The high bluish ridges on the horizon are like landmarks. The broad stretches of lake glisten blue, wondrously bright, way ahead in the distance as the road rises into the uplands. Perhaps within a couple of days they will freeze and get their first night's coat of ice.

By taking the Yli-Kitka short cut one can get direct from Posio straight to Salla. In between one can see the unforgettable beauty of Kuusamo's distant uplands, Käylä's border district church, Hautajärvi's chapel and Onkamojärvi, the village from which are visible nine arctic fells.

A short stay in Salla. A stop by the Salla church. But, oh dear! how grim the church roof is, and as black as sorrow. On a hot, bright summer day it makes no difference, as creation is in bloom, but in polar night scenery when the leaves have fallen from the trees and winter is settling in, the church, with its bell tower, is like a tower of doom.

But the River Kemijoki, the main stream of Peräpohjola, a river which has really brought people their livelihood, has changed. It is no longer a powerful wild rush of water which, at times of great flood when the snows melted on the fells and the bogs, snorted like a giant freed from its chains. That Kemijoki river no longer exists. At spring flood times it was the real ruler in these wilds. It would take with it houses and barns, saunas and cabins, it would flay and strip the great sand canyons like a child tears birch bark from gigantic trees. The scenery changed when seized upon by the waters of the main stream and crushed into their embrace. Ancient pines, thousands of years old, were torn loose like matchsticks and swept into the bedlam of the flood.

From Sodankylä the traveller is rushed across the wild rowards the west, and the landmarks of Kittilä are already visible, Aakenus, Kumputunturi, Levi-, Kätkä-, and Pyhätunturi and also the famous Pallas Fells are part of the Kittilä district. Then again, Muonio has its own — the arctic mountain Olostunturi. Here this distant tract of land ends at our joint border river, Muoniojoki, which further south at around the parish of Kolari, joins the River Tornionjoki.

Thus the round trip is over, completed in good company with Mother Nature as a travelling companion and with hospitable households with open doors to guests. But there have also been houses which were empty, and there still are. Too many have left these regions to flail their crops elsewhere. Too many meadows bear stubble hay awaiting the sharpened blade of the scythe. But the birds are there, the reindeer have a place to wade, the elks have the soft foliage of former gardens to chomp in their soft snouts, and the foxes have old stables under which to snuggle — where, once, a mother cat may have found a warm place to settle her litter.

Rundreise im Norden

Ich bin hier, in unmittelbarer Nähe des Ounasjoki, geboren — eines Flusses, der im hellen Fjällhochland entspringt und bei Rovaniemi in den Schoss des Kemijoki-Flusses mündet. Es heisst, der Ounasjoki und der Kemijoki seien zusammen mit sämtlichen Nebenflüssen insgesamt fast 3000 Kilometer lang. Sie bilden ein Wassersystem, welches Peräpohjola und Wald-Lappland beherrscht. Und dieses Land befruchtet, das in der Meinung vieler karg und unfreundlich ist. Meiner Meinung allerdings ist meine Heimat alles andere als karg und unfreundlich.

Wenn die Sonne hier den Sommer bewacht, beschreibt sie bei klarem Himmel viele Tage und Nächte lang ihre Bahn, ohne auch nur für einen Augenblick im Schosse der Berge oder Fjälls unterzugehen, ohne hinter den endlosen Rücken der Sümpfe und Aapamoore zu verschwinden. So taucht sie unser Haus einen ganzen Monat lang nachts über den Törmäsjärvi-See hinweg in Licht. Sie beginnt nämlich am 4. Juni, die Nacht durchzuwachen — und uns wachzuhalten — und erst im Juli verschwindet sie zum ersten Mal des Nachts wieder hinter dem Geröll der Koutas-Berggruppe in der Gemeinde Pello. Dann beginnen abends die herrlichen Farbsinfonien des Sonnenuntergangs, und sie wiederholen sich täglich, bis die Polarnacht anbricht, aber auch in ihr lodert die glühende Sonne hinter dem Horizont als feuriges Panorama, welches die Landschaft des Törmäsjärvi zu überirdischer Schönheit vergoldet.

"Der Wald bewegt sich", sagten einst die alten Bärenfänger von Kittilä, wenn sie hörten, dass die Bären zum Beutezug aufgebrochen waren. Denn das bedeutete, dass die gesamte sommerliche Schöpfung sich sozusagen auf ihre Hinterbeine stellte, um zu melden: der grosse Räuber ist unterwegs. Achtung alles Kleinvieh, dort kommt er tösend und packt sich das erste saftige Fleisch, das ihm über den Weg läuft.

"Der Wald bewegt sich, auch im Frühling und im Herbst", so ein Bewohner der Bruchwälder von Peräpohjola. Die grossen Umzügler kommen und gehen, die Natur erwacht zum Leben, es ist die Zeit der edlen Brunft, wenn alle, die es irgendwie noch schaffen, die ihnen auferlegte Aufgabe der Befruchtung erfüllen, zeugen, gebären, ihren Nachwuchs hier und jetzt für die kommenden Generationen aufziehen, um die Erhaltung der eigenen Art bis ans Ende der Welt zu sichern.

Und wenn dann die Natur ruhiger wird, um in ihren grossen Waldeinöden die Ankunft des Winters zu erwarten, dann haben jene Tage begonnen, in denen es für den Naturfreund höchste Zeit wird, zur Wanderung auf den Rentierpfaden aufzubrechen. Dann stehen die riesigen Wälder still wie grosse Säle vor Beginn einer Feier. Und eine Feier steht ja auch wirklich bevor: der Winter höchstpersönlich.

Aber ganz ist das Leben im Herzen der grossen Waldeinöde dennoch nicht erloschen. Aufgeschreckt durch den Schritt des Wanderers stiebt das Auerhuhn so heftig auf, dass die Erde fast zittert und bebt. Oder der Unglückshäher wirbelt vor dir zum Flug auf — wie ein grossäugiger Verführer, der sagen wollte: "folge mir doch", und er fliegt von Baum zu Baum, von Ast zu Ast.

Oder vielleicht gerätst du mitten in eine Rentierherde; es ist die Zeit der Rentierscheidungen, und der Mann aus Lappland hat seinen Reichtum zum ersten Mal in diesem Herbst ins Rentiergehege getrieben, um ihn in Augenschein zu nehmen. Lagerfeuer lodern am Rande des Geheges, der Duft starken Kaffees vermischt sich mit dem Geruch brennenden Kienholzes in der rauhreifgeschwängerten Luft. Hin und wieder hört man das gedämpfte Läuten von Rentierglocken, wenn der vor dem Gehege angeleinte Leitbock die Rentierflechten kaut, welche er unter der dünnen Schicht gefrorenen Bodens freigescharrt hat.

Wer einmal im Spätherbst aus der Höhe von Sodankylä nach Rovaniemi aufgebrochen und von dort weiter über Posio hinauf nach Salla gefahren ist, danach Kemijärvi, Pelkosenniemi, Savukoski, Sodankylä, Kittilä und Muonio in sich hineingeschlungen hat und schliesslich die offene Strasse Muonio—Torniojoki hinabgefahren ist, kann kaum umhin, den Pioniergeist zu preisen, mit welchem jene Orte in Peräpohjola und Wald-Lappland einst inmitten ausgedehnter Moorlandschaften und düsterer Ödwälder für den Ackerbau gerodet wurden.

Im Spätherbst, wenn dünner Schneereif die Landschaft zu verhüllen beginnt, vermittelt die Reise auf dieser gewaltigen Rundtour ein einzigartiges Bild davon, was diese Bauerndörfer in Peräpohjola und Wald-Lappland alles in sich bergen.

Wenn man seine Reise beispielsweise an einem Donnerstag beginnt, finden in diesem Bild auch alle Varianten der späten Ernte Platz. Die herbstliche Laichzeit erreicht ihren Höhepunkt: im Oktober werden in den Maränenseen die Herbstnetze ausgelegt, und die Fänge können wirkliche Petrusfänge sein. In den Häusern der abgelegenen Landdörfer qualmen an den Wochenenden die Saunas, und vielleicht erblickt man auch den Rauch geheizter Darren, denn in dieser Gegend wird auch Roggen angebaut, und der Roggen liebt die Trocknung durch Rauch.

An hellen Spätherbsttagen öffnen sich in diesen Strassendörfern vor den Augen prächtige Szenen, eine feierlicher als die andere. Die am Horizont bläulich schimmernden Berge sind wie Landzeichen. Ausgedehnte Seen leuchten schon von weither hellblau, wenn die Strasse auf einer Anhöhe anlangt. Vielleicht sind diese Seen schon zwei Tage später zugefroren, haben ihre erste dünne Eisdecke erhalten.

Über eine Abkürzung, die Yli-Kitka-Route, erreicht man Salla direkt von Posio. Unterwegs ein Anblick unvergesslicher Schönheit, das ferne Hochland von Kuusamo, dazu die Grenzregionskirche von Käylä und die Kapelle von Hautajärvi sowie Onkamojärvi, ein Dorf, in welches neun Fjälls hineinschauen.

Rast in Salla. Anhalten bei der Kirche. Aber wie düster ist das Kirchdach, schwarz wie ein Jammertal! An hellen Sommertagen stört das nicht weiter, denn die Schöpfung blüht. Aber in der Polarnacht, wenn die Bäume entblättert sind und der Winter seinen Platz einnimmt, ist das Dach zusammen mit dem Glockenturm wie der Turm des Jüngsten Gerichts.

Der Kemijoki, der Hauptfluss von Peräpohjola, hat sich verändert. Er ist nicht mehr der kraftvolle, wilde Strom, der während der grossen Überschwemmungen, wenn der Schnee auf den Fjälls schmolz, wie ein entfesselter Riese schnaufte. Jener Kemijoki existiert nicht mehr. Zu Zeiten des Frühlingshochwassers war er der wirkliche Herrscher der Waldödländer. Er riss Häuser und Scheunen, Saunas und Hütten mit sich, er schälte die Uferböschungen der Sandcañons wie ein Kind die Rindenstreifen einer Riesenbirke. Die Landschaft veränderte sich, wenn die Wässer des mächtigen Stroms sie packten und in ihrer Umarmung zerquetschten. Die uralten Föhren, die tausendjährigen, wurden wie Streichhölzer geknickt und stürzten in den flutenden Wahnsinn.

Von Sodankylä eilt die Strasse durch die Ödwaldlandschaft gen Westen, und schon kommen die Landzeichen von Kittilä in Sicht. Die Fjälls Aakenus, Kumputunturi, Levitunturi, Kätkätunturi und Pyhätunturi, ja auch die berühmte Pallastunturi-Fjällgruppe gehört zur Gemeinde Kittilä. Und auch Muonio hat seinen eigenen Fjäll, den Olostunturi. Hier endet dieser ferne Landstrich am Grenzfluss Muonionjoki, welcher sich später im Süden in der Höhe des Orts Kolari dem Torniojoki anschliesst.

Damit endet die Rundreise, eine Reise in guter Gesellschaft — die grosse Natur war als Reisegefährte dabei — auf der sich unterwegs die Türen der gastfreundlichen Stuben öffneten, um dem Besucher Einlass zu gewähren. Aber auch leere Höfe gab es und gibt es immer noch zu sehen. Zu viele Menschen sind zu fremden Landschaften aufgebrochen, um das dortige Korn zu dreschen, und auf zu vielen Wiesen wartet das Getreide umsonst auf die wohlgeschärfte Klinge der Sense. Aber dafür haben die Vögel ihr Auskommen und die Rentiere ihr Wasser zum Durchwaten, die Elche haben das weiche Laub ihrer alten Heimatwälder, nach dem sie mit ihren weichen Mäulern schnappen, und die Füchse haben die alten Ställe, auf deren Böden sie sich zusammenkuscheln können — an denselben Stellen, wo einst die Katzenmütter warme Schlupfwinkel für ihren Wurf gefunden haben.

The Nightless Night
Die nachtlose Nacht

One of the highlights of a trip to Lapland is to watch the midnight sun from some elevated point: the sun nears the skyline and moves towards the north, but just as it seems to touch the horizon it begins to rise again. The further south the observer lives the more memorable this experience is.

Astronomy provides an explanation for this phenomenon. The earth is inclined in relation to the plane of its orbit. When the northern hemisphere is leaning towards the sun, we have summer and bright nights. At Rovaniemi's latitude the sun is visible all night only during the last week of June. Farther north, at Sodankylä, one can see the midnight sun 40 days a year and at

Utsjoki, the northernmost community in Finland, it is visible for about three months.

The sunshine is not so strong at night as during the day. Since the sun is lower in the sky, its rays have to pass through the atmosphere at a more oblique angle, losing most of their energy. The midnight sun does not heat.

Zu den Höhepunkten einer Lapplandreise gehört es, die Bahn der Mitternachtssonne zu verfolgen: die Sonne nähert sich dem Horizont und wandert nach Norden, aber kaum, dass sie fast den Horizont streift, beginnt sie schon wieder zu steigen.

Die Mitternachtssonne ist ein astronomisches Phänomen. Die Erdachse steht in schrägem Winkel zur Umlaufbahn der Erde um die Sonne. Wenn die nördliche Halbkugel der Sonne zugeneigt ist, herrscht hier Sommer und die Nächte sind hell. In der Höhe von Rovaniemi kann man die Sonne nur in der Woche der Sommersonnenwende die ganze Nacht über sehen, in Sodankylä vierzig Tage und in Utsjoki drei Monate.

Des Nachts scheint die Sonne mit geringerer Intensität als tagsüber. Die Sonnenstrahlen fallen sehr schräg ein und müssen einen langen Weg durch die Atmosphäre zurücklegen, so dass sie einen Teil ihrer Energie verlieren. Daher hat die Sonne um Mitternacht kaum wärmende Wirkung.

In the Wilderness
In der Wildnis

Few houses in Lapland are built so deep in the wilderness. If only to facilitate communications, most people settled near a river or on a lakeshore.

Mitten im Wald gebaute abgelegene Häuser sind selten in Lappland. Gewöhnlich stehen die Häuser schon allein der Verkehrsverbindungen wegen am Ufer eines Gewässers.

Lapland has been inhabited for a very long time. The oldest archaeological finds are 8,000 years old, but the present Finnish population is of much more recent origin. The earliest permanent Finnish settlers arrived during the 18th and 19th centuries, either driving the Lapps further north or assimilating them. The mouths of rivers were settled first.

Nature dictated where a new house was built. The site chosen was nearly always by a lake or river; nowhere else was arable land to be found, and in summer the river was the only traffic artery. Apart from tillable fields, one also needed flood meadows and marshy bogs for hay production. The availability of fish and game was also an important factor in choosing the site for one's new home.

Beginning in the 1860s, logging diversified the Laplanders' means of livelihood. Forestry along with growing trade and transport also provided paid employment.

Wilderness habitation based on self-sufficiency is now almost a thing of the past.

Die Besiedlung Lapplands hat lange Traditionen: die ältesten menschlichen Spuren sind rund 8000 Jahre alt. Die heutige Besiedlung durch Finnen ist hingegen viel jünger. Erst im 18. und 19. Jahrhundert liessen sich die Finnen ständig in Lappland nieder, wobei sie die Samen entweder weiter nach Norden verdrängten oder sie assimmilierten. Zuerst liessen sich die Finnen an den Flussmündungen nieder, von wo die Besiedlung flussauf weiter landeinwärts vordrang.

Die Natur diktierte die Standorte der neuen Häuser. Fast immer wurde das Haus am Ufer eines Flusses oder Sees errichtet — anderswo war anbaugeeignetes Land kaum zu finden, und im Sommer waren die Flüsse die einzigen tauglichen Verkehrswege. Ausser Feldern benötigte man für die Heuproduktion auch Schwemmwiesen und feuchte Moore. Auch die Fische der Flüsse und Seen sowie das Wild der Ödwälder waren wichtige Faktoren bei der Wahl der Wohnstätte.

The River Kemijoki has played a vital role in the settlement of Lapland's trackless regions. The picture shows the River Jeesiöjoki (1). There are few lakes in the Kemijoki system and the headwaters flow tranquilly and directly (2). The river is still an important channel for log floating (3). The light area on the map was once submerged.

Der Kemijoki hat die Besiedlung des wegelosen Lapplands entscheidend beeinflusst. Im Foto der Fluss Jeesiöjoki (1). Die Flüsse fliessen an ihren Oberläufen ruhig und gradlinig (2). Der Kemijoki ist immer noch ein wichtiger Flössweg (3).
Das hellste Gebiet auf der Karte war einst von Wasser bedeckt.

Kemijoki

Kemijoki is the longest of Finland's rivers; the main river itself and its principal tributary have a combined length of 552 km and the catchment area of the system covers most of the administrative province of Lapland. The river begins as small streams in the eastern parts of Enontekiö and the northern parts of Kittilä, Sodankylä, Savukoski and Salla. Its easternmost headwaters are on the Soviet side of the border. The main watershed being south of the Saariselkä Ridge, the true fell areas are outside the catchment area of the Kemijoki system. The only larger group of fells in the area is the Pallastunturi—Ounastunturi chain. For most of its course, the Kemijoki flows through low-lying forests and peat bogs, swelling into a mightly river as it moves on. The headwaters are impressive rivers even close to their sources: Ounasjoki as soon as it leaves Lake Ounasjärvi and Kittinen once it has cleared the Porttipahdas reservoir.

The river basin contains few lakes, only about three per cent of the total area, and the flow volume can vary by a ratio of 50:1. Two major artificial lakes, Lokka and Porttipahdas, have been constructed for flow regulation purposes.

Der Kemijoki ist Finnlands längster Fluss; von der Quelle des Hauptflusses gemessen ist er 512 und von der des längsten Nebenflusses 552 Kilometer lang. Das Wassersystem des Kemijoki erstreckt sich über den grössten Teil der Provinz Lappland. Den Hauptteil ihrer Reise legen die Wässer des Hauptflusses durch tiefliegende Wald- und Moorlandschaft zurück, wobei sie sich allmählich zu einem grossen Strom vereinigen. Die Nebenflüsse des Kemijoki sind schon im Norden grosse Ströme: der Ounasjoki gleich nach seinem Ausfluss aus dem Ounasjärvi-See, der Kitinen, sobald er den Porttipahta-Stausee überwunden hat.

Im Einzugsbereich des Kemijoki gibt es nur wenige Seen. Lediglich drei Prozent der Oberfläche sind Seen, und aus diesem Grunde kommt es im Frühjahr zu starken Überschwemmungen. Stellenweise kann der Kemijoki während der Schneeschmelze bis zu fünfzigmal mehr Wasser führen als in trockenen Zeiten. Um dem Hochwasser entgegenzuwirken, wurden im Nordteil der Gemeinde Sodankylä zwei grosse Stauseen angelegt, der Lokka und der Porttipahta.

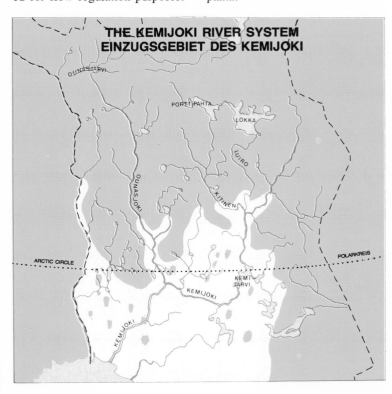

THE KEMIJOKI RIVER SYSTEM
EINZUGSGEBIET DES KEMIJOKI

Koilliskaira

The establishment of a national park in the trackless wilderness of the Koilliskaira area in the northern parts of the municipalities of Salla and Savukoski was proposed by a state committee in the early 70s. If this plan is implemented, Koilliskaira will become one of Europe's most important nature reserves.

With an area of about 1,700 sq. kilometres, the national park would be two-thirds the size of Luxembourg. The whole area is completely free of permanent private habitation.

The dominant feature in the landscape is of gently-sloping ridges. The only arctic fells are in the northern part bordering on Saariselkä and in the southeastern corner, where most of them reach heights of over 600 metres above sea level.

Most of the area is covered by forests, principally dry pinelands. Another feature typical of Lapland is the complete absence of lakes. There are, however, several smallish ponds.

Alongside forestry, reindeer herding is the most important source of livelihood in this part of the country (1). The vast, tranquil wilderness (2) impresses everybody who visits it. Nature uses every opportunity for growth that she can get: beard moss grows on living trees, while scabrous lichens cling to deadwood pines (4). Lichens (3) and mosses (5) thrive on fallen trees.

Es wird erwogen, in Koilliskaira, einer im Norden von Salla und Savukoski gelegenen weitläufigen, wegelosen Wildnis, einen Nationalpark zu gründen. Der Nationalpark Koilliskaira würde im Nordwesten an den Höhenrücken Saariselkä grenzen. Falls es zur Verwirklichung dieses Projekts kommt, wird Koilliskaira zu einem der bedeutendsten Naturschutzgebiete Europas.

Koilliskaira umfasst rund 1700 Quadratkilometer. Im ganzen Gebiet gibt es keine ständige menschliche Besiedlung.

Landschaftlich ist Koilliskaira vorwiegend leicht ansteigender Landrücken. Nennenswerte Fjälls erheben sich nur im Nordteil sowie in der Südwestecke des Gebiets, wo mehrere Fjälls über 600 Meter aufragen.

Der grösste Teil des Gebiets ist Wald, und zwar vorwiegend trockene Kiefernheide.

Koilliskaira ist auch insofern typisches Lappland, als dass es hier kaum Seen gibt, nur einige kleinere Teiche.

Neben Forstwirtschaft ist die Rentierzucht der Haupterwerbszweig in Koilliskaira (1). Koilliskaira beeindruckt mit seiner weitläufigen und friedlichen Wildnis (2). Die Natur nutzt alle Wachstumsmöglichkeiten. An lebenden Bäumen wachsen Bartflechten, an ausgedörrten Föhren die Krustenflechte (4). An faulenden Stämmen breiten sich Flechten (3) Moose aus (5).

2

1

3

5

The Land of Aapa Bogs
Das Land der Aapamoore

The flat terrain and cold, moist climate of Southern Lapland have led to peat bog formation on a massive scale. Between 40 and 60 % of the total area is covered by bogs and drainage has not diminished this to any significant extent.

The aapa bogs of Lapland are generally large and have distinct surface features, with fairly dry, long ridges of somewhat higher peat alternating with lower, water-logged mires. The tendon-like ridges run more or less in the same direction and rise a few tens of centimetres above the surrounding bog. The dividing line between the ridges and depressions is generally quite sharp. The hollows vary from pools a couple of metres deep to continuous expanses of sedge-covered mire. The mires are mostly very wet and swampy, but there is only a few centimetres of water.

The ridges resemble dams at right angles to the direction of water flow, and their effect is also frequently visible in the distinct height differences between adjoining pools. Aapa bogs play an important role in equalizing water flow rates and reducing flooding.

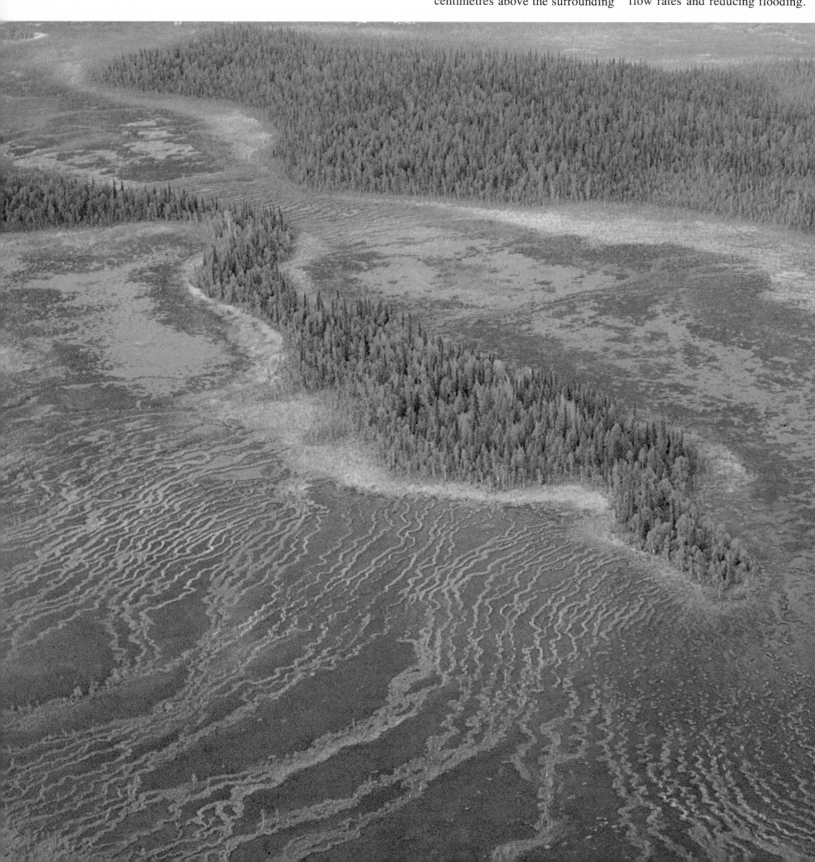

Im flachen Terrain und feuchtkalten Klima Südlapplands hat die Versumpfung gewaltige Ausmasse angenommen. Zwischen 40 und 60 Prozent der Fläche sind Moore.

Lapplands Aapamoore sind gewöhnlich weitläufig und haben eine klare Oberflächenstruktur, in welcher relativ trockene hohe Stränge und sumpfige Schlenken einander abwechseln. Die Stränge verlaufen als relativ gleichgerichtete, einige Dezimeter hohe Torfrücken quer durch das Moor. Die Formen der Schlenken wechseln von zwei Meter tiefen Senken bis zu von einheitlichen Seggendecken bewachsenen Seggenschlenken. Gewöhnlich sind die Schlenken sehr nass und nachgebend, aber ihr Wasserstand beträgt nur wenige Zentimeter.

Die Stränge verlaufen wie Dämme gegen die Strömungsrichtung des Wassers. Oft erkennt man ihre dämmende Wirkung auch am Gelände: der Wasserstand in benachbarten Schlenken kann sichtbar differieren. Aapamoore sind effektive Regulierer des Wasserstroms und wirken Überschwemmungen entgegen.

The watery aapa bogs of the River Kemijoki headwaters area are an excellent abode for birds, but an extremely difficult place for hikers to travel (1). Raised bogs are rare in Lapland, because the spring floods inhibit the growth of their most important plant, brown sphagnum moss (2). The birches on the ridges give the landscape a special appearance. The flora of these birch marshes is quite unusual (3). In the northern part of the Lapland forest zone the ridges are no longer parallel or concentric as in Northern Karelia, but broken up into a mottled pattern (4).

Die sumpfigen Aapamoore am Kemijoki bieten der Vogelwelt günstige Lebensbedingungen, sind aber für den Wanderer sehr schwer begehbar (1). Hochmoore sind in Lappland selten, da das Frühlingshochwasser das Wachstum ihrer wichtigsten Torfmoosart, des Spaghnum-Mooses, erschwert (2). Auf Strängen wachsende Birken lassen eine ungewöhnlich Landschaft entstehen. Derartige Birkenbrüche haben eine sehr spezifische Vegetation (3). Im Norden von Wald-Lappland verlaufen die Stränge kreuz und quer und überschneiden einander netzartig (4).

1

2

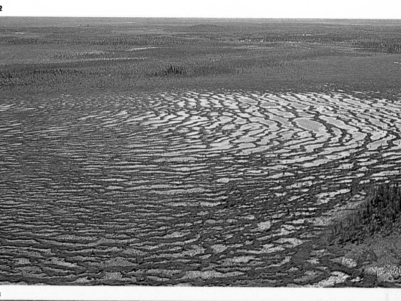

3

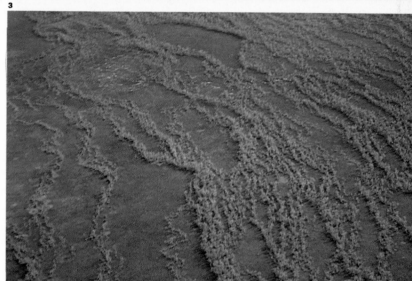

4

The Blooming Bog
Das Moor blüht

The flora and fauna of the aapa bogs are distinctive and rich. The alternation of waterlogged mires, intermediate surfaces and peat ridges, marshes and wildernesses, patches of forests and the small streams flowing through the bogs create a highly diverse mosaic capable of supporting many animal species and plant varieties. The transition from the nutritionally poor bogs of other regions to the limestone-based rich underlay of the marshy aapas also means that a more varied floral and faunal population can be maintained.

Most of the plants found on the aapa bogs are also found in the peatlands of Southern Finland, but there are also a number of

plants not found elsewhere. There are really only two distinctively northern varieties: aapa cotton grass and aapa sedge. Aapa cotton grass is a very conspicuous plant when it grows in large swards on the bogs. The plants on the raised peat ridges include cloudberry. The more waterlogged the bog the more northerly its flora.

Die Pflanzen- und Tierwelt der Aapamoore ist sehr spezifisch und reichhaltig, gegenüber der Fauna und Flora von Wäldern mit festem Waldboden sogar mannigfaltiger. Der Wechsel von sumpfigen Schlenken und Strängen, die Reisermoore an den Rändern und die Ödwälder, die inselartigen Waldungen und die quer durch die

Moore fliessenden Bäche mit ihren "Galeriewäldern" bilden ein sehr vielseitiges Mosaik, das als Lebensumwelt die Anforderungen vieler Tier- und Pflanzenarten erfüllt. Weiterhin tragen auch die wechselhaften Nährstoffbedingungen — von nährstoffarmen Mooren bis hin zu braunmoorartigen Aapamooren — zur Mannigfaltig-

keit der Fauna und Flora bei.

Die Pflanzenwelt der Aapamoore ist grösstenteils schon aus den südlicheren Mooren bekannt, aber vor allem in nährstoffreichen Mooren findet man Arten, die im Süden völlig fehlen. In kargen Aapamooren wachsen eigentlich nur zwei typisch nordische Arten: das Aapawollgras und die Aapasegge.

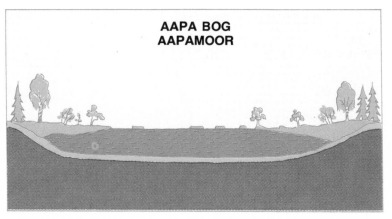

AAPA BOG
AAPAMOOR

1 2

Ground frost is a major factor in aapa bogs. The wet ground freezes to a considerable depth and plants winter best on hummocks (1). The cotton grass flowers in early summer (2). The centre of an aapa bog is lower than its edges.

Da der feuchte Boden der Aapamoore sehr stark gefriert, können die Pflanzen am besten auf Bülten überwintern (1). Das Wollgras blüht zum Sommeranfang (2). Die Mitte eines Aapamoores ist tiefer gelegen als die Moorränder.

Pyhätunturi

From Rovaniemi, the capital of Finnish Lapland, one still has to travel a long way north before reaching the arctic fells. The southernmost of the major fells is the Pyhätunturi chain, which stretches all the way to Sodankylä as a line of forested hills and culminates there in Luostotunturi, which is north of the treeline. Its distinguished, rugged profile can be seen from afar, although the range is not particularly high: at its highest point it rises to 375 m above the surrounding landscape and 540 m above sea level, but the flatness of the surrounding terrain and the steep sides of the hills create a striking impression. To the ancient Lapps, Pyhätunturi was a sacred mountain, which is just what its name means in Finnish.

The Pyhätunturi area was made a national park in 1938. There are now plans to extend this park to include the forests and bogs at its foot.

Pyhätunturi consists of erosion-resistant quartzite. Under the influence of freezing water, this type of rock easily cracks into angular blocks.

Pyhätunturi commands a magnificent view of the surrounding forests and peat bogs (1). Also the golden eagle finds a nesting place in the tranquil woods of the national park area (2). Pyhänkasteenlampi ("Baptism") Lake is near Isokuru (3).

Vom Pyhätunturi hat man einen weiten Ausblick über die umliegende Wald- und Moorlandschaft (1). Auch der Adler findet in den friedlichen Wäldern des Nationalparks geeignete Nistplätze (2). Der Teich Pyhäkasteenlampi mit Wasserfall am Ende der Fjällschlucht Isokuru (3).

3

2

Von Rovaniemi ist es noch ein langer Weg bis zu den ersten Fjälls. Der südlichste Hochfjäll, der Pyhätunturi an der Gemeindegrenze von Pelkosenniemi und Kemijärvi, ein vielgipfeliger Höhenzug, setzt sich in Form von waldbedeckten Bergen bis hin nach Sodankylä fort und ragt dort mit dem Fjäll Luostotunturi über die Baumgrenze hinaus. Sein charakteristisches, von steilen Fjällschluchten zerschnittenes Profil ist weithin sichtbar. Der Pyhätunturi ist nicht sonderlich hoch: er erhebt sich nur 375 Meter über seiner Umgebung und 540 Meter über dem Meeresspiegel. Aber die Ebenheit seiner Umgebung und seine steilen Formen verleihen ihm ein eindrucksvolles Äusseres. Er war einst ein Heiligtum der Samen, daher auch sein Name Pyhätunturi — Heiliger Fjäll.

Der Fels des Pyhätunturi ist gegenüber der Abtragung sehr widerstandsfähiges Quarzit. Unter dem Einfluss von gefrierendem Wasser zerbröckelt es leicht zu eckigen Stücken.

Pallastunturi

Yllästunturi (718 m) is the first in a chain of arctic fells stretching northwards towards the Norwegian border. The northernmost part of this chain, Pallastunturi and Ounastunturi together with the forests surrounding them, form Finland's second-largest national park.

The Pallastunturi Fells soar about half a kilometre above their surroundings (the highest peak, Taivaskero, is 807 m above sea level), and their eastern slopes are particularly steep. Nevertheless gentleness and roundness are the dominant features in the fells' shape. There is square kilometre after square kilometre of bare, stony high slopes and the overall impression is of a mountain wilderness. The birch zone is clearly marked, but on gentler slopes spruce and even pine grow almost all the way to the treeline.

Nearly 200 varieties of seed-bearing plants and pteriophytes have been identified — a large number for Finnish conditions.

There are also extensive forests and bogs.

Mit dem Fjäll Yllästunturi (718 m) in Kolari beginnt ein langer Fjällzug, dessen Nordteil, die Fjällgruppe Pallastunturi—Ounastunturi mitsamt ihrer Waldumgebung, als Nationalpark unter Naturschutz steht. Der Nationalpark Pallas—Ounastunturi ist der zweitgrösste Finnlands.

Die Gipfel der Pallastunturi-Gruppe überragen ihre Umgebung um einen halben Kilometer (der höchste Gipfel, der Taivaskero, liegt 807 Meter über dem Meeresspiegel), und sind vor allem an ihren Osthängen steil. Sonst dominieren an den Fjälls jedoch sanft ansteigende und gewölbte Formen. Baumlose Fjällspitzen gibt es quadratmeilenweise, und in der Landschaft liegt schon die Atmosphäre echten Fjällands. Die Fjällbirkenzone ist deutlich erkennbar, aber an sanft ansteigenden Hängen dringen die Fichten und Kiefern bis nahe an die Waldgrenze vor. Man hat im Nationalpark oberhalb der Waldgrenze fast zweihundert Samenpflanzen und Farne gefunden, was für finnische Verhältnisse viel ist.

Fell Chains
Fjällzüge

Most of Southern Lapland is so flat that one has to go all the way to the plains of Ostrobothnia to find a comparable topography. Most of the single arctic fells that one does find in this region consist of quartzite, which is extremely resistant to erosion.

Most of the fells barely rise above the treeline and the bareness of their summits is due more to rockiness than to elevation.

The longest chains of fells are Pyhätunturi-Luosto, Ylläs-Pallas-Ounas and its eastern branch Aakenus, Kätkä and Levi. The Pallas-Ounas chain gives a true impression of arctic fell country.

Südlappland ist grösstenteils flaches Terrain. Die südlichen Einzelfjälls bestehen zumeist aus Quarzit, einer sehr widerstandsfähigen Gesteinsart. Die meisten Fjälls dieser Gegend heben ihre Gipfel knapp über die Baumgrenze hinaus, und die Baumlosigkeit der Gipfel beruht oft mehr auf der Steinigkeit des Untergrunds denn auf der Höhe.

Längere Fjällzüge werden von den Fjälls Pyhätunturi—Luosto wie auch von der Kette Ylläs — Pallas — Ounastunturi und ihrem Ostausläufer, den Fjälls Aakenus, Kätkä und Levi, gebildet.

The Aapa Inhabitants
Die Bewohner der Aapamoore

The most conspicuous inhabitants of the aapa bogs are the birds, especially in summer, when Finland's own population is supplemented by northward-migrating species. Waders and ducks are most numerous, while the sparrow family receive little attention, if only because of their small size. Waders and ducks also dominate the nesting population.

Reindeer arrive in summer to eat the lush bog grasses. They also come to flee mosquitos, gnats and other insects, whose torments are kept to a tolerable level by the fresh bog breezes. Elk roam the fringes in search of food and the yellowing cloudberries in August can even entice bears.

Die auffälligsten Aapamoorbewohner sind die Vögel. Dies gilt besonders für den Frühsommer, wenn zu den Nistvögeln auch noch die nach Norden reisenden Zugvögel kommen. Am zahlenstärksten sind die Stelz- und Entenvögel vertreten, die auch unter den Nistvögeln dominieren.

Im Sommer kommen die Rentiere, um Moorgras zu fressen. Auch fliehen sie vor den Mücken in die Moore, denn über den Aapamooren weht ständig ein Wind, der die Insektenplage auf ein erträgliches Mass reduziert. Auf seiner Nahrungssuche kommt der Elch an die Moorränder, und Anfang August locken die Moltebeeren manchmal Bären an.

The watery aapa bogs in the northern regions are home to large bird populations. Cygnets swim in the ponds, learning to fly only as the colour display of autumn begins (1).

Joutsenenpesä Bog at the foot of Luostotunturi Fell (2) is a typical northern aapa fringed by forests of twisted trees (3).

Die sumpfigen Aapamoore des Nordens sind Heimstätten einer reichhaltigen Vogelwelt. Die auf den Teichen heranwachsenden Jungschwäne werden erst zur herbstlichen Ruska-Zeit flügge (1). Das Moor Joutsenenpesäaapa am Fusse des Luostotunturi-Fjälls (2) mit verkümmert wachsenden Randwäldern ist ein für Peräpohjola typisches Aapamoor.

A Mountain Stream

Wildnisbach

Lapland has few lakes, and so the rivers and streams, sometimes forming rapids, sometimes tranquil brooks, are the dominant water feature.

The headwaters of the rivers are important for fishing. Fish are often found in surprisingly small streams. Even in streams which during drier periods contain a barely noticeable trickle of water, one can find trout fingerlings. Another delicious member of the salmon family found in the headwaters is the grayling, easily recognizable by its handsome, sail-like dorsal fins. The preying pike lurking in still stretches and the burbot hiding on the bottom are also regular members of the fish population.

The streams also have unpleasant inhabitants. Millions of mosquito larvae float upside down in still pools as they wait to hatch, while another bloodsucking pest, the gnat, spends its larval stage in flowing waters, where it is an important part of the trout's diet.

The banks of the streams are often difficult to traverse.

Mal als Stromschnellen schäumende, dann wieder ruhig dahinfliessende kleine Flüsse und Bäche bilden die eigentümliche Wasserlandschaft des seenarmen Lapplands.

Die Oberläufe sind wichtige Fischwässer. Selbst in Bächen, wo in trockenen Zeiten nur ein kleines Rinnsal fliesst, leben noch fingerlange Grauforellen. Ein weiterer wichtiger Fisch der Oberläufe ist die Äsche, ein Lachsfisch, den man an seinen prächtigen segelähnlichen Rückenflossen erkennt. Auch der an ruhig fliessenden Stellen auf seine Beute lauernde Hecht und die am Grund versteckte Quappe gehören zum Fischbestand der Waldregion.

In den Bächen leben auch unangenehme Tiere: In den stillstehenden Tümpeln der Überschwemmungsbruchmoore schwimmen Millionen von Stechmückenlarven, die auf ihr Ausschlüpfen warten. Auch eine weitere blutsaugende Plage, die Kriebelmücke, verbringt ihre Larvenzeit im Wasser. Ihre Larven sind die wichtigste Nahrung der Grauforelle.

Saariselkä

Wide open spaces, the peace of the wilderness and ideal hiking conditions have made Saariselkä a popular attraction for tourists. The terrain is perfect for hikers, either springy pine barrens or level tundra moor. The arctic fells slope gently and are easy to climb. There are few bogs, and these are small and easily circumvented. Crystal-clear streams flow through the valleys, providing food for the lucky fisherman. The heaths provide dry firewood and many wilderness cabins have been built to provide shelter for wanderers.

Offene Landschaft, die Ruhe der Natur und ideale Wanderbedingungen haben aus Saariselkä ein beliebtes Ferienziel gemacht. Das Terrain ist vorwiegend von trockenen reiserbewachsenen Kiefernwaldböden oder ebener Fjällheide bedeckt. Die Fjälls steigen sanft an und sind leicht begehbar. Die wenigen Moore sind klein und leicht zu umgehen. Aus kristallklaren Bächen kann sich der Angler mit ein wenig Glück selbst versorgen. Im Saariselkä-Gebiet sind für die Wanderer mehrere Wildnishütten eingerichtet.

The arctic fell groups of Eastern Lapland, such as Saariselkä, Rautu, Aapis, Hammas, Viipus, Marasto, Muotka, Ruottir and Pais Fells were thrown up by block faulting which occurred in several stages towards the end of the Tertiary period. The edges of several fells stand out as almost vertical horsts, e.g. the southern wall of Saariselkä. The horsts also lean in different directions: Pais Fell to the South-West, Ruotti to the South-East and both Marasto and Viipus to the East. The deep valleys between the blocks are the lines along which the faulting occurred. The fells are excellent terrain for wilderness hiking.

Die Fjällgruppen Ostlapplands wie Saariselkä, Rautu-, Appis-, Hammas-, Viipus-, Marasto-, Muotka-, Ruottir- und Paistunturi sind zu Ende des Tertiärs bei Verwerfungen in mehreren Phasen über ihre Umgebung hinausgestiegen. Die Ränder vieler Fjällgruppen sind Bruchstufen, so z.B. der Südrand von Saariselkä. Die aufgestiegenen Horste sind in verschiedene Richtungen geneigt: der Paistunturi nach Südwest, der Ruottirtunturi nach Südost sowie der Marasto- und der Viipustunturi nach Osten. Die tiefen Täler zwischen den Horsten sind Bruchlinien. Saariselkä ist ein ausgezeichnetes Wandergelände.

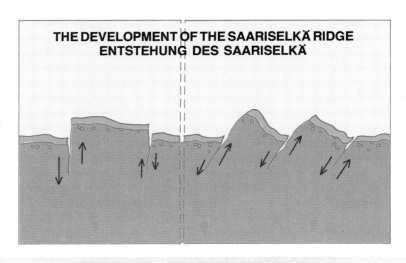

THE DEVELOPMENT OF THE SAARISELKÄ RIDGE
ENTSTEHUNG DES SAARISELKÄ

Autumn
Herbst

"Ruska", the extravagent display of colours in autumn, is one of the most beautiful sights in Lapland. This phenomenon is far less pronounced in Southern Finland, principally because there are more tree varieties there and these change into their autumn colours at different times. In Lapland there are only a few plants that change their colours in autumn: tundra birch, dwarf birch, bilberry, bog whortleberry and a couple of other berry bushes. All of these turn colour within a two-week period in early September.

The bright colours of the leaves are a sign that the plants are preparing for winter. Chlorophyll is withdrawn from the leaves and stored in the trunk and shoots. In the absence of chlorophyll the other pigments in the leaves, the reds and yellows, dominate.

The "ruska" changes are caused by the lengthening nights rather than by frost. These make the chlorophyll withdraw. Thus the "ruska" comes on schedule, whether the weather is cold or not.

"Ruska", die Zeit der herbstlichen Farbenpracht, gehört zu Lapplands herrlichsten Sehenswürdigkeiten. In Lappland wachsen nur wenige Ruska-Pflanzen: Fjällbirke, Blaubeere, Moorbeere und Alpen-Bärentraube. Sie erhalten ihre Herbstfarben Anfang September.

Die leuchtenden Farben der Blätter entstehen, wenn die Pflanzen im Herbst den grünen Farbstoff ihrer Blätter, das Chlorophyll, abbauen und ihn den Winter über in den Knospen und Stengeln speichern. Wenn das Grün verschwunden ist, kommen die anderen Farbstoffe, die gelben Karotine und die blauen oder violetten Anthozyane, zum Vorschein.

Eine weit verbreitete Vorstellung ist, dass Ruska durch den Frost ausgelöst würde. Tatsächlich hängt der Ruska-Beginn vom Licht ab. Wenn die Tage kurz genug und die Nächte dunkel sind, beginnt die Pflanze, unabhängig von der Temperatur, den Abbau und die Speicherung des Chlorophylls. Daher beginnt Ruska alljährlich fast zur gleichen Zeit, egal ob der Herbst warm oder kalt ist.

Stunted Birch
Fjällbirken

One of the most distinctive features of the arctic fell region is the zone of birch between the evergreen forests and the open, treeless area. The edge of a forest in these latitudes usually consists of softwood varieties, but due to the maritime climate of the arctic fells stunted birch also proliferate and are more numerous the more maritime the climate, i.e. in Kilpisjärvi and the northern part of Utsjoki. In the eastern part of Lapland, which has a more continental climate, the birch zone is less distinct and one even finds individual spruce growing at the edge of the bare zone.

The mountain birches are usually between two and five metres tall, either gnarled trees or multistemmed bushes. The trees in a stand are usually nearly all the same height. A characteristic feature is the vivid red of their autumn leaves — they turn yellow in the south.

Zu den wesenseigensten Zügen der Fjälls gehört die Birkenzone zwischen dem Nadelwald und der baumlosen Fjällspitze, denn normalerweise bilden Nadelbäume die Waldgrenze. Die Fjällbirken zeugen von der Maritimität des Klimas, und entsprechend wachsen die ausgeprägtesten Fjällbirkenwälder in den maritimsten Fjällgebieten — das sind in Finnland Kilpisjärvi und Nord-Utsjoki. Auf den im kontinentalen Klimabereich liegenden Einzelfjälls Ostlapplands ist die Birkenzone undeutlich, und noch direkt an der Waldgrenze wachsen Fichten.

Die Fjällbirke ist ein gewöhnlich zwei bis fünf Meter hoher krummstämmiger Baum oder mehrstämmiger Strauch. Eine Zeitlang sah man sie als eigene Baumart und dann wieder als Abart der Moorbirke an. Charakteristisch für die Fjällbirke ist ihre rote Herbstfarbe — die Herbstfarbe der Moorbirke ist gelb.

During the autumn "ruska" period, the stunted birch trees display a colourful splendour.

Zur Ruska-Zeit entfaltet sich die Fjällbirke zu herbstlicher Farbenpracht.

Winter Comes Early
Der Winter kommt früh

The first snow often falls while the autumnal colour display is still in progress, providing a white background for the reds and yellows.

Der erste Schnee fällt oft gleich nach Ruska, und sein Weiss betont die gelben, roten und blauen Farben. Im Bild der Pallastunturi.

Summer is brief at the latitude of Sodankylä. The growing period is only 127 days (181 in Helsinki); although its brevity is offset by the brightness and long days of summer. The nights start lengthening in August, and by September the summer is finally gone.

After the "ruska" colour display has spent itself, the darkest time of year comes again. Although the sun continues to rise above the horizon, the skies are mostly cloudy and the black earth absorbs light. Thus when the snow comes in November, the days seem to grow lighter. From 10th December to the early days of January the sun is not seen at all, but there are a couple of hours of twilight in the middle of the day.

In der Höhe von Sodankylä dauert die Wachstumsperiode nur 127 Tage; ihre Kürze wird allerdings teilweise durch die sommerliche Lichtfülle kompensiert. Im August werden die Nächte länger, und schon im September ist der Sommer endgültig vorbei.

Nach Ruska beginnt die dunkelste Zeit des Jahres. Obwohl die Sonne noch über den Horizont hinauskommt, ist der Himmel zumeist Zeit wolkenverhangen, und die schwarze Erde absorbiert das Licht. Wenn es im November schneit, scheinen die Tage heller zu werden. Zwischen dem 12. Dezember und Anfang Januar bleibt die Sonne vollständig unsichtbar, aber gegen Mittag herrscht für einige Stunden Dämmerlicht.

Yllästunturi

The highest peak in the Yllästunturi chain of arctic fells is 718 m above sea level. All in all, the Yllästunturi chain is one of the most imposing high points in Finland, since the relative height differences are rather great in this area for Finnish conditions.

The upper slopes of these fells are treeless. All that grows above the treeline are some stunted juniper bushes, a few shrubs, tundra grasses, mosses and lichens. The ground is rocky and jagged.

The wind plays an important part in restricting growth. The present treeline on Yllästunturi is 400—500 m above sea level. The climate would probably permit forest to grow above this altitude,

but the severe winds and rocky ground prevent the trees from advancing up the slopes. The edge of the forest consists of pines on Yllästunturi. The stunted birch zone characteristic of other arctic fells, especially in the Enontekiö area, is not very distinct on the fells belonging to the Yllästunturi chain.

Der höchste Gipfel des Yllästunturi-Fjälls erhebt sich 718 Meter über dem Meeresspiegel. Insgesamt gesehen ist diese Fjällgruppe eine der imposantesten Erhebungen Lapplands, denn die relativen Höhenunterschiede sind hier für finnische Verhältnisse gross.

Die Gipfelbereiche des Yllästunturi sind baumlos. Oberhalb der Baumgrenze wachsen nur flacher, in Bodennähe rankender Wacholder, krautstengelige Fjällpflanzen sowie Moose und Flechten. Die Oberläche ist steinig.

Als Faktor, der das Wachstum des Waldes begrenzt, ist der Wind von grosser Bedeutung. Zur Zeit verläuft die Waldgrenze am Yllästunturi in 400 bis 450 Meter Höhe.

Das Klima stände einem Waldwachstum auch in grösserer Höhe vermutlich nicht entgegen, aber der steinige Boden zusammen mit dem starken Wind verhindern, dass der Wald bis auf die höchsten Hänge klettert. Am Yllästunturi wird die Waldgrenze von Fichten gebildet. Die Fjällbirkenzone fehlt hier deutlich.

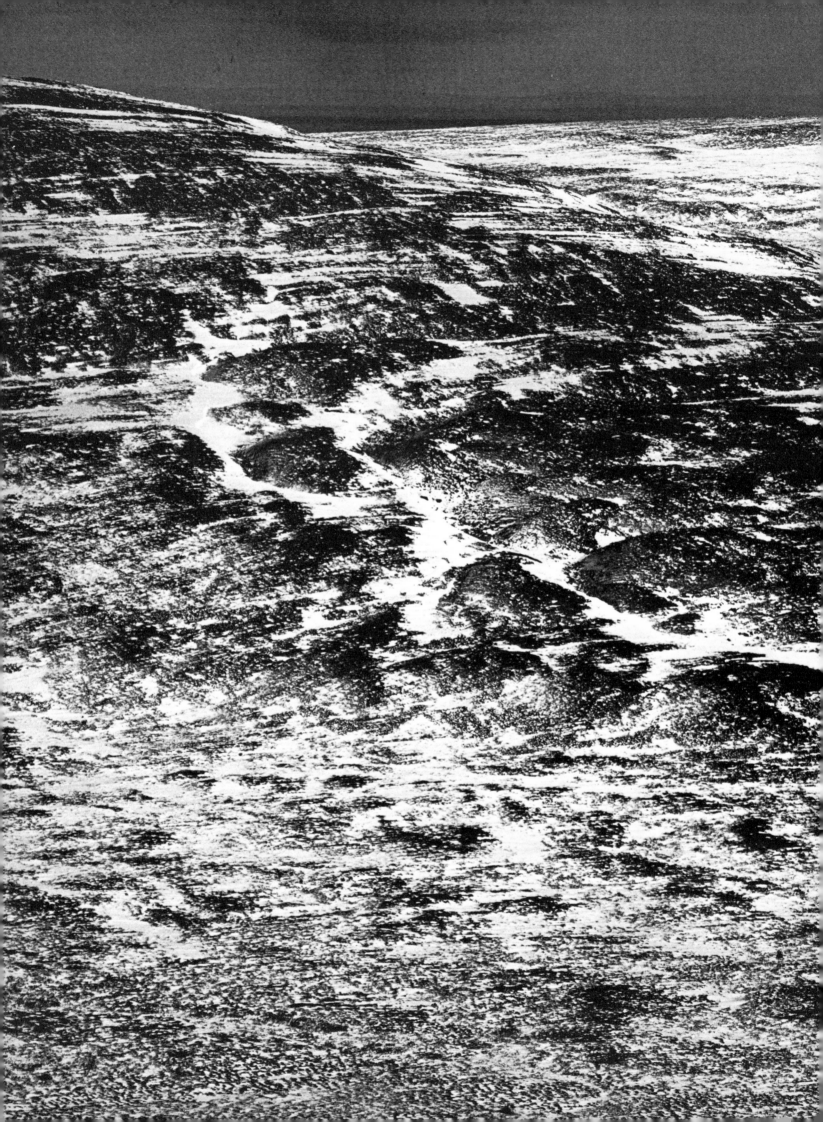

Lapland of the Fells
Fjäll-Lappland

My Home is in the Arctic Fells by/von Nils-Aslak Valkeapää

I am one of those Lapps who find it very difficult to explain where their home is. When I say that my home is where the pines no longer grow, I'm regarded as a smart aleck. And although circumstances are slightly different nowadays, I still feel that the arctic hills are my home — not any special point in them, nor even any particular fell, but all these hills. Both sides of them: night and day. Sunny skies and snowstorms. My home. Also home to many other of the Lapp people.

I dwell in my home, inside me is the place for the past to live. And this past is by no means brief, for my forefathers have been found to have worn, trampled this rocky North about 10,000 years ago. Those people thanks to whom the people of today are known: which are represented by a prototype: a Lapp. But even in the course of such a long time, this trampling has remained unnoticeable, so discreet that hardly any traces are left.

This is proof of the fact that they have lived in harmony with nature, that they have not imagined themselves as masters of nature. It also shows that they have not felt the need to emphasize themselves by attempting to create everlasting monuments, that it has not been necessary for them to be the biggest and most beautiful, to get more and the most. They have had the sun, the wind and the land.

So I wander this rocky arctic fell, feeling it is my home, a place to escape to, rely on. I also want my home to be left in peace by trespassers. I think this is a moderate request in a country where the Constitution protects domestic peace. In the same way as property.

Although, the concept of possessing, when it comes to that, is alien to the Lapps. They have just begun to adopt it. Especially the concept of owing land. The Lapps have always been of the opinion that land cannot be owned (nowadays their land is usually indicated by a sign reading "State land".)

To a Lapp, land is the root. It is enjoyed. One wanders on it. It is our home, our shelter, this rugged, rocky land. All of Finland was once our home, as the name Finlandia reveals, also Norway's Finmarken. The name Lapland shows it, and Finland.

And we cannot help it. We feel that these rocky tracts are our home. And not much remains of them. What has been declared a reserve for the Lapps by law is that only partially, because it contains a lot of privately-owned land, which connot be included in the reserve area meant for the Lapps. Representatives of a European culture and thought, who at some stage were driven here to make these unknown areas State lands. They were people running estates belonging to the Crown. Paid to live here. With the task of dwelling. Not any more. We have lost lands and waters. Saariselkä Ridge to a municipality. The orefields of Kiruna to the common weal. Lakes enlarged. Rapids harnessed for power. Our home has become "State land".

And when we went to school we were told our culture was primitive. That we ourselves were small and black.

The time has come to reappraise things. Perhaps the primitive is not primitive, for a culture that has lived in harmony with nature for thousands of years can not be primitive. And a culture that is able to live amid the nature of the Arctic without directly leaving traces in it? Is that not ingenious, a really sophisticated culture?

We have used this land and tried to be of use to it, too. When we have eaten meat or fish we have not wasted it. Why should we? When we have eaten, we have eaten with respect. And when we have died, it has been only right that nature received some benefit from us. And when we lived somewhere we dwelled in outdoor shelters built of evergreen poles or Lapp huts, and we didn't stay in the same place so long that nature suffered from it. Thus all these arctic fells became our home.

But "European" thinking proclaimed our life as primitive. It constructed buildings that remained where they were for good. Monuments. It taught technical, economical thinking. Reindeer raising became a source of raw material for the meat industry. And where "European"

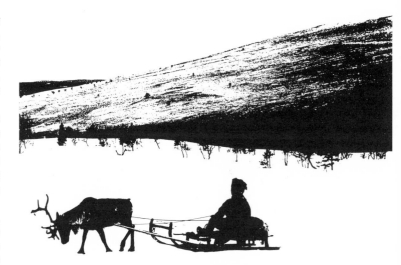

thinking reached, nature was marked forever. Also here in the arctic fells, a biologically sensitive area. Not even now is the importance of this area realized. Our children were taken away from nature very early. To become cultured. To learn the white man's thinking: faster, more, more efficiently. To regard our life in nature as primitive. They have taken everything away from us, up to and including names. Fin- and Lap-, but what about the name by which we are now known, Same? And what will happen to famous Finnish, Nordic, Scandinavian artists, if the Lapp culture ceases to exist? Where will they then draw their inspiration from?

And I see our arctic fells. I see our living environment and hear my heart beat: all this is my home and I carry it inside in my heart. These fjords, rivers, lakes, these biting frosts and hard weather. The day side and the night side of these arctic fells, joy and sorrow, sister and brother. All this is my home and I carry it in my heart. And should I start praising our nightless night, the beauty of the "kaamos" period of darkness, the orchardlike groves of stunted birch, the blue colour of the hills? For a home can be perfect only when it is swept by cleansing winds, fresh rains and spring floods.

And what would a home be like without life, without a sister's warm smile, without a brother's call to the barking dogs in the autumnally beautiful and powerful, snow-swirling reindeer's tail? Yes, all that is my home, my warmth throbs for it and it is what I carry with me, in my heart.

I think it might be bitter to be a colonialist. If things turn out like they did with us: nearly everything worth anything has been taken away from us. We have been pushed back into areas where others would not have managed to survive, and which have been regarded as a punishment. And now even these areas prove desirable, profitable, useful, something to be greedy about.

Now I have the time to wander these rocky tracts, for the fish are gone and the geese flocks of the Tarju lakes are but memories from my childhood. Somewhere inside me the chilling cold of a winter blizzard blows, because I see the door of my refrigerator hanging open and the food inside has disappeared with the wind. I can see that there are empty plastic bags floating in my bathtub and my bed has been littered with broken glass and empty beer cans. And my dining table has been cut into sections by asphalt roads, filling stations and whiskey puddles. My home.

And where is your conscience? Where?

Oh, you great Arctic hill, oh, my Home, my Mother, will you still shine my Sun, my God, will you still blow my Wind, my Freedom, will you still? Still?

And the October sky moves the clouds, makes the undergrowth sway, the wind soughs, the water still flows wildly in Pättikkä and we want nothing from others; we only want what is ours, our own.

Der Fjäll ist mein Zuhause

Ich gehöre zu jenen Samen, denen es schwer fällt zu erklären, wo sie ihr Zuhause haben. Wenn ich sage, dass mein Zuhause dort ist, wo keine Kiefern mehr wachsen, hält man mich für einen Klugschnacker. Und obwohl sich in letzter Zeit einiges verändert hat, fühle ich immer noch, dass der Fjäll mein Zuhause ist, keine bestimmte Stelle an einem Fjäll, nicht einmal ein bestimmter Fjäll, sondern all diese Fjälls. Ihre Nacht- und Tagseiten. Sonnige Himmel und Schneegestöber. Mein Zuhause. Auch das vieler anderer Samen.

Ich bewohne mein Zuhause, und in meinem Herzen bewahre ich einen Platz für die Vergangenheit. Und diese Vergangenheit ist gar nicht einmal so kurz, denn meine Vorväter nutzten diesen steinigen Norden nachweislich schon vor 10 000 Jahren ab. Jene Völker, in deren unser heutiges Volk seinen Ursprung hat: welche die Samen als Phänotyp repräsentieren. Aber selbst in solch langem Zeitraum ist die Abnutzung unmerkbar geblieben, so unmerkbar, dass man kaum Spuren zu erkennen vermag.

Das beweist, dass die Samen in Harmonie mit der Natur gelebt haben. Und dass sie nicht dem Irrglauben verfallen waren, Herrscher der Natur zu sein. Es beweist auch, dass sie es nicht für nötig befunden haben, sich selbst durch Schaffung ewiger Denkmäler zu erhöhen. Dass sie es nicht für nötig hielten, die Grössten und Schönsten zu sein. Mehr und am meisten zu bekommen. Denn sie hatten ja die Sonne. Den Wind. Und die Erde.

So wandere ich also durch diese steinigen Fjälls, empfinde sie als mein Zuhause, wohin ich fliehen, worauf ich mich verlassen kann. Und ich wünsche auch, dass mein Zuhause vor Eindringlingen geschützt bliebe. Das sollte wohl nicht zuviel verlangt sein in einem Lande, in welchem der Hausfriede grundgesetzlich geschützt ist. Wie auch das Eigentum.

Obwohl, was den Begriff Eigentum angeht: der ist den Samen allerdings fremd. Erst in jüngster Zeit hat man begonnen, ihn sich anzueignen. Nämlich die Vorstellung von der Möglichkeit, Land zu besitzen. Die Samen waren bisher der Ansicht, dass man Land nicht besitzen kann. Heute ist das Land der Samen zumeist mit dem Schild "Staatliche Domäne" gekennzeichnet.

Die Samen sehen im Land ihren Ursprung. Auf dem Land wandert man. Es ist unser Zuhause, unsere Zuflucht. Dieses karge, felsige Land. Der Name Finlandia erzählt davon, auch der Name Finnmark in Norwegen. Davon erzählt auch der Name Lappland.

Und wir können nicht dagegen an, wir fühlen, dass dieser steinige Boden unser Zuhause ist. Und viel ist von ihm nicht mehr übrig. Auch das, was per Erlass zur Heimat der Samen erklärt worden ist, ist dies nur zum Teil. Denn auf diesem Gebiet gibt es viel in Privatbesitz befindliches Land, das nicht zur Heimat der Samen gehören kann. Repräsentanten europäischer Kultur und Denkweise, die einst selbst in diese unbekannte Welt vorgeschoben wurden, um sie als staatliches Eigentum sicherzustellen. Bewohner staatlicher Domänen. Zum Wohnen besoldet. Ihre Aufgabe war das Wohnen. Heute nicht mehr. Wir haben unsere Länder und Gewässer verloren. Aus Saariselkä eine Stadt. Die Erzfelder von Kiruna zum Gemeinnutz. Die Seen grösser. Aus Stromschnellen Kraftwerke. Aus unserem Zuhause "Staatliche Domänen".

Und wenn wir zur Schule gingen, wurde uns erzählt, unsere Kultur sei primitiv. Dass wir klein und schwarz seien.

Es ist an der Zeit, die Dinge neu zu überdenken. Ob primitiv vielleicht doch nicht primitiv ist. Denn eine Kultur, die Tausende von Jahren in Harmonie mit der Natur gelebt hat, kann nicht primitiv sein. Und eine Kultur, welche die arktische Natur zu bewohnen vermag, ohne sichtbare Spuren zu hinterlassen, ist sie nicht genial, eine wirkliche Hochkultur?

Wir haben dieses Land genutzt, und wir haben versucht, unsererseits dem Lande zu Nutzen zu sein. Wenn wir Fisch und Fleisch assen, verschwendeten wir es nicht; warum hätten wir auch? Wenn wir assen, assen wir mit Respekt. Und wenn wir starben, war es nur billig, dass die Natur aus uns Nutzen ziehen konnte.

Und wenn wir irgendwo wohnten, wohnten wir unter Schutzdächern oder in Lappenzelten, und wir hielten uns nicht so lange an ein und derselben Stelle auf, dass die Natur darunter gelitten hätte. So sind all diese Fjälls unser Zuhause geworden.

Aber die "Europäische" Denkweise erklärte unser Leben für primitiv. Sie errichtete Bauwerke, die ewig an derselben Stelle stehen. Denkmäler. Lehrte, technisch zu denken, wirtschaftlich. Aus den Rentieren wurde Rohmaterial für die Fleischindustrie. Und wohin die "Europäische" Denkweise vordrang, dort liess sie auf Ewigkeit Spuren in der Natur zurück. Auch hier, in den Fjälls, in einer biologisch empfindlichen Landschaft. Unsere Kinder werden schon früh der Natur entzogen. Um Bildung zu erhalten. Die weisse Denkweise zu erlernen: schneller, mehr, effektiver. Damit sie unser Leben in der Natur als primitiv ansehen.

Sie haben uns alles genommen, einschliesslich unserer Namen. Finne und Lappe, aber wie steht es mit Same...? Und wie ergeht es den finnischen, schwedischen, norwegischen Künstlern, wenn die Kultur der Samen zu existieren aufhört? Woraus schöpfen sie dann ihre Inspirationen?

Und ich sehe unsere Fjälls, unsere Heimat, und ich höre mein Herz pochen: dies alles ist mein Zuhause, und dies trage ich in mir, in meinem Herzen. Diese Fjorde, Flüsse, Seen, diese Fröste, strengen Wetter. Die Nacht- und Tagseiten dieser Fjälls, Freude und Kummer, Schwestern und Brüder.

Dies alles ist mein Zuhause, und ich trage es in meinem Herzen. Sollte ich etwa in Lobpreisung unserer nachtlosen Nächte, der Schönheit der Polarnacht, unserer apfelbaumplantagenähnlichen Fjällbirkenwälder, des Blaus der Fjälls ausbrechen? Denn ein Zuhause kann nur vollständig sein, wenn es von reinigenden Winden, erfrischenden Regengüssen und Frühjahrsüberschwemmungen strapaziert wird.

Und was wäre ein Zuhause ohne Leben, ohne das Lächeln der Schwester, ohne den Ruf des Bruders, der den einem herbstlich schönen und kraftvollen, schneeaufstöbernden Rentier hinterdreinlaufenden bellenden Hunden gilt. Ja, dies alles ist mein Zuhause, hierfür pulsiert meine Wärme, und dies trage ich in mir, in meinem Herzen.

Ich überlege mir: es muss bitter sein, das Leben eines Kolonialisten zu führen. Wenn es so geht wie mit uns: man hat uns fast alles genommen, was irgendeinen Wert hatte. Wir sind in eine Gegend abgedrängt worden, in welcher die anderen nicht zurecht gekommen wären, welche als Strafe galt. Und jetzt erweist auch sie sich als erstrebenswert, nützlich, begehrenswert.

Jetzt habe ich Zeit, über dieses steinige Land zu wandern, denn die Fische sind verschwunden, und auch die Gänseschwärme auf den Tarju-Seen sind nur noch Kindheitserinnerungen. Irgendwo in mir staubt die eisige Kälte der winterlichen Schneestürme, denn ich sehe die Eisschranktür meines Zuhauses sperrangelweit offenstehen, und die Speisen, die einst darin lagen, sind in alle Winde verstreut. In meiner Badewanne sehe ich leere Plastikbeutel schwimmen, mein Bett ist mit zerbrochenen Flaschen und leeren Bierdosen übersät. Und mein Esstisch ist von Asphaltstrassen, Tankstellen und Whiskyseen zerrissen. Mein Zuhause.

Und wo ist euer Gewissen? Wo?

Du grosser Fjäll du mein Zuhause du meine Mutter scheinst du Sonne noch du mein Gott du mein Leben wehst du noch mein Wind wehst du noch? Noch?

Und der Oktoberhimmel lässt die Wolken treiben, die Reiser biegen sich, der Wind pfeift, noch fliessen die Wässer wild im Pättikkä, und wir wollen nichts von den anderen, wir wollen nur unser Eigenes, unser Eigenes.

Lake Inari
Der Inarisee

A long time before the most recent Ice Age, several thousands of square kilometres of the earth's crust subsided as the result of some natural catacyclasm in the northern part of Fennoscandia, just south of the present tree line. The ice sheets later completed what subsidence had begun and the result was the Inari lake basin, in which today one large lake is surrounded by well over a thousand smaller lakes and pounds.

The vast Lake Inari depression starkly contrasts the landscape in which it lies. To the south and west, chains of arctic fells stretch as far as the eye can see, while the labyrintine lake system itself is a bleak landscape dotted with stunted birch.

Schon lange vor den Wüten der letzten Eiszeit sackte im nördlichen Fennoskandia in unmittelbarer Nähe der heutigen Nadelwaldgrenze auf einer Tausende von Quadratkilometern umfassenden Fläche die Erde ab. Später vervollständigte das Inlandeis diese Formung der Landschaft. Als Ergebnis entstand das Gebiet des Inarisees, auf dem heute neben dem grossen Hauptsee weit über tausend kleinere Teiche glitzern.

Die Senkung des riesigen Inarisees unterscheidet sich deutlich von ihrer Umgebung. Die sowohl im Süden als auch im Westen aufragenden Fjällrücken reichen bis über den Horizont hinaus. Das gesamte Seenlabyrinth hingegen ist relativ ebene, vor kargen Geröllufern gezeichnete Wildnis.

Lake Inarijärvi is about a thousand square kilometres. It measures forty by eighty kilometres and reaches a maximum depth of 100 metres. There are about three thousand islands in all. The best known of these is Ukonsaari (in the picture on the right), which is an ancient sacrificial site.

Der Inarisee nimmt eine Fläche von reichlich 1000 Quadratkilometern ein. Der See ist rund 40 Kilometer breit und etwa 80 Kilometer lang; seine grösste Tiefe beträgt 100 Meter. Die Zahl der Inseln des Inarisees liegt bei 3000. Die bekannteste von ihnen ist Ukonsaari, eine vorzeitliche Opferstätte.

Lemmenjoki

The nature conservationist associates the name of Lemmenjoki with an extensive national park, while to the historian it conjures up memories of the fabulous gold rush of bygone days.

Even today, Lemmenjoki is a truly genuine wilderness landscape. Here the traveller finds relatively untouched forests in which lichen-covered pine groves alternate with silver willows, steep-walled gorges, wilderness lakes, bogs with lush growths of vegetation and rocky fell upland.

For the hiker in search of varying, untouched landscapes, the Lemmenjoki area is a paradise, and will remain so, because it is now a national park covering nearly two thousand square kilometres. Lemmenjoki National Park is the largest in Finland and certainly one of the most important nature reserves in the whole of Europe.

Der Naturschützer denkt beim Namen Lemmenjoki an den grössten Nationalpark Finnlands, der Historiker an den Goldrausch vergangener Jahre.

Bis zum heutigen Tage ist die Landschaft um den Fluss Lemmenjoki echte Wildnis. Hier findet man relativ unberührte Wälder, wo flechtenbewachsene Kiefernwaldungen, helle Birkenwälder, steile Flusstäler, Wildnisseen, üppig bewachsene Moore und schieres Fjällplateau einander abwechseln.

Für den Wanderer ist das Gebiet des Lemmenjoki ein Paradies. Um ihre Natur zu erhalten, wurde diese Landschaft zum Nationalpark erklärt. Später ist der Nationalpark erweitert worden, und heute umfasst sein Gebiet fast 2000 Quadratkilometer. Damit ist er Finnlands grösster Nationalpark und eines der grössten Naturschutzgebiete des Kontinents.

The scenery varies considerably in Lemmenjoki National Park. The river valley contains pine forest, which gradually yields to stunted birch and finally treeless upland.
Both bears and eagles live in the park. There is a motor-boat service along the River Lemmenjoki.
There are only a few geologically-ancient river valleys in Finland. These were carved out by flowing water before the Ice Age.
The ice sheets changed the shapes of most valleys. Wherever the ice flowed in the same direction as the valley the original V-shape was replaced by an almost U-shaped, trough-like profile.

Die Natur des Nationalparks Lemmenjoki ist mannigfaltig. Im Flusstal wächst Kiefernwald, und weiter oben trifft man auf Fjällbirken, deren Bestand mit steigender Höhe immer lichter wird und schliesslich in baumlose Fjällspitzen übergeht. Im Park sind sowohl der Bär wie auch der Adler zuhause.
In Finnland existieren nur wenige geologisch alte, schon vor der letzten Eiszeit von fliessendem Wasser ausgehöhlte Flusstäler. Die meisten Täler haben durch das Inlandeis eine neue Form erhalten. In Fällen, in denen das Eis in Talrichtung geflossen ist, hat sich das Querprofil des Tals zu einem fast U-förmigen offenen Trogtal gewandelt.

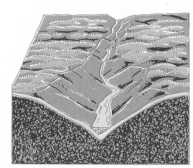

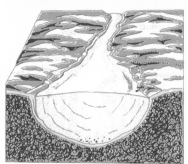

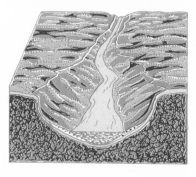

Sevettijärvi

The ponds dry up in late summer (1). The old "Outer Lapland" trail was a waterway and iceway route linking Inari with Northern Norway (2), via Sevetti.

Die Teiche trocknen im Spätsommer aus (1). Die alte Hinter-Lappland-Strasse führte als Wasser- und Eisroute von Inari an Sevetti vorbei zur Finnmark (2).

The Skolts, who form a distinct tribe within the Lapp nation, have had to abandon their homelands beyond the eastern border at least twice. The Government financed their re-construction effort after the Second World War, and thus a new Skolt village was established at Sevettijärvi in the Inari district.

The typical features of the district are sandy pine heaths and flat tundra birch groves, but above all the impression is of bleakness. The gentle profiles of the arctic fells are scarred by sheer walls of broken rock and the same moonscape can be seen by the lakeshores.

The Skolts were given their own reindeer area when they were resettled in Sevettijärvi, but the rocky ground can not support many animals. Fishing is one means of supplementing incomes.

Die als eigener Stamm dem Volk der Samen angehörenden Skoltlappen haben mindestens zweimal ihre jenseits der Ostgrenze liegende Heimat verlassen. Heute leben sie in Nordost-Inari im neuen Skoltlappendorf Sevettijärvi.

Sandige Kiefern- und ebenmässige Fjällbirkenwälder charakterisieren diesen Landstrich, aber am auffälligsten ist die Kargheit der Landschaft. An den sanften Berghängen dehnen sich vegetationslose Geröllfelder aus. Auf die gleiche "Mondlandschaft" stösste man auch an den Seenufern.

Als die Umzügler sich in Sevettijärvi niederliessen, erhielten ihre Rentiere ein eigenes Weideland, aber da die Erträge aus der Rentierzucht in dieser kargen Umwelt nicht sehr üppig sind, beziehen die Skoltlappen einen Teil ihres Auskommens durch Fischfang.

1

The Kevojoki Canyon
Der Cañon des Kevojoki

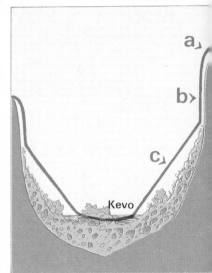

In Kevo Canyon (3) the arctic buzzard (1) and other eastern species depend on the lemming (2) and other small mammals for nourishment.

Der Tierbestand des Kevo-Cañons (3) ist sehr wechselhaft. Ob der Bussard (1) und andere Raubvögel hier nisten, hängt wesentlich vom Bestand des Lemmings (2) und anderer Kleinsäuger ab.

Kevo Canyon in the Utsjoki district is Finland's mightiest river gorge. It developed millions of years ago in a fissure in the rocky crust and was scoured and deepened during the last Ice Age.

The flora of the Kevo area is subalpine, but the two-month period of uninterrupted daylight during the summer reminds one of the northern arctic regions. The diversity of the flora also stems from the combined effect of the climate and the soil typography. There are pine groves, small patches of meadows and at the highest elevations grasses, mosses and lichens excellently adapted to arctic conditions.

Kevo Canyon is a nature reserve. Hikers must keep to the marked trails following the icy-cold river. The trail starts at Karigasniemi and Luobmusjärvi — where all creation began, according to a folk myth — and continues nearly 40 km, passing mighty walls of rock and waterfalls, one of which — Fielluköngäs — is nearly 30 m high.

Der Kevo-Cañon in Utsjoki ist Finnlands imposantestes Flusstal. Es entstand vor Jahrmillionen durch Abbröckeln der Felsen, und die letzte Eiszeit vervollständigte diese Landschaftsformung.

Von seiner Vegetation her gehört dieses Gebiet zur subalpinen Zone, aber die zwei sommerlichen Monate ständigen Lichts lassen mehr an die Nordpolarlandschaft denken.

Die Mannigfaltigkeit der Vegetation hat ihre Ursache im Zusammenwirken von Klima und Bodenbeschaffenheit: Kiefernwaldungen, üppige Wiesenflecken und ganz oben eine Polstervegetation, die auch strengen arktischen Bedingungen widersteht.

Der Kevo-Cañon ist heute ein Naturpark. Durch ihn führt ein markierter Wanderpfad, der in der Nähe von Karigasniemi beim Luobmusjärvi-See von der Landstrasse abzweigt und auf vierzig Kilometern im Tal dem Fluss folgt. Unterwegs kommt man an mächtigen Felswänden und Wasserfällen vorbei.

Beneath the sheer cliffs (b), debris weathered from the granulite rocks of the upper slope (a) has formed landslide piles on the valley floor.

Die Verwitterungsprodukte des Granulitfelses am Oberhang (a) bilden unter der steilen Felswand (b) auf dem Talgrund Rutschkegel (c).

Utsjoki

The dominant tree in the Utsjoki area is stunted tundra birch.
Mieraslompolo is a pretty Lapp village in traditional style.

Der dominierende Waldtyp in Utsjoki ist der Fjällbirkenwald. Das Dorf Mieraslompola ist ein schönes und harmonisches Samendorf.

Beyond the northern limit of soft-wood trees begins the tundra, which stretches across the whole of our continent as a belt of fluctuating breadth. Where Finland is concerned, this zone is at its broadest in the Utsjoki area. The characteristic features of a tundra landscape are bleak, treeless arctic hills, capped with snow all the year round, and ice-cold streams, rivers and lakes, the surfaces of which are but fleetingly freed of their icy shackles. Stunted birches with twisted stems dot the partially permafrost-bound palsa bogs.

Stretching eastwards and south-wards from Teno, Utsjoki is Finland's northernmost municipality. Most of its area consists of gently undulating, bleak tundra, on which only a few "exotic" northern birds thrive. Mammals are also few, the most typical — and from the point of view of man most important — being the reindeer. It finds its nourishment from Iceland moss lichen growths and in stunted birch groves. And behind the reindeer comes man, a Lapp, who like every other creature depends on the bounty of nature for his livelihood.

———

Nördlich der Nadelbaumgrenze beginnt die Tundra, die als wechselnd breite Zone dem oberen Rand unseres Kontinents folgt. In Finnland erreicht diese Zone ihre grösste Breite auf dem Gebiet der Gemeinde Utsjoki. Die typische Tundralandschaft charakterisieren karge baumlose Fjällflächen, weisse Schneeflecken, die auch dem Sommer widerstehen, sowie ewig kalte Bäche, Flüsse und Seen, welche sich höchstens für einen Augenblick ihrer Eisdecke entledigten. Weiterhin gehören zum Wesen der Tundra Wälder mit verkrüppelt wachsenden krummstämmigen Fjällbirken und dazwischen hier und da vom ewigen Eis beherrschte Palsamoore.

Utsjoki, Finnlands nördlichste Gemeinde, ist grösstenteils leicht gewellte, spärlich bewachsene Tundra. Hier leben nur wenige "exotische" nordische Vogelarten. Auch der Säugetierbestand ist gering. Das typischste und für den Menschen wichtigste Säugetier ist das Ren. Es findet seine Nahrung auf den flechtenbewachsenen Böden sowie in den windgepeitschten Geröllfeldern.

The Tenojoki Salmon River
Der Lachsfluss Tenojoki

The River Tenojoki rises in Norway, meanders as two separate streams until it crosses the Finnish border to the north of Karigasniemi and receives an infusion of extra strength from the River Inarijoki. Then it again swings north, recrosses the border near Finland's northernmost point and finally flows into the Arctic Ocean.

The River is 360 km in length. It contains salmon, which swim upstream from the ocean towards their spawning grounds. The Tenojoki is a tranquil river. Between the bleakest of gravelly shores, it winds its way through a valley, which is fringed in places by gentle birch-clad slopes and elsewhere by steep arctic fells covered, even in summer, with snow.

Der in Norwegen beginnende Tenojoki trifft im Norden von Karigasniemi auf die finnische Grenze. Dort erhält er einen zusätzlichen Schub durch den Inarijoki. Sein gewundener Lauf bildet bis zu Finnlands nördlichstem Punkt die Landesgrenze, fliesst dann weiter nach Norden und mündet schliesslich ins Eismeer.

Der Fluss ist 360 Kilometer lang und lachsreich. Nachdem er vom Eismeer in den Fluss gestiegen ist, schwimmt der Lachs zum Oberlauf, wo er seinen Laichplatz aufsucht. Der Tenojoki fliesst ruhig. Eingerahmt von kargen Kiesufern schlängelt er sich durch sein Tal, das stellenweise von sanft ansteigenden Fjällbirkenhängen und dann wieder von steilen Fjälls mit ganzjährig schneebedeckten Gipfeln gesäumt ist.

2

Palsa Bogs
Palsamoore

In the upland area of Enontekiö, Inari and Utsjoki, the mean annual temperature is just a little bit on the wrong side of zero, Celsius. This is one of the reasons for the existence of a type of peat bog called a "palsa". During cold summers unmolten permafrost cores or lenses develop in the peat layer, causing mounds several decimetres above the surrounding terrain. From this "seed" a hummock gradually grows, just as the permafrost core gains in strength.

For all their bleakness, palsa bogs are rich. They are treeless, but dense shrubbery is often found at the bases of the mounds, and the landscape varies from watery mires to hay-grown marshes. The fauna is also highly varied.

Auf dem Hochland von Enontekiö, Inari und Utsjoki bleibt die jährliche Durchschnittstemperatur knapp unter dem Gefrierpunkt. Dies ist eine Voraussetzung für die Entstehung von Palsamooren. In kalten Sommern bilden sich in der Torfschicht Eislinsen, die nicht schmelzen, sondern die Erdoberfläche um einige Dezimeter anheben. Aus diesem Kern wächst allmählich die Bülte, wobei zugleich die Eisschicht in ihrem Inneren dicker wird.

Die Palsamoore sind baumlos, aber oft wuchert gleich am Ansatz der Riesenbülte dichtes Gestrüpp. Sumpfige Schlenken, grasbewachsene Weissmoore und Tümpel sorgen für Abwechslung in der Moorlandschaft.

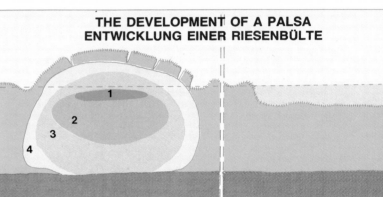

**THE DEVELOPMENT OF A PALSA
ENTWICKLUNG EINER RIESENBÜLTE**

Finland's biggest palsas are nowadays some 7 metres high (1). The core of a palsa is permanently frozen and ice-hard even in summer, but northern bog flora grows in great profusion around the bases of the mounds (2). One of the most delicious fruits growing on palsa bogs is the cloudberry (3). The permafrost core of a palsa mound gradually swells during cold periods. However, the peat surface finally ruptures and the core melts when the climate again becomes warmer.

Finnlands grösste Riesenbülten erheben sich rund sieben Meter über ihrer Umgebung (1). Der Permafrostkern des Hügels bleibt auch im Sommer eisenhart, aber um die Bülte wuchert üppigste Moorvegetation (2). Zu den Gaben der Torfmoosbülten gehört die Moltebeere (3).

Die Eislinse im Kern der Riesenbülte hat sich in kalten Klimaperioden allmählich ausgedehnt und den Torfhügel angehoben, dessen Oberfläche schliesslich rissig wird. Wenn das Klima wärmer wird, schmilzt der Eiskern und der Hügel sackt in sich zusammen.

1

Malla was made a nature reserve because of the richness of its scenery and flora, which is the entire arctic fell area in microcosm. The pioneers returning after the Ice Age included various varieties of saxifrage, such as yellow mountain saxifrage (1). The exotic alpine plants include Lapland rhododendron (2) and the furry lauseworth (3). The lime-rich soil encourages moss campion (5) and mountain avens (4), which grows in swards square kilometres in extent.

Entscheidend für die Gründung des Naturparks Malla war seine Vielseitigkeit, die sich in der gesamten Vegetation des Hochfjällgebiets niederschlägt. Als sich zu Ende der letzten Eiszeit der Gletscher zurückzog, waren einige Steinbrecharten die ersten Pioniere, so der Fetthennen-Steinbrech (1). Zu den alpinen "exotischen" Arten gehören die Lappländische Alpenrose (2) und das haarige Alpen-Läusekraut (3). Auf kalkhaltigem Untergrund wachsen Stengelloses Leimkraut (5) und Silberwurz (4).

2

4

Malla

Malla, Finland's oldest nature reserve, begins at the cairn marking where the borders of Finland, Norway and Sweden meet.

The reason for establishing Malla (in 1938), was twofold: one wanted to isolate a convenient area for the use of scientists and at the same time preserve some of the high arctic fells in as virgin a state as possible. Today we can appreciate the foresight of those conservationists. The hiking trails are flanked by litter and even many of the protected plants have disappeared from beside the beaten tracks. In Malla, however, the nature remains well preserved.

Malla was originally chosen because of its representative fell nature and the variety of its scenery. Just a few short steps take the observer from one zone to another — and from one season to another. The waterside birch groves display summer at its finest while the alpine slopes higher up are still awakening to spring and the summits are cloaked in their permanent mantle of snow.

Finnlands ältester Naturpark, der 1938 gegründete Naturpark Malla, dehnt sich vom Dreiländereck Norwegen—Schweden—Finnland nach Osten aus.

Als man Malla unter Naturschutz stellte, verfolgte man zwei Absichten: man wollte für die Forschung ein geeignetes Gebiet absondern und ein Stück Hochfjälland möglichst unberührt erhalten. Schon heute ist zu erkennen, wie weitsichtig die Naturparkgründer waren. Die Fjälls an den allgemeinen Wanderrouten sind mit Abfällen übersät, und neben den ausgetretenen Pfaden sind auch viele unter Naturschutz stehende Pflanzen vernichtet worden. Die Natur von Malla hingegen ist gut erhalten.

Mit nur wenigen Schritten kommt man in Malla von einer Vegetationszone in die andere. Gleichzeitg erlebt man auch den Jahreszeitenwechsel. In den Birkenhainen am Seeufer zeigt sich der Sommer von seiner besten Seite, an den alpinen Oberhängen trifft er gerade erst ein, und hoch oben herrscht noch Winter.

The High Fells
Die Hochfjälls

The "panhandle" belonging to Finland and stretching between Sweden and Norway contains a small area of high arctic fells, which continue as a steep alpine range in Norway and Sweden.

In Finland, the traveller meets the high fells just shortly before the frontier. The first and most conspicuous is Saana, from which the Yliperä chain stretches about fifty kilometres. Finland's highest peak, Halti, is at the extreme end of the chain. There, a peak just on the Norwegian side of the border soars to 1,328 metres.

Stunted birch grow up to the treeline at 700 m, above which there are bare, rocky slopes, snow-covered all the year round.

Bei der Grenzziehung verblieb in der äussersten Ecke Finnlands ein kleines Stück Hochfjälland, das sich in Norwegen und Schweden mit steilen, alpenähnlichen Fjälls als Kjölen-Gebirge fortsetzt.

Auf Hochfjälls trifft man erst kurz vor der Grenze: der erste und ansehnlichste ist der Saana. In der Nordecke des finnischen Fjällhochlands ragt die höchste Erhebung des Landes auf, der Halti. Auf ihm verläuft in 1328 Meter Höhe die finnisch-norwegische Grenze.

Die von Fjällbirken gebildete Waldgrenze verläuft in 700 Meter Höhe. In den Mulden der Oberhänge bleibt den ganzen Sommer über Schnee liegen.

The figures in the map
refer to the page numbers.
Die Zahlen in der Karte beziehen
sich auf die Textseiten.

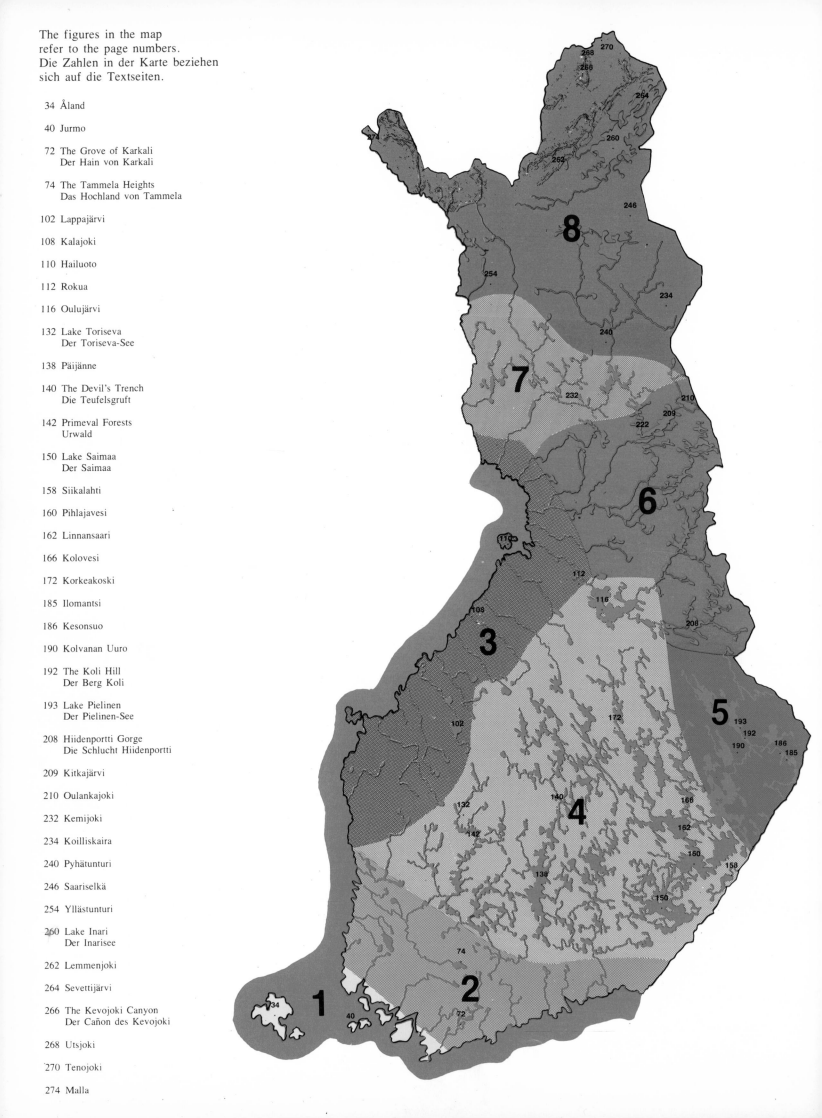

The Division Geographical used in this Book:

1. THE ARCHIPELAGO
The archipelago off the south-west coast of Finland is one of the unique areas of the world. Here one finds most of the scenic elements present in the Finnish landscape: treeless islets, wooded islands, arboured meadows, farmland and a labyrinth of water and land with its special flora and fauna.

2. THE FINNISH HEARTLAND
Most of Finland has been uplifted from the sea in the course of only a few millenia. Islands and skerries have gradually changed into mainland and hills; straits and open expanses of water into fertile alluvial plains. The Finnish Heartland is the traditional cultured part of the country at its most fertile.

3. THE PLAINS OF OSTROBOTHNIA
The extensive cultivated plains are an impressive sight in this region. The colourful plain dotted with grey hay-barns stretches to the horizon, and the green and golden checkerboard pattern is broken only by the rivers, which have carved out deep courses for themselves in the clayey soil.

4. THE FINNISH LAKELAND
The tens of thousands of lakes and ponds in this region form an intricate labyrinth of water bodies, with large open spaces of water found here and there. The fields are small and the areas once burned over to create agricultural land are now covered by stately stands of silver birch, although evergreen trees dominate the region as a whole.

5. THE KARELIAN HILLS
Forested hills interspersed with lakes and small strips of cultivated land are the characteristic elements of the Karelian hill country's landscape. Some of the hills are relicts of the ancient Karelian fold mountains, while the retreating ice sheets scoured out lakes and bays oriented in the direction the glaciers moved.

6. KAINUU-KOILLISMAA
The western part of the Kainuu region contains extensive marshy moors, large peat bogs and small lakes. The eastern part, by contrast, is upland, with wooded hills, clean lakes and swift rivers. Here, too, one finds the famous wilderness areas of Kuhmo, Kiutaköngäs Falls, Ruka and many other splendid sights.

7. FOREST LAPLAND
The scenery of forest Lapland is a blend of bleak forests and open expanses of peat bogs. The arctic fell chains of Ounasselkä and Salla-Saariselkä add variety to the periphery of the region. Here one can admire the bleak beauty of the aapa bogs, the extravagant colour display of the splendid "ruska" period in autumn and the yellowly glowing patches of cloudberries.

8. LAPLAND OF THE FELLS
The most massive scenic views in Finland open up before one on the arctic fell plateaus of Lapland. The timber line lies far below and the wind has stripped the summits bare in many places. Lower down one finds stunted alpine birch and palsa bogs. One is close to the tundra belt.

Die geografische Einteilung Finnlands in diesem Buch:

1. SCHÄREN-FINNLAND
Finnlands südwestliche Schärenwelt ist eine der ungewöhnlichsten Landschaften der Welt. Dort trifft man die meisten der finnischen Landschaftstypen an: baumlose Klippen, bewaldete Schären, laubbaumbestandene Wiesen, Ackerland sowie Labyrinthe aus Wasser und Land mit einer spezifischen Tier- und Pflanzenwelt.

2. KERN-FINNLAND
Der grösste Teil Finnlands ist im Laufe von wenigen Jahrtausenden dem Meer entstiegen. Aus den einstigen Inseln und Klippen sind Hügel und Anhöhen geworden, aus den Sunden und offenen Seenflächen fruchtbare Tonebenen. Kern-Finnland ist eine traditionelle finnische Kulturlandschaft.

3. DIE TIEFEBENE VON ÖSTERBOTTEN
Weitläufige Anbauebenen prägen hier die Landschaft. Die vielfarbige Tiefebene, die mit grauen Scheunen übersprenkelt ist, setzt sich bis zum Horizont fort, und die grünen und goldgelben Felder werden nur von Flüssen unterbrochen, die ihr Bett tief in den Tonboden eingefurcht haben.

4. SEEN-FINNLAND
Hier in der finnischen Seenplatte bilden Zehntausende von Seen und Teichen ein Wasserlabyrinth, das nur selten von grossen offenen Seenflächen unterbrochen wird. Die Ackerflächen sind klein, und auf den einstigen brandgerodeten Schwenden wachsen heute Birkenwälder. Allerdings beherrschen auch hier Nadelwälder das Landschaftsbild.

5. BERG-KARELIEN
Bewaldete Berge, zwischen ihnen schimmernde Seen und kleine Ackerflächen bilden die wesenseigene Landschaft Berg-Kareliens. Ein Teil der Berge sind Relikte des alten Karelischen Faltengebirges, und das Inlandeis hat auf seinem Rückzug in Fliessrichtung Seen und Buchten in den Boden eingefurcht.

6. KAINUU-KOILLISMAA
Im Westen von Kainuu dominieren weitläufige Weissmoore, grosse Reisermoore und Teiche. Der Osten wiederum ist Hochebene mit bewaldeten Bergen, sauberen Seen und reissenden Flüssen. Hier findet man die bekannte Wildnis von Kuhmo, die Kiutaköngäs-Fälle, den Fjäll Ruka und andere berühmte Sehenswürdigkeiten.

7. WALD-LAPPLAND
Die Landschaft von Wald-Lappland ist eine Kombination aus kargen Wäldern und offenen Mooren. Am Rande des Gebiets bringen die Fjällketten Ounasselkä und Salla-Saariselkä Abwechslung in das Landschaftsbild. In Wald-Lappland erfreuen die karge Schönheit der Aapamoore, die farbenprächtige Ruska-Landschaft und gelb leuchtende Moltebeerenfelder das Auge.

8. FJÄLL-LAPPLAND
Von der Fjällhochebene Hinterlapplands öffnen sich Finnlands massivste Landschaften. Die Waldgrenze bleibt tief unten zurück, und der Wind hat vielerorts die Fjällgipfel kahl gepeitscht. Weiter unten verkrüppelte Birkenwälder und Palsamoore — die Tundra ist nicht mehr weit.

Picture Credits/Bildquellen:

All pictures by Matti A. Pitkänen, except (page nos. in boldface):
Alle Fotos von Matti A. Pitkänen, ausser (Seitenzahlen fett gedruckt):

16 Teuvo Suominen **26—27** Arno Rautavaara (1, 2+4) **29** Arno Rautavaara (above/oben) **31** Seppo Keränen (3) **32** Seppo Keränen (above/oben) **39** Mauri Korhonen (2+3) **44** Mauri Korhonen (1) **59** Seppo Keränen (3) **60—61** Jorma Luhta (large picture/grosses Bild) **64** Arno Rautavaara (3+4) **72** Arno Rautavaara (1) **79** Mauri Korhonen **80** Arno Rautavaara (1) **83** Arno Rautavaara **95** Arno Rautavaara (3), Kari Soveri (4) **111** Hannu Hautala (2) **115** Jorma Luhta (2+3) **131** Hannu Hautala (3) **136** Hannu Hautala (1), Jorma Luhta (2), Mauri Korhonen (3) **142** Mauri Korhonen **143** Hannu Hautala (3+4) **158** Hannu Hautala **159** Kari Soveri (3+4) **187** Seppo Keränen (3), Jorma Luhta (4) **188** Teuvo Suominen (2) **202** Martti Montonen **212—213** Mauri Korhonen **217** Teuvo Suominen (2) **236—237** Rauno Ruuhijärvi **240 Gatefold/Klappseite** Teuvo Suominen (2) **242** Jorma Luhta (1) **266** Teuvo Suominen **272** Teuvo Suominen (3) **274** Mauri Korhonen (1), Teuvo Suominen (2+3), Arno Rautavaara (4+5).

Diagrams by Teuvo Berggren, based on the following sources:
Grafische Darstellungen von Teuvo Berggren, auf Grundlage folgender Quellen:
23 National Board of Survey/Finnisches Landvermessungsamt **43** Atlas över Skärgårds-Finland **44** Hulten: Atlas över växternas utbredning i Norden **47** Suomen geologinen kartta **72** National Board of Survey/Finnisches Landvermessungsamt **74** National Board of Survey/Finnisches Landvermessungsamt **78** T. Aartolahti: Suomen geomorfologia (Helsinki 1977) **80** Suomen geologinen kartta **83** Tellus 3—5, en naturgeografisk tv-serie om vår planet **93** M. Eronen **98** National Board of Survey/Finnisches Landvermessungsamt **100** National Board of Survey/Finnisches Landvermessungsamt **103** National Board of Survey/Finnisches Landvermessungsamt **108** T. Aartolahti: Suomen geomorfologia (Helsinki 1977) **112** U. Häyrinen: Suo **123** National Board of Survey/Finnisches Landvermessungsamt **133** R. Uusinoka **146** Tellus 3—5, en naturgeografisk tv-serie om vår planet **161** National Board of Survey/Finnisches Landvermessungsamt **162** National Board of Survey/Finnisches Landvermessungsamt **166** National Board of Survey/Finnisches Landvermessungsamt **184** M. Mielonen: Thesis/Dissertation **201** R. Uusinoka **221** Suomen geologia **233** Suomen geologia **239** U. Häyrinen: Suo **247** R. Uusinoka **266** R. Uusinoka **272** T. Aartolahti: Suomen geomorfologia (Helsinki 1977)